Contents

PRECAUTIONS TO AVOID POSSIBLE EXPOSURE TO EXCESSIVE MICROWAVE ENERGY

a) Do not attempt to operate this oven with the door open since open-door operation can result in harmful exposure to microwave energy. It is important not to defeat or tamper with the safety interlocks.

b) Do not place any object between the oven front face and the door or allow soil or cleaner residue to accumulate on sealing surfaces.

c) Do not operate the oven if it is damaged. It is particularly important that the oven door close properly and that there is no damage to the: (1) Door (bent), (2) hinges and latches (broken or loosened), (3) door seals and sealing surfaces.

d) The oven should not be adjusted or repaired by anyone except properly qualified service personnel.

Recipes Developed and Tested in the Thermador Test Kitchen

Directed By: Madeleine Burger Brown, Director of Home Economics - Engineering Department

Assisted By: Michael Snyder, Staff Home Economist
Sandy Stave, Consulting Home Economist

Editors: Mary M. Powers
Marcia Redding

Book Design: Josh Young

Photography: George de Gennaro Studios

Food Stylist: Mable Hoffman

Hand Model: Traci E. Brown

© Thermador/Waste King Division, Norris Industries, Los Angeles, California 90040
ISBN: 0-912656-67-0, Library of Congress Catalog Card No. 76-52256, Printed in U.S.A. 1977

Micro-Thermal Cooking

The Best of Two Worlds

As the new owner of a Thermatronic II Micro-Thermal oven you will be using one of the most advanced cooking appliances ever designed. We expect that you will enjoy the adventure of learning to use your oven as much as we have enjoyed the adventure and challenge of developing this cookbook.

Whether you are an experienced microwave oven user or just beginning, this cookbook has been designed to guide you through the basics of microwave cooking and into the fascinating world of micro-thermal cooking. However, for you to fully understand and enjoy the fabulous Thermatronic II oven, we urge you to read carefully the Care and Use manual and the introductory information in this cookbook.

We have chosen several recipes we call Beginning Basics to guide you in learning the five most often used cooking techniques. These recipes are indicated with this mark (•) next to the recipe title in the index. They are a sampling of easy-to-prepare dishes to get you started cooking with and enjoying your Thermatronic II oven.

As you gain experience and confidence, you will develop your own cooking techniques and establish your own guidelines. It will become easy to convert your own favorite recipes to the Thermatronic II. We encourage you to experiment! Our recipes are meant as a starting point, but since we have incorporated many of our own favorites, we hope they will also become yours.

Please write us with your questions and comments. We wish you much cooking success and long time enjoyment with the Thermatronic II Micro-Thermal oven.

Home Economics Staff

The Basics

BASICS OF THERMATRONIC II COOKING

The Thermatronic II cookbook has been designed specifically to guide you in learning to cook with three microwave power levels, either with or without conventional oven heat. All the recipes use microwave energy for all or part of the cooking operation. It is important to become familiar with the Microwave Cooking Techniques discussed later in the book. These techniques apply both to cooking with microwave only and to cooking with microwaves combined with heat. Remember too, the Thermatronic II is also a fine conventional oven and broiler for all oven uses that do not utilize microwave energy. However, recipes for conventional cooking are not included in this book.

Five basic cooking procedures are used in the recipes for this cookbook:

Microwave Only
Microwave and Bake Simultaneously
Microwave and Bake, Then Bake Only
Bake Only, Then Microwave and Bake
Microwave and Broil Simultaneously

Each of these procedures is described in the following pages. Check information, charts and pictures describing suitable utensils for each type of cooking. Become familiar with the information compiled here for ease in preparing the recipes contained in the cookbook and later for adapting your own favorite recipes to the Thermatronic II.

The primary advantages of microwave cooking are speed and convenience, cooking foods as quickly and easily as possible. Many foods cook very well with microwave energy only. Some foods, especially vegetables, are actually better cooked with microwave energy than when cooked on the cooktop. Other foods, however, lack palatability if cooked with just microwave energy. The combination of microwave energy with bake or broil heat, speeds cooking and adds browning and crisping for flavor and eye appeal.

It will become evident that other cooking operations are possible beyond the five options offered, depending on the food being prepared and the end result desired. For example, a vegetable dish would be prepared using microwave power only; then broil heat could be added at the end, with or without continuing the microwave process, to brown and crisp the surface. Or a food may start cooking quickly on High power, then simmer on Low. Let experience and imagination be your guide in helping you to use the Thermatronic II to its fullest potential.

Beginning Basic Recipes are indicated with this mark (•) in the index. These recipes have been selected to help the new Thermatronic II user become acquainted with the basic cooking techniques and advantages of the oven. Try several of these recipes to gain experience and confidence in microwave only and microwave and heat cooking.

MICROWAVE ONLY

Microwave only cooking is used to duplicate cooktop cooking but with faster, often superior, results. The types of food most often cooked with microwave energy alone are vegetables, sauces, beverages, candies, pudding, egg dishes, defrosting and reheating.

The Thermatronic II oven has three microwave power levels, Low, Medium and High, which offers great cooking flexibility.

When deciding which microwave power to use, consider the type of food to be prepared and the desired end result. Most vegetables are best when cooked as quickly as possible on High. With other foods, however, the fastest is not always the best. Delicate foods, like cheese, will toughen and separate if cooked too quickly, so Low power is most suitable. Breads and rolls heated too quickly become tough. By taking a little more time and warming the rolls on Medium, the heating time will still be fast and the rolls will be warm with less chance of overcooking. Try several recipes from this cookbook to become acquainted with the way different foods react to microwave energy.

General uses for each power level, without heat, include:

Low—Delicate sauces and desserts, cheese dishes, dissolve gelatin, soften butter and cream cheese. Defrost meat, fish, poultry and most other foods.

Medium—Reheat breads, cakes, rolls, thick soups, stews, spaghetti. Cook poultry, hot dogs, heat sandwiches. Defrost and cook entrees in cooking pouches.

High—Vegetables, heating liquids and thin soups, candy, shellfish, fruits, puddings, ground beef, fish and melting butter. Defrost and cook vegetables in cooking pouches.

Steps to Cooking:

1. Place food in oven on shelf position indicated in recipe; close door.
2. Press microwave selector to Low, Medium or High power.
3. Set microwave cooking time on timer.
4. Move latch lever to left to Microwave position, to start cooking.
5. The Microwave timer chimes a few seconds before the end of the time set on the timer and continues until the timer reaches "0." Then both the chime and Microwave energy turn off.

MICROWAVE AND BAKE SIMULTANEOUSLY

A bake heat is used along with microwave energy to speed cooking, yet achieve the browning and crisping associated with conventional baking. The addition of microwave energy speeds baking significantly, often saving half to two-thirds of the cooking time. Low and Medium powers are most often combined with a bake heat, which is 25° to 50°F higher than in a similar conventional recipe, to brown food sufficiently. If, at the end of the cooking time indicated in a recipe, the interior of the food tests done but is not brown enough, turn off the oven and microwave power and allow food to stand in hot oven a few minutes to continue browning. This saves energy and avoids overcooking the food.

When setting the oven to preheat for any microwave and heat cooking operation, set the oven selector and thermostat, then select the microwave power. This starts the fan for air circulation and the best browning results.

Check food for doneness after minimum cooking time in recipe. Remove the food from the oven to check it. While checking the food, keep the oven door closed to confine the heat in the oven.

General uses for this technique include:

Low Power and Bake—Yeast breads, angel food and sponge cakes, some fruit-crust desserts, and bread pudding. Roasting beef, pork, and lamb. Many convenience foods.

Medium Power and Bake—Many cookies, some cake and bread mixes, fruit-crust desserts, and meatballs. Roasting poultry. Convenience food entrées, casseroles, and TV dinners.

High Power and Bake—Quiche.

Steps to Cooking:

1. Press oven selector to Bake.
2. Set oven thermostat to temperature indicated in recipe.

3. Press microwave selector to Low, Medium or High power.*
4. Allow oven to preheat if indicated in recipe.*
5. Place food in oven on shelf position indicated in recipe; close door.
6. Set microwave cooking time on timer.
7. Move latch lever to left to Microwave position.
8. The microwave time will start to chime a few seconds before the end of the time set. Microwave cooking stops when the chime stops; oven heat will continue until the oven selector is pressed Off.

* Always select a microwave power when setting the oven to preheat. This starts the fan for air circulation and even browning. Microwave energy will not start until the door is latched.

MICROWAVE AND BAKE, THEN BAKE ONLY

An alternative to the microwave and bake procedure is simultaneous microwave and bake for part of the cooking time, followed by baking only. Many foods will overcook or toughen or not brown sufficiently if both microwave and bake are used for the entire cooking time. Breads and cakes containing a large proportion of heavy ingredients such as fruit, nuts or cheese, produce best results if microwave and bake are used first, then bake heat alone to finish the cooking. The microwave timer will turn off the microwave energy and the oven will continue to bake automatically. At the start of cooking, set the Minute Minder to signal at the end of the *total* cooking time.

This technique is generally used for:

Low Power and Bake, Then Bake—Heavy, fruity cakes; breads, muffins, chiffon cakes, less tender cuts of meat, foods to be simmered and some convenience foods.

Medium Power and Bake, Then Bake—Some quick breads and convenience foods.

Steps to Cooking:
1. Press oven selector to Bake.
2. Set oven thermostat to temperature indicated in recipe.
3. Press microwave selector to Low, Medium or High power.*
4. Allow oven to preheat if indicated in recipe.*
5. Place food in oven on shelf position indicated in recipe; close door.
6. Set microwave cooking time on timer. Set Minute Minder for total cooking time.
7. Move latch lever to left to Microwave position.
8. When microwave timer chimes, and microwave energy is turned off, leave food in oven for desired additional baking time. The door latch does not need to be released. The microwave power stops automatically when the timer reaches "0" but the oven will continue to bake with heat only.
9. If set, Minute Minder will signal end of total cooking time.

* Always select a microwave power when setting the oven to preheat. This starts the fan for air circulation and even browning.

BAKE ONLY, THEN MICROWAVE AND BAKE

Many foods are best when baked first, then finished with a combination of microwave energy and baking heat. Most light batter cakes, quick breads and muffins respond well to this technique. The batter begins cooking and is "set" with a bake heat usually 25° to 50°F higher than in conventional baking. Then microwave power is added for a short time to finish the cooking. In cakes and quick breads, the key to success is not to turn on the microwave energy too soon. Depending on the quantity of batter, 10 to 20 minutes and occasionally longer, of bake heat is required before adding microwave power. The reduction in total cooking time is less dramatic than for many foods cooked with heat and microwave power, but significant time is still saved.

Since the microwave energy is turned on after cooking begins, set the microwave timer at the start of cooking, then set the Minute Minder to remind yourself to move the latch lever to the left to start the microwave cooking at the appropriate time.

Preheat the oven with a microwave power selected. The microwave power selector should remain pressed during entire baking time for good air circulation and best browning.

General uses for this technique are:

Bake Only, Then Low Power and Bake—Pound cake.

Bake Only, Then Medium Power and Bake—Most cakes, both scratch and mixes, and quick bread mixes.

Steps to Cooking:

1. Press oven selector to Bake.
2. Set oven thermostat to temperature indicated in recipe.
3. Press microwave selector to Low, Medium or High power.*
4. Allow oven to preheat if indicated in recipe.*
5. Place food in oven on shelf position indicated in recipe; close door.
6. Set microwave cooking time on timer, but DO NOT latch the door.
7. Bake for desired length of time; set Minute Minder.
8. When Minute Minder chimes move latch lever to left to Microwave position, to start microwave energy.
9. Microwave timer will chime to signal end of cooking time.

* Always select a microwave power when setting the oven to preheat. This starts the fan for air circulation and even browning.

MICROWAVE AND BROIL SIMULTANEOUSLY

This cooking technique simulates broiling because the heat radiates entirely from the upper element and food is cooked and browned very quickly. The addition of microwave energy hastens the cooking. The door must be closed when using microwave energy, therefore this technique is not identical to broiling with heat only which is always done with the door ajar.

The Thermatronic II also offers several broil settings to correspond to the type of food being prepared. You may select High, Medium or Low Broil, or any temperature in between on the thermostat. As long as the Oven Selector is set to Broil, the heat will radiate from the upper element only down onto the surface of the food. Add Low, Medium or High microwave power, according to how fast you want the food to cook.

The two-piece Thermatronic II broil pan must be used for broiling high fat foods. Fat then drips away from the food and is confined in the lower part of the pan to diminish splattering and crisp the food. Broiling is usually a short cooking operation. Longer cooking with the metal broil pan would be inefficient because metal blocks the circulation of microwaves. Food cooked with microwave energy and broil heat on the metal broil pan usually needs to be turned over, since the microwaves cannot penetrate to the bottom of the food.

Food may also be broiled in a glass-ceramic dish. This food may not need to be turned over, because microwaves can penetrate through the glass-ceramic and cook from the bottom.

The Microwave and Broil technique may be used for:

Low Microwave and Broil—Many appetizers, chops, patties, fish (turned), lobster and shellfish. Some frozen convenience foods with crisp coatings—onion rings and french fries.

Medium Microwave and Broil—Poultry, thick pieces of beef, pork and fish.

High Microwave and Broil—Bacon appetizers.

Steps to Cooking:
1. Place food in oven on shelf position indicated in recipe; close door.*
2. Press oven selector to Broil.
3. Set oven thermostat to High, Medium or Low Broil, or Broil temperature indicated in recipe.*
4. Press microwave selector to Low, Medium or High power.*
5. Set microwave cooking time on timer.
6. Move latch lever to left to Microwave position.
7. Microwave timer will chime to signal end of cooking time.

* Some recipes indicate to preheat the broil element a few minutes. If broil element is to be preheated, leave the door ajar for the time specified, then place the food in the oven, close the door and continue with Step 5 above.

MICROWAVE COOKING TECHNIQUES

A microwave oven has special features that make it different from a conventional oven. You won't have to learn to cook all over again, just remember foods cook faster, so check more often. You can use utensils you never before used for cooking. Testing for doneness is still done the same way it always has been done; a toothpick tells when cakes or breads are done, or a fork pierced into vegetables indicates if they are soft.

Use cooking times as a guide; they are approximate, because food preferences and amounts being cooked differ. A vegetable cooked tender-crisp may be just right for one person and under-cooked for another. The size, shape and material of the cooking dish can make a difference. A large, deep casserole will heat food slower than a large, shallow casserole of the same capacity.

Arrangement

When cooking one item, place it in the center of the shelf. To cook multiple items: Place two side by side, three in a triangle, four in a square, five in a circle, without placing any item in the center. Always leave at least one inch of space between each item. Microwaves are more attracted to the corners and outer edges of the food, therefore, these areas cook more rapidly.

Cover

In microwave cooking, as in conventional cooking, casseroles are often covered to retain moisture and to speed cooking. When cooking with micro-wave only, a glass lid, plastic wrap, waxed paper or paper towels make a good cover. When a bake temperature is added to microwave cooking, a heat-proof glass cover must be used. Be careful of steam when removing covers. Unless a recipe specifies a cover, leave the dish uncovered.

Rotate, Stir or Turn-Over

Depending on the food, one of these techniques may be necessary. When cooking conventionally, heat can be adjusted or food stirred to distribute the heat and cook evenly. During microwave cooking, the same thing is done, but in a different manner. A pie crust or delicate food is rotated 1/4 to 1/2 turn during baking. A casserole may be stirred halfway through the cooking time to bring the slower cooking center food to the faster cooking outside edges. A topping may then be added and the casserole returned to the oven to finish cooking. A roast is often turned over after half the roasting time.

Some recipes require that the food be rotated or stirred more than once, however, the recipe will state this. Remember, during the last half of cooking, the food will require the most attention. Turn the light on and check the food through the window; if necessary, open the door to check more carefully.

Shield

Often times, foods are not evenly shaped. Foil can be used to shield uneven or small parts of food that may overcook before the bulk of the food is done. For example, small pieces or strips of foil can be used to wrap poultry wings, legs and neck openings or the smaller end of a roast. Watch for signs of over-cooking as the food is turned over or checked for doneness; shield any area necessary at that time. Foil can be held in place with a tooth-pick.

Standing Time

Some cooking continues within the food after it has been removed from the oven. All food should have a standing time (rest), after cooking to allow for this continued cooking. The amount of time varies depending on the density, size, amount, and moisture content of the food. If a food appears just about done, before adding extra cooking time, give the food a few minutes of standing time. Approximate standing times are:

1 to 5 minutes for small or individual items.
5 to 10 minutes for chicken pieces, cakes, sauces and most vegetables.
10 to 15 minutes for main dishes, whole chicken, small roasts, potatoes and foods that are quite dense.
15 to 20 minutes for large turkeys or roasts.

Add extra cooking time slowly, 1 to 2 minutes at a time, to avoid overcooking. More time can always be added, but overcooked food cannot be repaired.

INFLUENCES ON COOKING TIME

Volume

The larger the food or the more items of food, the longer it will take to defrost, heat or cook. With one small item, all the microwave energy is being used for cooking it alone. When two or more items are being cooked, they must share the energy. The increase in time is not proportional to the increase in volume. In other words, twice the amount of food will not necessarily take twice as much time to cook. The increase in time varies according to the food and may be one-half to three-fourths longer than the time required to cook the original quantity. With combination cooking, the increase in time will be less than for microwave only cooking, due to the addition of heat.

Starting Temperature

The colder the food, the longer it will take to cook or heat. Reduce cooking time slightly if food that is normally cold at the start of cooking, for example, meat or fish, has warmed to room temperature.

Density

A dense, compact food, like a roast, will take longer to heat or cook, than a porous food, like bread. With porous food, the microwaves can readily penetrate throughout. With denser food items, the microwaves penetrate the outer portion, then the center is heated by conduction from the depth of microwave penetration. With dense items, it may be necessary to use a standing time, or a lower power setting, or both, to allow the center to cook without the edges being overcooked.

Fats and Sugar

Fats and sugar heat very fast with microwave power. Cheese on top of a casserole will heat more readily than the filling; the icing on top of a coffee-cake may be starting to melt when the bread portion is just warm. Use of a lower microwave power or adding topping after half of cooking time will keep the topping from overcooking before the casserole is cooked.

CONVERTING RECIPES

After you become familiar with the Thermatronic II oven and have prepared several recipes from this cookbook it should be easy to convert your recipes to microwave or combination cooking. Here are some guidelines to follow to help convert microwave or conventional recipes to Thermatronic II cooking:

Most food items normally cooked on the cooktop will use only microwave energy. Some of these are vegetables, candy, soups, eggs, sauces, sautéing and melting.

Foods which need browning will use either a combination of microwave and bake or microwave and broil. These include foods which are normally cooked in the oven such as: Breads, cakes, cookies, meat and seafood, some desserts and convenience foods.

As a general rule, to convert any recipe, whether conventional or microwave, find a similar recipe in the cookbook and use general preparation methods, microwave power, oven temperature and cooking time for a similar quantity of food.

Recipes written for use in other microwave ovens can be cooked in the Thermatronic II, but the relationship between our Low, Medium and High power settings and the settings on other brands of microwave ovens must be established. It will be necessary to determine by comparing cookbooks how the microwave power on another microwave oven corresponds to Low, Medium and High. Then prepare the recipe on the appropriate power setting in the Thermatronic II.

Recipes written for the highest power on a 600-700 watt microwave oven can be cooked on High in the Thermatronic II. Cooking time on High may be 1 to 2 minutes longer for each 10 minutes of cooking time with microwave only. If using Thermador recipes designed for Low or Medium power in another Thermador microwave oven add 1 to 2 minutes for each 10 minutes of cooking time at the corresponding power level.

Many microwave only recipes from other sources can probably be improved by adding heat. Experience, a similar recipe and experimentation will be the best guide.

SELECTING UTENSILS FOR MICROWAVE ONLY COOKING

The most suitable cooking utensils will allow microwaves to pass through, yet remain reasonably cool. Some utensils will either absorb or reflect microwaves; interfering with cooking time, causing uneven cooking, or damaging the utensil. Glass, paper, ceramic, and some plastics make good microwave cooking and heating utensils.

Glass—Oven or heat-proof glass and glass-ceramic dishes are the most commonly used microwave cooking utensils. These types of utensils should be used for any food item that is cooked longer than 5 minutes.

China, ceramics, pottery and earthenware can be used for reheating or cooking small amounts of food for a short time. Dishes with a metal trim —gold, silver—should not be used as the trim can be damaged.

Centura dinnerware, Cook-n-Serve covers and the Corelle closed handle cups should not be used in microwave cooking. These dishes absorb microwave energy and can become too hot to handle. Eventually these dishes may crack or break.

Paper—This includes such things as plates, towels,

napkins, freezer wrap, waxed paper and cartons. Paper dishes are ideal for reheating, however avoid cooking foods more than 4 to 5 minutes on paper. Plastic coated paper dishes are recommended to retard absorption of juices. Paper towels placed under food are good absorbers for moisture and/or grease. Paper towels or waxed paper placed over food will reduce spattering.

Plastics—Plastics must be used with caution. Use only plastics that can withstand heat from the food, such as semi-rigid freezer containers or dishwasher safe plastics (heat-proof). Soft plastics may melt or distort if used for cooking; or if used for heating foods with high sugar or fat content. Plastic dishes should be used only for heating foods, as transfer of the heat from the food may distort some containers. Some plastics absorb enough energy to cause charring. Melamine Ware is an example of this type of plastic. This type of plasticware quickly becomes too hot to handle and is not recommended for use with microwave cooking.

Cooking bags designed to withstand freezing, boiling and oven heat may be used in the microwave oven. However, DO NOT use metal twist ties. Close bags with string. Make a slit "X" in all cooking bags and pouches to allow steam to escape.

Plastic wrap is ideal for covering dishes when a lid is not available. Cover dish loosely making a puncture to allow steam to escape, but still keep the heat in.

Straw—A straw basket can be used for the short time it takes to heat rolls or coffeecake.

Wood—Wooden spoons can withstand short periods

COOKING UTENSIL SELECTION CHART			
	Recommended For		
Utensil	**MICROWAVE ONLY**	**MICROWAVE & BAKE**	**MICROWAVE & BROIL**
Oven or Heat-proof glass	Yes	Yes	No
Glass-Ceramic	Yes	Yes	Yes
China, ceramics, pottery, earthenware (no metal trim)	Yes, as specified	No, unless oven or heat proof	No
Paper	Yes	Limited	No
Plastics	Limited	Limited	No
Straw or Wood	Limited	No	No
Metal	Limited	Limited	Limited
TV Trays—7/8-inch deep	Yes	Yes	Yes
Foil	Limited	Limited	Limited
Broil Pan	No	Yes, as specified	Yes, as specified
Angel Food Pan	No	Yes	No
Bundt-type Pan	No	No, use glass	No
Cookie Sheets	No	No	No
Muffin Pan	No	Yes, 6 count	No
Pie Pan	No	Yes, as specified	No
8″ x 8″ x 2″	No	Yes, as specified	No
13″ x 9″ x 2″	No	No	No
Conventional—Meat thermometer	No	No	No
Microwave—Meat thermometer	Yes	Yes, if heat resistant	Yes, if heat resistant
Temp-Matic Meat thermometer	Yes	Yes	Yes
*MD12 Wire Rack (7 Bars)	Yes	Yes.	Yes
	Yes	Yes	Yes

*Available from Thermador.

UTENSIL GUIDE

This guide describes sizes and shapes of utensils used in testing the recipes in this cookbook.

GLASS

When recipe calls for:	Use heat-proof ovenware or glass-ceramic dishes:
9-inch pie plate	9" x 1-1/4"
10-inch pie plate	10" x 1-1/2"
1-quart loaf dish	8-3/4" x 5" x 2"
1-1/2-quart loaf dish	8-1/2" x 4-1/2" x 2-1/2"
2-quart loaf dish	9" x 5" x 3"
1-1/2-quart round cake dish	8-1/4" x 1-1/2"
2-quart square cake dish	8" x 8" x 2"
1-1/2-quart oblong baking dish	10" x 6" x 1-3/4"
2-quart oblong baking dish	11-3/4" x 7-1/2" x 1-3/4"
2-3/4-quart oblong baking dish	12" x 7-1/2" x 2"
3-quart oblong baking dish	13-1/2" x 8-3/4" x 1-3/4"
1, 2 or 4-cup liquid measure	1, 2 or 4-cup glass measure

METAL

When recipe calls for:	Use *only* these metal utensils or racks:
Broil Pan	Thermatronic II two-piece Broil Pan comes with oven.
9" pie pan	9" x 1-1/2"
1-3/4-quart square cake pan	7-3/4" x 7-3/4" x 1-7/8"
Muffin Pan	6-count muffin pan
Roasting Pan	Glass-ceramic baking dish with metal rack included MD12 or Lower half of broil pan with conventional roasting rack for food items 18 pounds or larger.

of microwave energy. Wooden bowls or boards are not recommended for use as microwaves evaporate the natural moisture in the wood, causing splitting or cracking.

Metal—In general, we do not recommend using metal utensils for cooking. Metal reflects microwaves, therefore the microwaves can only reach the food from the top of the container. However, there are some instances when metal can be used selectively with good results:

1. Aluminum foil can be used to prevent or slow the cooking or heating of an area. If a portion of a roast, legs or wings on poultry or other food item is cooking too fast, cover the area with a small piece of foil. This is often referred to as shielding.

2. Such things as skewers or clamps, may be used if there is a larger amount of food in proportion to the metal.

3. TV dinners and convenience foods can be heated in their foil trays if the containers are no deeper than 7/8-inch. Otherwise, the food should be transferred to a glass dish or paper container for heating.

Bonded Adhesive Handles—Some cups, mugs and casserole covers have handles attached with glue. These handles may come off if the dishes are used with microwave energy.

Lacquer Ware—Lacquer ware may crack or become discolored if heated in the microwave oven.

Thermometers—Most thermometers should not be used in a microwave oven, as the microwaves are attracted to the mercury, causing them to become inaccurate. There are some thermometers now available that can be used with microwave; and if they are also heat resistant, they can be used with heat.

Microwave Yes

Microwave No

SELECTING UTENSILS FOR COMBINATION COOKING

The most suitable cooking utensils for combination cooking must transmit microwaves and be oven-proof. For a few selected foods, metal utensils may be used.

Glass—Oven-proof baking dishes or glass-ceramic utensils are the most commonly used cooking utensils for combination cooking. Earthenware dishes may be used when starting with a cold oven. Gradual heating is recommended as sudden temperature changes can cause earthenware dishes to crack or break. Do not use earthenware with Broil heat. Any other type of glass and china should be used for MICROWAVE ONLY cooking.

Paper—Paper may scorch or burn; however, there are some exceptions, such as cupcake liners, or baking boxes designed specifically to be used in conventional ovens. All other paper products should be used for MICROWAVE ONLY cooking.

Plastics—Plastics may melt or burn if used with combination cooking. Use with MICROWAVE ONLY cooking.

Metal—With combinaton cooking, some metal utensils are used with delicate foods because the metal utensil slows down the amount of microwave energy being absorbed by the food. For some recipes, glass (oven-proof) dishes are not available. Use metal utensils only in recommended recipes. The addition of the Bake or Broil heat helps to overcome the microwave intereference that a metal utensil creates. This permits the use of the metal broil pan, some metal cooking utensils, and convenience food trays for heating pre-cooked foods.

Combination Yes

Combination No

Appetizers

Microwave only cooking is excellent for heating many quick hor d'oeuvres. This book contains a few easy dip and appetizer recipes that can be prepared quickly with microwave power, such as Nachos and Hot Bean Dip. Any recipe that simply heats food or melts cheese can be easily adapted for use in the Thermatronic II oven. Therefore, we have tried to concentrate on a variety of recipes that show the advantages of combined cooking techniques, such as microwave and broil. Try several of these recipes before converting your favorite similar foods to combination cooking. Many appetizers can be prepared ahead and refrigerated until guests arrive, then quickly cooked with a minimum of time spent in the kitchen at the last minute.

As can be seen when glancing through the appetizer recipes, two types of utensils are used in the microwave-broil operation. The two-piece Thermatronic II broil pan is used for cooking high fat foods, such as Bacon-Wrapped Water Chestnuts, so that fat will drip away from the food and be confined in the lower part of the pan. Appetizers cooked on the two-piece broil pan usually need to be turned over for best cooking results. Low fat microwave-broil foods may be prepared in a glass-ceramic baking dish, or on a microwave, oven-proof roasting rack with tray.

High, Medium or Low microwave power is used according to the specific food. Most sauces are cooked on High power, while thicker dips cook on Medium and are stirred occasionally so that outside edges do not cook too quickly. Meatballs are cooked on Medium power, with Bake heat to add browning. Low power is used for delicate foods, such as cheese, or where conventional baking or broiling needs to be hastened just a little.

Tijuana Quiche is an exception. Our tests showed best results are attained when it is baked with heat and High microwave power, then allowed to stand in a hot oven to set the center.

Mushrooms with Crab Stuffing

Microwave Power:	High	Low
Oven Selector:	Off	Broil
Oven Temperature:	Off	High Broil
Shelf Position:	2	3

3/4 lb. large fresh mushrooms
2 tablespoons butter
2 green onions, finely chopped
1/2 teaspoon seasoning salt
1 can (7-oz.) crabmeat, drained

1 pkg. (3-oz.) cream cheese, softened
3 tablespoons Parmesan cheese
Dash Worcestershire sauce
Dash salt and pepper
Chopped parsley or green onion stems

Wash mushrooms and remove stems. Arrange caps, stem side up, in 2-3/4-quart glass-ceramic baking dish and set aside. Finely chop stems, combine with butter and onions in 2-quart bowl. Cook with Microwave on High, 3 to 4 minutes or until onions are tender, stirring once. Stir in remaining ingredients. Fill mushroom caps with crabmeat mixture, piling high. Move shelf to 3rd position. Broil at High Broil, with Microwave on Low, 7 to 9 minutes. Garnish with chopped parsley or green onion stems. Makes about 24 mushrooms.

To make ahead:
Prepare and fill mushroom caps, then refrigerate. When ready to serve, Broil as instructed.

Sesame-Curry Chicken Wings

Microwave Power:	High	Off	Medium
Oven Selector:	Off	Broil	Broil
Oven Temperature:	Off	High Broil	Medium Broil
Shelf Position:	2	2	3

2 lbs. chicken wings
1/2 cup soy sauce
3 tablespoons honey
2 tablespoons water
2 teaspoons cornstarch

2 teaspoons lemon juice
1/2 teaspoon curry powder
1/4 teaspoon ground ginger
1/3 cup sesame seeds, lightly toasted

Cut wings at joints, separating double-bone section, tip and single-bone section (drumstick). Discard tips. Set wings aside. Combine remaining ingredients, except sesame seeds in a 4-cup liquid measure. Stir with a fork to dissolve cornstarch. Cook sauce with Microwave on High, 2-1/2 to 3 minutes, until mixture boils and thickens, stirring once. Cool. Pour over chicken, marinate several hours; drain. Toast sesame seeds with oven on High Broil, about 5 minutes. Stir often and watch carefully so seeds do not over brown. Dip each wing in toasted sesame seeds, one side only. Place seed side up in a 2-3/4-quart oblong glass-ceramic baking dish. Broil at Medium Broil with Microwave on Medium, 9 to 12 minutes. Do not turn. Makes about 26 pieces.

Honey-Orange Glazed Spareribs, Mushrooms with Crab Stuffing, Sesame-Curry Chicken Wings

Honey-Orange Glazed Spareribs

Microwave Power:	High	Low
Oven Selector:	Off	Bake
Oven Temperature:	Off	375°F, not preheated
Shelf Position:	2	2

Sauce:

1 tablespoon cornstarch
2 tablespoons honey
3 tablespoons soy sauce
1/2 teaspoon garlic powder

1/4 teaspoon ground ginger
1/4 cup orange juice
1/4 cup sherry (optional, omit sherry and increase orange juice 1/4 cup)

2-1/2 to 3 lbs. spareribs, cut into individual pieces

Sauce:

In a 2-cup liquid measure, combine sauce ingredients. Cook with Microwave on High, 2 minutes; stir. Continue to cook and stir for an additional 2 to 3 minutes, until thick and transparent.

Place cut-up ribs in a 3-quart oblong baking dish. Place dish in oven with handles right to left. Bake at 375°, not preheated, with Microwave on Low, 10 minutes. Remove from oven; turn and redistribute ribs. Return to oven, handles right to left. Bake at 375° with Microwave on Low, 10 minutes more. Remove from oven, spoon off fat. Spoon sauce over ribs and return to oven, handles right to left. Bake at 375° with Microwave on Low, 10 minutes. Check and redistribute sauce, if necessary. Bake with Microwave on Low an additional 8 to 12 minutes. Allow to cool 10 minutes before serving. Makes about 20 ribs.

Hot Bean Dip

Microwave Power:	High
Oven Selector:	Off
Oven Temperature:	Off
Shelf Position:	2

4 slices bacon, diced
1 can (17-oz.) refried beans or
   1 can (16-oz.) red kidney beans,
   drained and mashed
1 tablespoon finely chopped green pepper

1 teaspoon instant minced onion
1 to 2 teaspoons taco sauce
1/4 teaspoon garlic salt
1/8 teaspoon pepper
1/2 cup dairy sour cream

Cook bacon in 1-1/2-quart casserole with Microwave on High, 5 to 8 minutes; drain. Add remaining ingredients to bacon; blend well. Cover; heat with Microwave on High, 5 to 6 minutes, until hot, stirring once. Serve with tortilla chips. Makes about 1-1/2 cups.

Fiesta Stuffed Mushrooms

Microwave Power:	High	Low
Oven Selector:	Off	Broil
Oven Temperature:	Off	High Broil
Shelf Position:	2	4

16 fresh medium mushrooms
1/4 cup butter
3 tablespoons finely chopped green pepper
3 tablespoons finely chopped onion
1/4 teaspoon whole rosemary, crushed

1 cup fresh bread crumbs (1/4-inch cubes)
1/2 teaspoon salt
1/4 teaspoon garlic powder
1/8 teaspoon pepper

Wipe mushrooms with a damp cloth. Remove stems and chop fine; set aside. Melt butter in 2-cup liquid measure, with Microwave on High, 3/4 to 1 minute. Brush mushrooms lightly with melted butter; place in 2-3/4-quart oblong glass-ceramic baking dish. Sauté chopped stems, green pepper, onion and crushed rosemary in remaining butter until tender, 2-1/2 to 3 minutes, with Microwave on High. Add bread crumbs, salt, garlic and pepper; mix thoroughly. Fill mushroom caps, mounding mixture high in center. Move oven rack to 4th position (highest) and Broil at High Broil with Microwave on Low, 4 to 6 minutes depending on size of mushrooms. Makes 16.

Tijuana Quiche

Microwave Power:	High	High
Oven Selector:	Off	Bake
Oven Temperature:	Off	350°F, preheated
Shelf Position:	2	2

1 cup half and half
1/4 teaspoon salt
1/8 teaspoon cumin
Dash cayenne pepper
3 eggs, beaten

1 cup shredded Monterey Jack cheese
1 cup shredded Cheddar cheese
1 can (4-oz.) diced green chiles
1 (9-inch) baked pie shell

In a 2-cup liquid measure, combine half and half, salt and spices. Heat with Microwave on High, 2 to 3 minutes until hot, but not boiling. Preheat oven. Pour hot mixture slowly into beaten eggs, stirring constantly. Stir in cheeses and chiles. Pour into pie shell. Bake at 350° with Microwave on High 3 minutes. Turn dish one half turn; continue to Bake at 350° with Microwave on High, 2 to 4 minutes or until filling is almost set in the center. Turn oven Off. Allow pie to stand in hot oven 15 minutes or until center is completely set. Serve warm. Cut into small wedges for appetizers or 6 to 8 large wedges for a main dish.

Hot Minced Clam Dip

Microwave Power:	Medium
Oven Selector:	Off
Oven Temperature:	Off
Shelf Position:	2

1 pkg. (8-oz.) cream cheese
1 can (7-1/2-oz.) minced clams, drained
1 tablespoon lemon juice
1 tablespoon finely minced green pepper

1 green onion, finely minced
1 teaspoon Worcestershire sauce
1/2 teaspoon salt
1/8 teaspoon ground pepper

Place cream cheese in a 1-quart bowl, soften with Microwave on Medium, 1 to 1-1/2 minutes until soft enough to mix easily. Add remaining ingredients and combine thoroughly. Heat with Microwave on Medium, 3 to 4 minutes, stirring twice. Serve with crackers or chips.

Quick Hot Clam-Cheese Dip

Microwave Power:	Medium
Oven Selector:	Off
Oven Temperature:	Off
Shelf Position:	2

2 jars (5-oz. each) sharp process cheese spread
1 jar (6-1/2-oz.) minced clams, not drained

2 teaspoons freeze dried chives
1/4 cup dry white wine

Combine cheese spread, clams and chives in a 1-1/2-quart glass bowl. Cook with Microwave on Medium, 4 to 6 minutes, stirring often, until hot. Do not boil. Stir in wine, continue to cook with Microwave on Medium, 1 minute. Serve hot with chunks of French bread for dipping.

Nachos

Microwave Power:	Low
Oven Selector:	Off
Oven Temperature:	Off
Shelf Position:	2

Tortilla chips
Jalapeño peppers or taco sauce or chile salsa

Sharp Cheddar cheese, grated
Monterey Jack cheese, grated

Place a layer of chips (about 15) on a paper or glass plate. Place a thin layer of pepper on each chip or sprinkle with sauce or salsa. Sprinkle with cheese. Heat with Microwave on Low, 1-1/2 to 2 minutes until cheese is melted. Serve while hot. Makes about 15.

International Meatballs

BASIC MEATBALLS

Microwave Power:	Medium
Oven Selector:	Bake
Oven Temperature:	450°F, not preheated
Shelf Position:	2

1 lb. lean ground beef	1/2 teaspoon salt
1 egg, beaten	1/4 teaspoon nutmeg
1/4 cup milk	1/4 teaspoon garlic powder
1/3 cup fine dry bread crumbs	1 teaspoon Worcestershire sauce
2 teaspoons instant minced onion	1/8 teaspoon pepper

Combine all ingredients. Form into 1-inch balls. Place in a 2-quart oblong baking dish. Bake at 450° with Microwave on Medium, 6 to 9 minutes or until completely cooked. Turn meatballs over once about halfway through the cooking time. Place meatballs in serving dish. Reserving drippings for later use. Serve meatballs plain or with one of following sauces. Makes 25 to 30 meatballs.

Swedish Meatballs

Microwave Power:	High	Low
Oven Selector:	Off	Off
Oven Temperature:	Off	Off
Shelf Position:	2	2

1 recipe Basic Meatballs	1/8 teaspoon pepper
Drippings from cooked meatballs	1 cup beef broth or 1 beef bouillion cube
2 tablespoons flour	dissolved in 1 cup hot water
1/4 teaspoon salt	3/4 cup dairy sour cream
1/4 teaspoon paprika	

Prepare Basic Meatballs; set aside. Stir flour, salt, paprika and pepper into drippings in same 2-quart oblong baking dish used to cook meatballs. Blend well, making a paste. Stir in beef broth, blending well. Cook with Microwave on High, 1 to 2 minutes or until mixture bubbles, stirring once. Stir in sour cream. Turn Microwave to Low and cook 1-1/2 minutes. Stir and cook 1 to 2 minutes longer or until sauce is hot. Add meatballs and cook with Microwave on Low, 2 to 3 minutes or until heated through, stirring once.

Texas Barbecue Meatballs

Microwave Power: High
Oven Selector: Off
Oven Temperature: Off
Shelf Position: 2

1 can (8-oz.) tomato sauce
1/4 cup catsup
1/4 cup cider vinegar
2 tablespoons brown sugar, firmly packed
1 teaspoon instant minced onion

1 teaspoon prepared mustard
1 teaspoon Worcestershire sauce
1/4 teaspoon salt
1/8 teaspoon liquid smoke
1 recipe Basic Meatballs, uncooked

Combine all ingredients, except Basic Meatballs, in a 4-cup liquid measure. Cook with Microwave on High, 6 to 8 minutes, stirring often. Sauce will thicken during cooking. Prepare Basic Meatballs. Drain drippings and pour barbecue sauce over meatballs. Cook with Microwave on High, 2 to 3 minutes or until sauce is hot.

Polynesian Pineapple Meatballs

Microwave Power: High
Oven Selector: Off
Oven Temperature: Off
Shelf Position: 2

3 tablespoons brown sugar
2 tablespoons cornstarch
1/2 teaspoon ground ginger
1/8 teaspoon garlic powder
1 can (20-oz.) chunk pineapple in
   heavy syrup, reserve syrup

1/3 cup soy sauce
1 beef bouillion cube dissolved in
   3/4 cup water
2 tablespoons dry white wine
1-1/2 teaspoons lemon juice
1 recipe Basic Meatballs, uncooked

Mix brown sugar, cornstarch, ginger and garlic in small bowl. Drain pineapple, reserving 1/2 cup syrup. In a 4-cup liquid measure combine syrup, soy sauce, bouillion, wine and lemon juice. Stir in cornstarch and brown sugar mixture. Cook with Microwave on High, 5 to 6 minutes, stirring often. Stir in pineapple. Cook with Microwave on High, 2 to 3 minutes longer. Set aside. Prepare Basic Meatball recipe according to directions substituting 1/4 teaspoon ginger for nutmeg and 1 teaspoon soy sauce for Worcestershire sauce. Drain drippings and pour pineapple-teriyaki sauce over meatballs. Cook with Microwave on High, 2 to 3 minutes to heat sauce and pineapple. Can also be served with rice as a main dish.

Bacon-Wrapped Water Chestnuts

Microwave Power:	High
Oven Selector:	Broil
Oven Temperature:	High Broil, not preheated
Shelf Position:	3

1 can (8-1/2-oz.) water chestnuts, drained
8 slices bacon, cut in half
1/4 cup soy sauce
1 tablespoon sugar

2 tablespoons water
1/2 teaspoon ground ginger
1/4 teaspoon garlic powder

Wrap each water chestnut in half slice of bacon. Secure with toothpick. Combine remaining ingredients in 8-inch square dish and marinate bacon-wrapped water chestnuts for several hours. Drain, arrange on top of Thermador two-piece broil pan. Set broil pan at 3rd shelf position. Broil at High Broil with Microwave on High, 3 to 4 minutes; turn over. Continue at High Broil with Microwave on High, 2 to 3 minutes or until bacon is crisp. Serve hot. Makes about 16 pieces.

Quick Mini Pizzas

Microwave Power:	Low
Oven Selector:	Bake
Oven Temperature:	500° F, preheated
Shelf Position:	2

6 English muffins, sliced in half
1 can (10-1/2-oz.) pizza sauce
1 teaspoon oregano, crushed
1 cup grated Cheddar cheese

1 cup grated Monterey Jack or mozzarella cheese
Thinly sliced mushrooms, green pepper, onion, pepperoni, or favorite pizza toppings

Arrange English muffin slices on Thermatronic II two-piece broil pan, cut-side up. For crisp pizzas, toast muffins on High Broil 2 to 3 minutes, or until lightly toasted. For soft pizzas omit toasting. Preheat oven to 500°. Spread each muffin half generously with pizza sauce and sprinkle with crushed oregano. Sprinkle cheeses over muffins, reserving about 1/2 cup. Arrange favorite toppings on each muffin; top with reserved cheese. Bake at 500° with Microwave on Low, 4 to 6 minutes or until cheese melts and pizzas are hot and bubbly. Serve whole or cut into quarters for appetizers. Makes 12 whole or 48 wedges.

Beverages

Beverages and water for hot drinks are heated with microwave power only, usually on High. Microwaves reheat coffee quickly to serving temperature in a cup, maintaining a fresh flavor. Although microwave heating of beverages does not save a great deal of time, the advantage is in being able to heat beverages in paper, glass, pottery or china cups, pitchers or punch bowls.

Allow more time to heat cold liquids than room temperature liquids. The larger the quantity of liquid, the longer it will take to heat. One large container of a beverage will take more time to heat than the same quantity heated simultaneously in several cups. If heating several cups of beverage at a time, place the cups on a glass tray or ceramic plate to remove easily from oven.

Milk beverages heat fast with microwaves and the necessity of scrubbing a sticky pan is eliminated. Milk should just be hot, not boiled.

Coffee Reheating Table

Microwave Power:	High
Oven Selector:	Off
Oven Temperature:	Off
Shelf Position:	2

Amount	Time
1 - 6-ounce cup	1-1/2 to 2 minutes
2 - 6-ounce cups	2-1/2 to 3 minutes
4 - 6-ounce cups	4 to 4-1/2 minutes
6 - 6-ounce cups	5-1/4 to 5-3/4 minutes

The Microwave oven reheats room-temperature coffee back to drinking temperature without boiling, so the coffee still tastes fresh.

Hot Cocoa

Microwave Power:	High
Oven Selector:	Off
Oven Temperature:	Off
Shelf Position:	2

2 teaspoons cocoa	Pinch salt
2 teaspoons sugar	3/4 cup milk
2 tablespoons water	1 marshmallow (optional)

Mix cocoa, sugar, water and salt together in 8-ounce glass mug. Heat with Microwave on High, 30 seconds. Stir. Add milk and mix. Heat with Microwave on High, 2 to 2-1/2 minutes or until serving temperature. Add marshmallow last 15 seconds, if desired. Makes 1 serving.

Mulled Cider

Microwave Power:	High
Oven Selector:	Off
Oven Temperature:	Off
Shelf Position:	2

1 qt. (4 cups) apple cider
2 tablespoons brown sugar, firmly packed
2 cinnamon sticks

3 whole cloves
1/2 lemon, sliced
1 orange, sliced

In large heat-proof glass dish combine all ingredients except the orange slices; mix well. Heat with Microwave on High, 7 to 9 minutes, or until hot. Strain and garnish with orange slices. Makes four 1-cup servings.

Boysenberry Refresher

Microwave Power:	High
Oven Selector:	Off
Oven Temperature:	Off
Shelf Position:	2

Pulp from 1 recipe Boysenberry Jam
Equal amount of water

1/4 cup sugar, or to taste
Lemon-lime soda

Measure pulp from Boysenberry Jam, add an equal amount of water and pour into a 3-quart casserole. Cook uncovered just until bubbly with Microwave on High.* Strain through a fine sieve. Mix in sugar. Bring just to a boil with Microwave on High.* Pour into a scalded jar and refrigerate. To serve, mix equal portions of juice and soda.

*Time depends on amount of pulp and water, or juice. Turn oven light on and watch for bubbles.

Hot 'N Spicy Cranburgundy Punch

Microwave Power:	High
Oven Selector:	Off
Oven Temperature:	Off
Shelf Position:	2

2 cups water
1 cup sugar
16 whole cloves
1 cinnamon stick, crushed
1/2 cup lemon juice

2 cups cranberry juice cocktail
2 cups boiling water
1 cup Burgundy or 1 additional cup of water
1 lemon, sliced, studded with whole cloves

In 4-cup liquid measure, combine 2 cups water, sugar, cloves and cinnamon. Cook with Microwave on High, 8 to 10 minutes. Mixture should come to a boil and boil rapidly for 5 minutes. Strain into 4-quart glass bowl; add remaining ingredients except lemon slices. Heat with Microwave on High, 4 to 5 minutes, just to serving temperature; do not boil. Garnish with lemon slices. Makes nine 6-ounce servings.

Hot Grape Punch

Microwave Power:	High
Oven Selector:	Off
Oven Temperature:	Off
Shelf Position:	2

1-1/2 cups grape juice
1-1/2 teaspoons brown sugar, firmly packed
1 teaspoon lemon juice

1 cinnamon stick, broken in half
5 whole cloves
1/2 cup Burgundy

Mix all ingredients except wine in 4-cup liquid measure. Heat with Microwave on High, 4 to 5 minutes, until almost boiling. Let steep 5 minutes; strain. Add wine and serve. Makes four 1/2-cup servings.

Cappuccino

Microwave Power:	High
Oven Selector:	Off
Oven Temperature:	Off
Shelf Position:	2

2 cups milk
6 teaspoons (1/2-oz.) semi-sweet chocolate,
   grated
2 to 4 teaspoons sugar

3 teaspoons instant coffee powder
4 oz. brandy
Whipped cream, sweetened

Heat milk in 4-cup liquid measure with Microwave on High, 5 to 6 minutes, until hot. Stir in 4 teaspoons grated chocolate; reserve 2 teaspoons. Stir in sugar and coffee. Pour into 4 serving cups; add 1 ounce brandy to each cup. DO NOT stir. Top with sweetened whipped cream and sprinkle each serving with 1/2 teaspoon of reserved chocolate. Makes four 1/2-cup servings.

Mocha Hot Chocolate

Microwave Power:	High
Oven Selector:	Off
Oven Temperature:	Off
Shelf Position:	2

1/2 cup water
1/2 cup semi-sweet chocolate pieces

1 tablespoon instant coffee powder
2-1/2 cups milk

Pour water into a 2-quart covered glass casserole. Bring to a boil with Microwave on High, 1 to 2 minutes. Add chocolate pieces and coffee. Stir together; cover. Melt chocolate with Microwave on High, 1-1/2 to 2 minutes. Mix thoroughly. Stir in milk; cover. Continue heating with Microwave on High, 4 to 5 minutes or until heated through. Makes four 6-ounce servings.

Hot Cranberry Punch

Microwave Power:	High
Oven Selector:	Off
Oven Temprature:	Off
Shelf Position:	2

4 cups cranberry juice cocktail

1 can (6-oz.) frozen lemonade
concentrate, undiluted

1-1/4 cups grape juice

1-1/2 cups water

2 cinnamon sticks, crushed

10 whole cloves

1 orange, sliced

Combine all ingredients, except orange slices, in a 3-quart casserole. Heat, just to boiling, with Microwave on High, 11 to 13 minutes, stirring occasionally. Let stand 10 minutes. Remove spices and serve garnished with orange slices. Makes eight 6-ounce servings.

Quick Breads

A combination of baking heat and microwave energy does an excellent job on quick breads and usually cuts the baking times by one third to one half. Baking temperatures are often 25° to 50° F higher than conventional baking to achieve browning in the shortened baking time.

Generally two procedures are used to bake quick breads. Very heavy batters that contain a large proportion of nuts, fruit, cheese, or a small amount of liquid, are baked with microwave power for the first part of baking; then the microwave power is turned off and bake heat only is used to finish the baking. Light, very liquid batters are usually baked with heat only first to set the batter, then microwave power is added to finish the baking. A few exceptions follow methods that simply proved to be the best way to bake that particular bread.

Metal pans have been used in some recipes to achieve the best results for those foods, however glass baking dishes are recommended for the majority of recipes and should be used exclusively unless otherwise specified.

At the end of the baking time, if additional browning is desired, turn oven and microwave off and allow bread to stay in hot oven until sufficiently browned.

Muffins are baked quite successfully in metal muffin pans. Again, heavy, fruity batters are microwave and baked first, then just baked; light batters are baked first to set, then microwave power is added to finish the cooking. The time savings over conventional baking is less for muffins, and the texture is often improved. Try making muffins from a quick bread mix for fast results. Be careful not to overmix muffins.

Spicy Apple Bread

Microwave Power:	Off	Low
Oven Selector:	Bake	Bake
Oven Temperature:	425°F, preheated	425°F
Shelf Position:	2	2

1-1/2 cups sifted flour
1 cup sugar
1 teaspoon baking soda
1/2 teaspoon cinnamon
1/4 teaspoon cloves
1/4 teaspoon nutmeg

1/2 cup (1 stick) melted butter
1 egg, slightly beaten
1/2 cup cold coffee
2/3 cup grated apple
1/3 cup chopped raisins
1/2 cup chopped walnuts

Sift dry ingredients together. Melt butter and combine with egg and coffee. Combine liquid with dry ingredients, mix until just moistened. Gently stir in apples, raisins and nuts. Pour into greased 1-1/2-quart glass loaf pan. Bake at 425° for 5 minutes, then continue baking at 425° with Microwave on Low, 8 to 10 minutes or until bread tests done. Makes 1 loaf.

Date-Nut Bread

Microwave Power:	High	Low	Off
Oven Selector:	Off	Bake	Bake
Oven Temperature:	Off	400°F, preheated	400°F
Shelf Position:	2	2	2

3/4 cup water
3/4 cup dates, pitted and snipped
1 egg
2 tablespoons salad oil
1/4 cup brown sugar, firmly packed
1/2 cup nuts, chopped

1-1/4 cups sifted flour
1/2 teaspoon salt
1/2 teaspoon soda
1/2 teaspoon cinnamon
1/4 teaspoon nutmeg

In 2-cup liquid measure, bring water to a boil with Microwave on High. Stir in dates and let cool. Preheat oven. Slightly beat egg in medium mixing bowl. Blend in oil, sugar, nuts and date mixture. Sift together remaining dry ingredients; add to oil mixture. Stir just to combine. Pour batter into a greased 1-1/2-quart METAL loaf pan. Place in oven with handles left to right. Bake at 400° with Microwave on Low, 9 minutes. Turn Microwave Off; continue to Bake at 400°, 9 to 12 minutes or until golden brown and bread tests done. Allow to cool 10 minutes before removing from pan. Makes 1 loaf.

Spicy Apple Bread

California Orange Bread

Microwave Power:	Off	Low
Oven Selector:	Bake	Bake
Oven Temperature:	425°F, preheated	425°F
Shelf Position:	2	2

2/3 cup sugar	2 cups sifted flour
1/3 cup shortening	1 teaspoon baking powder
2 eggs	1/2 teaspoon salt
2 tablespoons coarsely grated orange peel	1/2 teaspoon baking soda
1 cup orange juice with pulp (about 2 oranges)	1/2 cup chopped walnuts

Cream sugar and shortening together. Add eggs, one at a time. Blend well after each addition. Stir in peel and orange juice. Sift dry ingredients together, add to creamed mixture. Combine just until blended. Mix in nuts. Pour batter into a greased 2-quart loaf dish. Bake at 425° for 10 minutes, then add Microwave on Low, 7 to 8 minutes, or until loaf tests done. Makes 1 loaf.

Pineapple Date-Nut Bread

Microwave Power:	High	Low	Off
Oven Selector:	Off	Bake	Bake
Oven Temperature:	Off	400°F, preheated	400°F
Shelf Position:	2	2	2

2 tablespoons butter	1/2 teaspoon salt
1 egg	1 cup snipped dates
1 teaspoon vanilla	1/2 cup chopped nuts
2 cups sifted flour	1 teaspoon baking soda
1/2 cup sugar	1 can (8-oz.) crushed pineapple,
1 teaspoon baking powder	not drained

In a 1-cup liquid measure melt butter with Microwave on High, 45 seconds to 1 minute. Add egg and vanilla and beat with a fork. Preheat oven. In a medium bowl combine flour, sugar, baking powder, salt, dates and nuts. Add egg mixture. Stir. Dissolve soda in pineapple and add to flour mixture. Stir just to moisten. Pour into a greased 1-1/2-quart loaf dish. Bake at 400°, with Microwave on Low, 9 minutes. Turn Microwave Off and continue to Bake at 400°, 12 to 15 minutes or until toothpick tests clean. Allow to cool 20 minutes before removing from pan. Cool completely before slicing. Makes 1 loaf.

California Sunshine Bread

Microwave Power:	High	Low	Off
Oven Selector:	Off	Bake	Bake
Oven Temperature:	Off	400°F, preheated	400°F
Shelf Position:	2	2	2

1 cup sugar
2 cups sifted flour
2 teaspoons baking powder
1 teaspoon baking soda
3/4 teaspoon salt
3 tablespoons butter

1 egg
1 cup applesauce
1 medium orange, cubed (do not remove peel)
1/2 cup raisins
3/4 cup nuts

Combine sugar, flour, baking powder, soda and salt in a large bowl; set aside. Melt butter in a 1-cup liquid measure with Microwave on High, 30 to 45 seconds. Preheat oven. Pour butter into blender jar. Add egg, applesauce, orange, raisins and nuts; blend until well mixed. Add to dry ingredients and mix thoroughly. Pour into a greased 2-quart loaf dish. Bake at 400° with Microwave on Low, 10 minutes. Turn Microwave Off. Continue to Bake at 400°, 17 to 20 minutes or until bread tests done with a toothpick. Cool for 1 hour on a wire rack; remove from loaf dish and continue to cool. Allow to stand 12 hours before slicing. Makes 1 loaf.

Very Banana Bread

Microwave Power:	Low	Off
Oven Selector:	Bake	Bake
Oven Temperature:	400°F, preheated	400°F
Shelf Position:	2	2

1/2 cup (1 stick) butter
1-1/4 cups sugar
2 eggs
3/4 cup mashed bananas (2 to 3 small)
1-3/4 cups sifted flour

3/4 teaspoon baking soda
1/2 teaspoon baking powder
1/2 teaspoon salt
1/2 cup chopped nuts
1/4 cup buttermilk

Cream butter with sugar, beat in eggs, one at a time, then beat in bananas. Combine flour, soda, baking powder, salt and nuts. Alternately add flour mixture and buttermilk to creamed mixture. Pour into a greased 2-quart loaf dish. Bake at 400° with Microwave on Low, 10 minutes. Turn Microwave Off. Continue to Bake at 400°, 6 to 9 minutes or until bread tests done with a toothpick. Makes 1 loaf.

Create Your Own — Bran Muffins

Microwave Power:	Low	Off
Oven Selector:	Bake	Bake
Oven Temperature:	475°F, preheated	475°F
Shelf Position:	2	2

3 cups sifted all-purpose flour
2 cups whole wheat flour
2-1/2 cups sugar
5 teaspoons baking soda
2 teaspoons salt

5 cups (1 15-oz. box) raisin bran cereal
4 eggs, beaten
1 cup oil
1 qt. buttermilk

Optional additions:

2 cups textured cereal, such as granola or
   1 cup wheat germ

and/or 1 to 2 cups cut-up dried fruits
   (dates, apricots, apples, raisin) or coconut

In a 4-quart bowl mix the flours, sugar, soda, salt and cereal thoroughly. Using a 5-quart bowl beat the eggs; add the oil and buttermilk. Beat until well blended. Add the dry ingredients and combine just until mixed. Use 6-count METAL muffin pans only. Do not use larger size. Two 6-count METAL muffin pans may be baked simultaneously. Grease muffin pans and fill 2/3 full.

Bake one 6-count METAL muffin pan at 475° with Microwave on Low, 2 minutes, turn Microwave Off and continue to Bake at 475°, 7 to 8 minutes or until as brown as desired. Makes 6 muffins.

Bake two 6-count METAL muffin pans at 475° with Microwave on Low, 3 minutes, turn Microwave Off and continue to Bake at 475°, 7 to 9 minutes or until as brown as desired. Makes 12 muffins.

The remaining batter may be refrigerated up to two weeks, in a covered container. Do not stir the batter after it has been refrigerated. If you transfer the batter into a smaller container, scrape without stirring.

To bake refrigerated batter:
For one 6-count METAL muffin pan, add 1 minute to Microwave time and 1 minute to browning time.
For two 6-count METAL muffin pans, Microwave time remains the same, add 1 minute to browning time.

Nut or Fruit Quick Bread from a Mix

Microwave Power:	Off	Low
Oven Selector:	Bake	Bake
Oven Temperature:	450°F, preheated	450°F
Shelf Position:	2	2

1 pkg. (15 to 17 oz.) Nut or Fruit Quick Bread Mix

Prepare mix according to package directions. Pour batter into greased 1-1/2-quart or 2-quart glass loaf dish. Place dish in oven with handles right to left. Bake at 450°, 15 minutes, then add Microwave on Low and continue to bake at 450°, 5 to 8 minutes, or until a toothpick inserted in center comes out clean. Cool on a wire rack 15 minutes before removing from pan. Allow to cool completely before slicing. Makes 1 loaf.

Streusel Coffeecake

Microwave Power:	Low
Oven Selector:	Bake
Oven Temperature:	450°F preheated
Shelf Position:	2

3 cups sifted flour
2 cups sugar
1/2 teaspoon nutmeg
1/2 teaspoon cloves
3/4 teaspoon cinnamon
3/4 cup shortening

1 teaspoon salt
1 cup raisins
1/2 cup chopped walnuts
2 cups buttermilk
2 teaspoons baking soda

Combine first six ingredients in large mixer bowl. Mix at medium speed until crumbly. Reserve 1/2 cup for topping. Stir in salt, raisins and nuts. Measure buttermilk and add soda. Add to flour mixture; blend thoroughly. Pour into a greased 3-quart oblong glass baking dish. Sprinkle top of batter with 1/2 cup of reserved mixture. Bake at 450° with Microwave on Low, 12 to 14 minutes, or until golden brown and cake tests done. Makes 15 pieces.

Onion-Cheese Bread

Microwave Power:	High	Low	Off
Oven Selector:	Off	Bake	Bake
Oven Temperature:	Off	450°F, preheated	450°F
Shelf Position:	2	2	2

3 tablespoons instant minced onions
1/2 cup water
2 tablespoons butter
1 egg
1/2 cup milk

1 cup grated Cheddar cheese
1-1/2 cups biscuit mix
2 tablespoons melted butter
2 teaspoons poppy seed

Mix onions with water to reconstitute. Drain well. Melt butter in a 2-quart glass mixing bowl. Add onion and cook with Microwave on High, 1 minute. Preheat oven. Beat in egg with a fork. Stir in milk and 1/2 cup cheese. Add biscuit mix, stir just to combine. Spread in a greased 8-inch round glass cake dish. Drizzle melted butter over surface; top with remaining cheese and sprinkle with poppy seed. Bake at 450° with Microwave on Low, 3 minutes. Rotate dish 1/4 turn and continue to Bake at 450° with Microwave on Low, 3 minutes. Turn Microwave Off and continue to Bake at 450°, 5 to 8 minutes or until golden brown. Makes 6 to 8 wedges.

Southern Buttermilk Biscuits

Microwave Power:	Low	Low	Off
Oven Selector:	Off	Bake	Bake
Oven Temperature:	Off	525°F, preheated	525°F
Shelf Position:	3	3	3

2 tablespoons butter or shortening
2 cups sifted flour
1 teaspoon baking powder

1/2 teaspoon salt
1/4 teaspoon baking soda
1 cup buttermilk

Soften butter or shortening with Microwave on Low about 1/2 minute. Preheat oven. Combine flour, baking powder, salt and soda. Cut in butter or shortening and stir in buttermilk to form a soft dough. Turn out onto a floured surface. Knead 5 to 6 times and pat into a 7-inch circle. Cut into circles with a biscuit cutter and place into a lightly greased 2-quart square baking dish. Bake at 525° with Microwave on Low, 3-1/2 minutes. Turn Microwave Off and continue to Bake at 525°, 6-1/2 to 9 minutes or until golden brown. Serve hot. Makes 9 to 11, 2-1/4-inch biscuits.

Muffins from a Mix

Microwave Power:	Off	Low
Oven Selector:	Bake	Bake
Oven Temperature:	475°F, preheated	475°F
Shelf Position:	2	2

1 pkg. (13 to 15 oz.) muffin mix*

Prepare muffins according to package directions. Use two 6-count METAL muffin pans, greased or lined with cupcake papers. Fill 1/2 to 2/3 full, according to package directions. Place 2 muffin pans in oven with 1-inch between. Bake at 475°, 9 minutes. Then add Microwave on Low and continue to bake, 1 to 3 minutes or until muffins test done. Remove from pans immediately. Makes 12 muffins.

*Muffin mixes may vary in size and yield. This method developed with mixes from 13 ounces to 15 ounces, yielding 12 muffins. One pan of 6 muffins from a mix will bake at the same time, temperature and microwave power as two pans.

Corn Bread from a Mix

Microwave Power:	Off	Low
Oven Selector:	Bake	Bake
Oven Temperature:	450°F, preheated	450°F
Shelf Position:	2	2

1 pkg. (15-oz.) Corn Bread Mix

Prepare mix according to package directions. Pour batter into a greased 8-inch square baking dish. Bake at 450°, 10 minutes, then add Microwave on Low and continue to Bake at 450°, 1-1/2 to 2 minutes or until a toothpick inserted in center comes out clean. Serve hot. Makes 16 pieces.

Aunt Em's Corn Bread

Microwave Power:	Low	Off
Oven Selector:	Bake	Bake
Oven Temperature:	475°F, preheated	475°F
Shelf Position:	2	2

2 eggs	**1 cup sifted flour**
2/3 cup buttermilk	**1/2 teaspoon salt**
1/4 cup oil	**2 teaspoons baking powder**
1 cup cornmeal	**2 to 4 tablespoons sugar**
	1/2 teaspoon baking soda

In a medium bowl, beat egg slightly. Stir in buttermilk and oil. Combine dry ingredients and add to egg mixture. Stir just until moistened. Pour into a greased 8-inch square **METAL** pan. Bake at 475° with Microwave on Low, 1 minute. Rotate pan 1/4 turn and Bake with Microwave on Low, 1 minute longer. Turn Microwave Off and continue to Bake 7 to 10 minutes, or until bread tests done with a toothpick. Makes 9 pieces.

Chile Relleno Corn Bread

Microwave Power:	High	Low	Off
Oven Selector:	Off	Bake	Bake
Oven Temperature:	Off	450°F, preheated	450°F
Shelf Position:	2	2	2

1/4 cup butter	1 tablespoon baking powder
2 eggs	1-1/2 teaspoons salt
1 cup (8-oz. can) whole kernel corn, drained	1 can (4-oz.) peeled green chiles
1 cup dairy sour cream	1 cup grated Cheddar cheese
1 cup yellow cornmeal	

Melt butter in a 1-1/2-quart mixing bowl with Microwave on High, 45 seconds to 1 minute. Preheat oven. Beat in eggs, corn and sour cream. Combine cornmeal, baking powder and salt. Stir in dry ingredients until well blended. Pour half the batter into a greased 8-inch square glass baking dish. Place the chiles and half the cheese over batter. Spread with remaining batter and top with remaining cheese. Bake at 450° with Microwave on Low, 2 minutes. Rotate dish 1/4 turn and continue to Bake with Microwave on Low, 2 minutes. Turn Microwave Off, Bake 11 to 14 minutes, or until golden brown. Makes 9 pieces.

Cheese Olive Roll-ups

Microwave Power:	High	Low	Off
Oven Selector:	Off	Bake	Bake
Oven Temperature:	Off	500°F, preheated	500°F
Shelf Position:	3	3, remove glass insert	3

5 tablespoons butter
3 cups biscuit mix
1 tablespoon instant minced onion
3/4 cup milk
1/3 cup mayonnaise

1/8 teaspoon dillweed, crushed
Few dashes cayenne
1-1/2 to 2 cups grated Cheddar cheese
1 can (2-1/4-oz.) sliced olives, drained

Melt 2 tablespoons butter with Microwave on High, about 45 seconds; set aside. Soften remaining 3 tablespoons butter with Microwave on High, about 20 seconds. Remove glass insert and preheat oven. Cut the softened butter into biscuit mix and onion. Stir in milk to make a soft dough. Turn out onto a floured surface, knead 5 to 6 times and roll into a rectangle, 12 x 16 inches. Combine mayonnaise, dill and cayenne; spread onto surface of dough and sprinkle with cheese and olives. Roll up from short side; pinch to seal and cut into twelve 1-inch slices. Arrange in a greased 2-quart oblong baking dish placing largest rolls in corners and smallest rolls toward the center. Brush with reserved melted butter. Bake at 500° with Microwave on Low, 3-1/2 minutes. Turn Microwave Off and continue to Bake at 500°, 5 to 7 minutes or until center tests done with a toothpick and rolls are golden brown. Makes 12 rolls.

Yeast Breads

The basic baking method for yeast breads in the Thermatronic II oven is a simultaneous Low power and bake heat for the entire cooking time. Higher bake temperatures are used to achieve browning in the shortened baking time. If the bread tests done—sounds hollow when tapped and an inserted toothpick comes out clean—but is not sufficiently browned, turn off the oven and allow bread to stand in hot oven a few minutes until browned.

Many of these bread recipes follow the conventional or straight dough methods. Water or other liquid is heated to 105°F to 115°F (for best results use a thermometer) to dissolve active dry yeast. Water or other liquid should be heated to 80°F to 90°F for compressed yeast. If milk is pasturized it need not be scalded, but is heated very hot to melt butter and dissolve sugar. This helps insure all ingredients to be warm, so yeast will grow properly. Also try the short-cut recipes and hot roll mix recipes.

The amount of flour used in many recipes is not exact because moisture will vary, requiring slightly different amounts of flour each time the recipe is prepared. Add last flour slowly until dough is no longer sticky. Knead in additional flour if necessary. Knead dough thoroughly until it is very smooth. Oil or grease dough to keep it from drying out and cover with a dry towel to rise. Let dough rise until doubled or until a dent remains when top is pressed gently. Punch dough down. Form loaves, let rise again but do not let rise too much. Bubbles in the surface of the dough are an indication of too much rising. If this occurs, for best results, punch dough down and reshape loaves, let rise again. A dough with fruit, nuts or whole wheat flour will take longer to rise than a plain dough.

Bake yeast breads in well greased (do not use oil) glass baking dishes only. Place dishes in oven with handles placed right to left. If more than one loaf is baking at a time, allow at least one inch of space all around each dish. Cool bread about 5 minutes, then remove from dish and cool on a wire rack out of any drafts. For easy slicing of warm bread, cut with an electric knife. Try several recipes from this book before converting your own favorite yeast bread recipes for use in the Thermatronic II.

Dark Wheat Germ Bread

Microwave Power:	High	Low
Oven Selector:	Off	Bake
Oven Temperature:	Off	425°F, preheated
Shelf Position:	2	2

1-1/2 cups warm water
2 pkg. active dry yeast
3 tablespoons sugar
2-1/2 teaspoons salt
1/3 cup butter
1/3 cup molasses

3/4 cup milk
1 cup wheat germ
3 cups unsifted whole wheat flour
3 cups unsifted white flour
1 egg yolk, beaten

Heat 1/4 cup of water with Microwave on High, about 1/2 to 3/4 minutes to 105° to 115°. Pour into mixing bowl, sprinkle yeast on water, let stand a few minutes; then stir until dissolved. In a 4-cup liquid measure combine remaining 1-1/4 cups water, sugar, salt, butter and molasses. Heat with Microwave on High, 2 to 3 minutes, until butter begins to melt. Cool to lukewarm. Heat milk with Microwave on High, 2 to 3 minutes. Pour hot milk over wheat germ. Cool to lukewarm. Stir cool water-butter mixture and wheat germ mixture into yeast. Combine wheat and white flours, add half to other ingredients, beat until smooth. Stir in remaining flour to form a soft dough. Turn onto a lightly floured board, knead until smooth and elastic. Place smooth side down in an oiled bowl; flip over to oil all sides of dough. Cover with a damp towel. Let rise in a warm place, free from drafts until doubled—about 1-1/2 hours. Punch down and divide into two equal portions. Shape into loaves and place in two greased 2-quart glass loaf dishes. Cover; let rise in a warm place until doubled—about 1 hour. Brush tops with beaten egg yolk. Place dishes in oven with handles right to left. Bake at 425°, with Microwave on Low, 8 to 11 minutes or until loaves test done. Cool on wire racks 5 minutes. Remove from dishes, continue to cool on wire racks. Makes 2 loaves.

Christmas Stollen, Dark Wheat Germ Bread, Swedish Cardamom Braid

Christmas Stollen

Microwave Power:	High	Low
Oven Selector:	Off	Bake
Oven Temperature:	Off	400°F, preheated
Shelf Position:	2	2

1 cup milk
1/2 cup (1 stick) butter
1/2 cup sugar
1 teaspoon salt
2 pkgs. active dry yeast
1/4 cup warm water (105° to 115°F)

4-1/2 cups sifted flour
3/4 teaspoon nutmeg
1-1/4 teaspoons cinnamon
1/2 cup seedless raisins
1/2 cup diced mixed candied fruit
1/4 cup chopped almonds

Confectioner's Frosting:
1 cup powdered sugar (sift if lumpy)

2 tablespoons milk

In a 4-cup liquid measure heat milk and butter with Microwave on High, 3 to 4 minutes until milk is hot and butter melts. Stir in sugar and salt; cool to lukewarm. In large bowl of electric mixer sprinkle yeast over warm water. Let stand a few minutes, then stir to dissolve. Stir milk mixture into yeast mixture. Add 2 cups of flour and mix until smooth with electric mixer. Add nutmeg, cinnamon, raisins, candied fruit and almonds. Mix at low speed, slowly adding 2 more cups of flour. Scrape down sides of bowl as needed. Stir in remaining 1/2 cup of flour to form a soft dough. Turn dough onto a lightly floured board, knead 10 minutes. Place dough smooth side down in an oiled bowl, flip dough over to oil all sides. Cover with a towel; let rise in a warm place—about 1-1/2 hours or until doubled. Punch dough down and turn onto lightly floured board. Knead lightly about 1 minute. Cut dough in half, form into two balls. Place both in a greased 3-quart oblong baking dish. Cover. Let rise about 1 hour. Bake at 400° with Microwave on Low, 10 to 13 minutes or until loaves are brown and sound hollow when tapped. Cool 5 minutes in baking dish. Remove bread to wire rack; continue to cool 10 to 15 minutes. Frost loaves with Confectioner's Frosting and decorate with candied fruits, if desired. Makes 2 round loaves.

Confectioner's Frosting:
Combine sugar and milk in a small bowl. Stir until smooth.

Swedish Cardamom Braid

Microwave Power:	High	Low
Oven Selector:	Off	Bake
Oven Temperature:	Off	450°F, preheated
Shelf Position:	2	2

2 pkg. active dry yeast
1/2 cup warm water (105° to 115°F)
1/2 cup milk
3/4 cup butter
1 teaspoon salt
1/2 cup sugar

2 eggs, beaten
5 to 5-1/2 cups sifted flour
1-1/2 teaspoons ground cardamom
1/2 cup golden raisins
1 egg white, beaten
2 tablespoons sugar

In a large mixing bowl, sprinkle yeast over warm water. Let stand a few minutes; then stir to dissolve. Heat milk in a 2-cup liquid measure with Microwave on High, 1-1/2 to 2 minutes. Add butter, salt and sugar to hot milk, let stand to melt butter. Then cool. To yeast mixture add cooled milk mixture, eggs, 3 cups flour and cardamom. Beat until smooth with mixer at low speed. Stir in raisins and enough remaining flour to make a soft dough. Turn dough onto a lightly floured board. Knead until smooth and elastic, about 3 to 5 minutes. Turn smooth side down into an oiled bowl; flip over to coat all sides of dough. Cover. Let rise in a warm place, free from drafts, until doubled in bulk—about 1 to 1-1/4 hours. Punch dough down and turn onto lightly floured board. Divide dough in half, then divide each half into thirds. Roll each third into a strip 10 inches long. Braid three strips together to form a loaf; pinch ends together and tuck under slightly. Place each loaf in a greased 2-quart oblong baking dish or a 2-quart glass loaf dish. Cover; let rise until doubled—about 45 minutes to 1 hour. Brush top of each loaf with egg white beaten with 2 tablespoons sugar. Sprinkle with additional sugar, if desired. Place dishes in oven with handles right to left. Bake at 450° with Microwave on Low, 7 to 9 minutes or until loaves test done. Cool on a wire rack 5 minutes. Remove from dishes and continue to cool on wire rack. Makes 2 loaves.

Milk & Egg Bread

Microwave Power:	High	Low
Oven Selector:	Off	Bake
Oven Temperature:	Off	450°F, preheated
Shelf Position:	2	2

1/2 cup milk	1 pkg. active dry yeast
1-1/2 tablespoons sugar	1/4 cup warm water (105° to 115°F)
1-1/2 tablespoons butter	1 egg
1 teaspoon salt	2-3/4 to 3 cups sifted flour

In a 2-cup liquid measure heat milk with Microwave on High, 2 to 3 minutes, or until it is just below boiling (190° to 200°F). Add sugar, butter, and salt; cool to lukewarm. In large bowl of electric mixer sprinkle yeast over water. Let stand a few minutes; stir to dissolve. Add cooled milk mixture and egg. Add 2 cups of flour slowly, while beating at low speed. Stir in enough remaining flour to form a soft dough. Turn onto a lightly floured board and knead 10 minutes, kneading in additional flour if necessary, until dough is smooth and elastic. Place dough smooth-side down in an oiled bowl; flip over to coat all sides. Cover; let rise in a warm place until doubled—3/4 to 1 hour. Punch dough down and knead about one minute. Shape into a loaf. Place in a greased 2-quart loaf dish. Let rise until dough reaches top of dish—about 1/2 hour. Brush top with soft butter. Bake at 450° with Microwave on Low, 6 to 8 minutes. Cool in dish on a rack 5 minutes, remove bread from dish, continue to cool on a rack. Makes 1 loaf.

Rich Raisin Bread

Microwave Power:	Low
Oven Selector:	Bake
Oven Temperature:	450°F, preheated
Shelf Position	2

Follow directions for Milk and Egg Bread. Allow dough to rise once; punch down. Then knead 2/3 cup raisins into dough. Knead about 5 minutes or until raisins are well distributed throughout dough. Shape into a loaf and place in a greased 2-quart loaf dish. Let rise until dough just reaches top of dish—about 45 minutes. Brush top with soft butter and sprinkle with sugar. Bake at 450° with Microwave on Low, 7 to 9 minutes. Cool in dish on a rack; remove bread from dish and continue to cool on a rack. Makes 1 loaf.

Jewish Challah Bread

Microwave Power:	**Low**
Oven Selector:	**Bake**
Oven Temperature:	**450°F, preheated**
Shelf Position:	**2**

Follow directions for Milk and Egg Bread. Allow dough to rise once; punch down. Knead dough lightly a few times, then divide into thirds. Form each part into a strand about 12 inches long. Place lengthwise in a well greased 3-quart oblong baking dish. Braid loosely; pinch ends together and tuck under. Brush top with soft butter. Let rise until doubled—about 30 to 40 minutes. Brush top with one egg yolk beaten with 1 tablespoon water. Sprinkle poppy seeds or sesame seeds over top. Bake at 450° with Microwave on Low, 6 to 8 minutes. Cool bread on a wire rack. Makes 1 loaf.

Defrosting Frozen Bread Dough

Microwave Power:	**Low**
Oven Selector:	**Off**
Oven Temperature:	**Off**
Shelf Position:	**2**

1 loaf (1 lb.) frozen yeast bread dough

Wrap frozen loaf loosely in paper towels or waxed paper. Place in 1-1/2-quart loaf dish. Defrost with Microwave on Low, 2 minutes. Turn dough over after 1 minute. Let stand 10 minutes. If dough is unworkable, defrost with Microwave on Low, 15 to 30 seconds longer. Let stand 10 minutes.

Baking Frozen Bread Dough

Microwave Power:	**Low**
Oven Selector:	**Bake**
Oven Temperature:	**400°F, preheated**
Shelf Position:	**2**

1 loaf (1-lb.) frozen yeast bread dough

Place loaf of frozen bread dough in greased 1-1/2-quart glass loaf dish. Prepare loaf as package directs. Let rise until doubled in size. Bake at 400° with Microwave on Low, 6 to 8 minutes or until bread sounds hollow when tapped.

For 2 loaves let rise, then Bake at 400° with Microwave on Low, 8 to 11 minutes.

For individual loaf (5-3/4-ounces) let rise, then Bake at 425° with Microwave on Low, 4 to 5 minutes.

Garlic-Parmesan Bubble Loaf from Hot Roll Mix

Microwave Power:	Low
Oven Selector:	Bake
Oven Temperature:	400°F, preheated
Shelf Position:	2

1 pkg. (13-3/4-oz.) Hot Roll Mix   1/2 teaspoon garlic powder
1/3 cup butter or margarine, melted   2/3 cup grated Parmesan cheese

Prepare Hot Roll Mix Basic Recipe dough according to package directions. Let dough rise once; punch down. Knead a few times on a floured board. Divide dough in half and divide each half into 16 pieces. Form each piece into a ball. Dip balls in melted butter mixed with garlic powder; then dip in Parmesan cheese. Arrange balls in layers in a well-greased 2-quart loaf dish. Let rise until doubled—45 to 60 minutes. Bake at 400° with Microwave on Low, 6-1/2 to 9 minutes, or until loaf is brown and tests done. Makes 1 loaf.

Hot Roll Mix — Pan Rolls or Cloverleaf Rolls

Microwave Power:	Low
Oven Selector:	Bake
Oven Temperature:	475°F, preheated
Shelf Position:	2

1 pkg. (13-3/4-oz.) Hot Roll Mix

Prepare Hot Roll Mix Basic Recipe dough according to package directions. Let dough rise once; punch down. Knead a few times on a floured board. Divide dough into 15, for large rolls, or 24, for small rolls, and shape into balls. Place in a greased 3-quart oblong baking dish. Do not bake rolls in a METAL pan or METAL muffin pans. For Cloverleaf Rolls, dip scissors in flour and cut each ball in half, then in quarters, cutting through almost to bottom. Let rise until doubled—30 to 45 minutes. Bake at 475° with Microwave on Low, 5 to 7 minutes. Makes 15 or 24 rolls.

Quick Sticky Pecan Rolls

Microwave Power:	High	Low	Off
Oven Selector:	Off	Bake	Bake
Oven Temperature:	Off	450°F, preheated	450°F
Shelf Position:	2	2	2

1 pkg. active dry yeast
1/4 cup sugar
2 cups biscuit mix

1 to 1-1/4 cups sifted flour
2/3 cup milk
1/4 cup butter

Syrup:
1/2 cup brown sugar, firmly packed
1/4 cup butter

2 tablespoons dark corn syrup

Filling:
1/4 cup butter, melted

1/3 cup brown sugar, firmly packed

3/4 cup chopped pecans

Combine yeast, sugar, biscuit mix and 1 cup flour in a large mixing bowl. In a 2-cup liquid measure combine milk and 1/4 cup butter. Heat with Microwave on High, 2-1/2 to 3 minutes, to heat milk and melt butter. Cool mixture slightly (120° to 130°). Add liquid slowly to flour mixture while beating at low speed of an electric mixer. Continue to beat until a soft dough is formed, adding up to 1/4 cup additional flour if dough is too sticky. Turn dough onto a lightly floured board, knead about ten times. Let dough rest while preparing syrup.

Combine brown sugar, 1/4 cup butter and corn syrup in a 4-cup liquid measure. Cook with Microwave on High, 2 to 3 minutes or until mixture boils rapidly. Set aside to cool slightly.

Roll out dough to a rectangle about 1/2-inch thick. Brush with 1/4 cup melted butter, then spread brown sugar evenly over all. Starting at wide edge roll up dough, pinching edge to seal. Cut into rolls about 3/4-inch thick.

Pour slightly cooled syrup into bottom of a well greased 2-quart oblong baking dish. Sprinkle with chopped pecans. Place rolls about 3/4-inch apart on top of syrup and nuts. Cover; let rise in a warm place 30 to 45 minutes or until doubled. Bake at 450°, with Microwave on Low, 5 to 7 minutes, or until a toothpick inserted in rolls comes out clean. Turn Microwave Off and Bake an additional 2 to 3 minutes if needed for browning. Cool on a wire rack 5 minutes, then invert dish onto a cookie sheet or large platter. Let dish stand inverted 1 minute then lift off. Cool slightly and serve. Makes 12 to 14 rolls.

Whole Wheat Batter Bread

Microwave Power:	Low	Off
Oven Selector:	Bake	Bake
Oven Temperature:	450°F, preheated	450°F
Shelf Position:	2	2

1 pkg. active dry yeast
1-1/4 cups warm water (105° to 115°F)
2 tablespoons butter
1-1/2 teaspoons salt

2 tablespoons honey, brown sugar
  or light molasses
1-1/2 cups unsifted whole wheat flour
1-1/2 cups sifted white flour

In large bowl of an electric mixer, sprinkle yeast over warm water. Let stand a few minutes; stir to dissolve. Add butter and salt. Add honey, brown sugar or light molasses and whole wheat flour. Beat two minutes. Then gradually add white flour; beat until smooth, scraping side of bowl often. Cover bowl and let rise in a warm place until doubled—about 1 hour. Stir batter down; spread into a greased 2-quart loaf dish. Smooth top of dough with an oiled spatula. Let rise until dough reaches top of dish. Bake at 450° with Microwave on Low, 6 to 7-1/2 minutes or until loaf sounds hollow when tapped. Brush top loaf with melted butter. Turn Microwave Off, continue to Bake at 450°, 2 to 3 minutes or until nicely browned. Cool dish on wire rack 5 minutes; remove from dish. Continue to cool on wire rack. Makes 1 loaf.

White Batter Bread

Microwave Power:	Low	Off
Oven Selector:	Bake	Bake
Oven Temperature:	450°F, preheated	450°F
Shelf Position:	2	2

1 pkg. active dry yeast
1-1/4 cups warm water
  (105° to 115°F)
2 tablespoons butter

1-1/2 teaspoons salt
2 tablespoons sugar
3 cups sifted flour

In large electric mixer bowl, sprinkle yeast over warm water. Let stand a few minutes; stir to dissolve. Add butter, salt, sugar and 2 cups of flour. Beat two minutes, then gradually add remaining flour; beat until smooth, scraping sides of bowl often. Cover bowl and let rise in a warm place until doubled—about 45 minutes. Stir batter down; spread into a greased 2-quart loaf dish. Smooth top of dough with an oiled spatula. Let rise until dough reaches top of dish. Bake at 450° with Microwave on Low, 6 to 7-1/2 minutes or until loaf sounds hollow when tapped. Brush top of loaf with melted butter. Turn Microwave Off, continue to Bake at 450°, 2 to 3 minutes or until nicely browned. Let dish cool on wire rack 5 minutes; remove from dish. Continue to cool on wire rack. Makes 1 loaf.

Really Quick Yeast Biscuits

Microwave Power:	High	Low
Oven Selector:	Off	Bake
Oven Temperature:	Off	450°F, preheated
Shelf Position:	2	2

2/3 cup milk
1 pkg. active dry yeast
2 tablespoons sugar

2 tablespoons butter, melted
2 to 2-1/2 cups biscuit mix

Heat milk to lukewarm (105° to 115°) with Microwave on High, about 1 minute. Sprinkle yeast over milk, let stand a few minutes; stir to dissolve yeast. Combine yeast-milk mixture, sugar, butter and 2 cups biscuit mix in a bowl. Gradually stir in enough additional biscuit mix to form a soft dough. Turn out on a lightly floured board; knead a few times until smooth and elastic. Roll out to 1/2-inch thick, cut with biscuit cutter. Place biscuits in a greased 2-quart oblong baking dish with sides touching, but not crowded. Let rise until doubled—about 20 to 30 minutes. Bake at 450° with Microwave on Low, 4 to 6 minutes, or until biscuits test done. Makes 12 to 15 biscuits.

Basic Rapidmix White Bread

Microwave Power:	High	Low
Oven Selector:	Off	Bake
Oven Temperature:	Off	450°F, preheated
Shelf Position:	2	2

5 to 6 cups sifted flour
3 tablespoons sugar
2 teaspoons salt
1 pkg. active dry yeast

1 cup milk
1 cup water
1/4 cup butter

In a large bowl of an electric mixer, combine 2 cups flour, sugar, salt and yeast. In a 4-cup liquid measure, combine milk, water and butter; heat with Microwave on High, 4 to 5 minutes or until liquid is very hot and butter starts to melt. Cool to 120° to 130°. Pour into flour mixture; beat at medium speed 2 minutes, scraping side of bowl often. Add 1 cup flour, beat 2 minutes. Slowly add 1-1/2 cups flour, beating at high speed, to form a thick batter. Stir in enough additional flour to form a soft dough. Turn dough onto a floured board; knead until smooth and elastic, about 10 minutes, kneading in additional flour if necessary. Place dough in a greased bowl, smooth side down; flip over to grease all sides. Cover; let rise in a warm place until doubled—about one hour.

Punch down; turn onto a lightly floured board and knead a few times. For a finer grained bread, punch dough down and let rise again in bowl until doubled—about 1 hour. Divide dough in half and shape into loaves. Place each loaf in a greased 1-1/2-quart loaf dish. Brush tops of loaves with melted butter. Cover; let rise until dough is about 1/2 inch from top of dish. Place both loaf dishes in oven with handles right to left. Bake at 450° with Microwave on Low, 7-1/2 to 9 minutes, or until loaves sound hollow when tapped and are nicely browned. Let loaves cool 5 minutes in baking dishes; turn out and cool on wire rack. Makes 2 loaves.

Almond Butter Kuchen

Microwave Power:	High	Low
Oven Selector:	Off	Bake
Oven Temperature:	Off	425°F, preheated
Shelf Position:	2	2

3/4 cup milk
1/2 cup (1 stick) butter
1/2 cup sugar
1-1/2 teaspoons salt

2 pkgs. active dry yeast
1/2 cup warm water (105°-115°F)
1 egg
4 cups sifted flour

Topping:
1/2 cup (1 stick) butter, melted
1/2 cup sugar
1 tablespoon flour

1/2 teaspoon almond extract
1/3 cup chopped almonds

Heat milk in a 4-cup liquid measure with Microwave on High, 2-1/2 to 3 minutes or until milk reaches 190° to 200°. Add butter, sugar and salt; cool to lukewarm. In large bowl of electric mixer sprinkle yeast over water. Let stand a few minutes, then stir to dissolve yeast. Add cooled milk mixture and egg to yeast mixture. Beat at low speed, adding flour, one cup at a time, to form a soft dough. Scrape down sides of bowl forming a large ball. Cover bowl; set in a warm place free from drafts. Let rise until doubled—about 1 hour. Press dough down. Spready evenly into a greased 3-quart oblong baking dish. Use a butter spatula for easy spreading.

Combine topping ingredients and pour over dough. Then with fingers make deep indentations all over top, spacing about one inch apart. Cover; let rise until doubled—about 45 minutes. Just before baking, make more indentations as described above. Bake at 425° with Microwave on Low, 8 to 10 minutes or until coffee cake tests done. Cool slightly, cut into 24 pieces. Serve warm.

Cinnamon Coffee Braid

Microwave Power:	High	Low
Oven Selector:	Off	Bake
Oven Temperature:	Off	450°F, preheated
Shelf Position:	2	2

Dough:

3/4 cup milk	1 pkg. active dry yeast
1/4 cup sugar	1 egg
1/4 cup (1/2 stick) butter	3 to 3-1/4 cups sifted flour
1 teaspoon salt	1/2 teaspoon cinnamon
2 tablespoons warm water (105° to 115°F)	

Filling:

1/4 cup (1/2 stick) soft butter	1-1/2 teaspoons cinnamon
1/2 cup sugar	1/4 teaspoon allspice

Topping:

2 tablespoons soft butter	3/4 teaspoon cinnamon
1/4 cup sugar	

In a 2-cup liquid measure heat milk with Microwave on High, 1-1/2 to 2 minutes or until milk is just below boiling (190° to 200°F). Add sugar, butter and salt; cool to lukewarm. Pour water into large bowl of an electric mixer. Sprinkle yeast over water and let stand a few minutes; stir to dissolve. Add cooled milk mixture to yeast, add egg, 2 cups flour and cinnamon. Beat until smooth, then stir in enough remaining flour to form a soft dough. Turn dough onto a lightly floured board and knead until smooth and elastic. Place smooth-side down in an oiled bowl, flip over to coat all sides. Cover and let rise in a warm place until doubled—about 1 hour. Punch down and let rise again. Punch down and divide into thirds.

Roll out each part into a rectangle about 1/8-inch thick. Spread each with soft butter listed in Filling ingredients. Combine sugar, cinnamon and allspice for filling; sprinkle on each rectangle. Roll up each piece tightly from long side; pinch dough together at seam. Place in greased 3-quart oblong baking dish. Braid pieces together tightly; pinch ends together and tuck under.

Brush with soft butter listed in Topping ingredients. Combine sugar and cinnamon for topping and sprinkle over dough braid. Let rise until doubled—about 30 minutes. Bake at 450° with Microwave on Low, 7 to 9 minutes, or until bread tests done. Cool on wire rack. Makes 1 loaf.

Cakes

Most types of cakes may be prepared in the Thermatronic II with very good results. Cakes baked with a combination of heat and microwave often have a finer grain and moister texture than conventionally baked cakes. Total baking times are cut 1/3 to 1/2, depending on the type of cake. Higher oven temperatures are used to achieve good browning in the shorter baking times.

Best results are obtained with glass baking dishes, except in a few specific recipes, like chiffon cakes, where metal pans are used. In any recipe, baking time will vary according to the size of baking dish being used. To prepare dish, grease bottom only, unless otherwise specified. Layer cake dishes should be greased and lined with a piece of waxed paper cut to fit the bottom of the dish. Place square and oblong dishes in oven with handles positioned right to left. Two round layer dishes should be positioned one to the rear and to one side, the other to the front and to the opposite side, with at least one inch of space all around each dish.

Cakes prepared from "scratch" will give the best results if recipes are followed exactly and carefully. Use room temperature ingredients. Cream shortening, sugar and eggs thoroughly; beat all ingredients for length of time specified in recipe. Thick batter cakes produce the best results. Try a few "scratch" recipes from this cookbook before converting your own favorites to the combination oven.

Generally, a bake time, in a preheated oven, 25°F or more above conventional bake times are used to "set" the cake batter. Then microwave power is added to quickly finish the cooking. For example, in a standard shortening cake, two 8-inch layers are baked at 375°F for 18 minutes or one 3-quart oblong layer at 375°F for 20 minutes, then Medium microwave power is added for 1 to 3 minutes or until the cake tests done. As a rule-of-thumb, a too high bake temperature or a too short bake time, or both, will result in unevenly shaped cakes, bubbled tops, cracks and boiled-up centers. Other types of cakes are baked with different methods. Consult specific scratch or mix recipes.

Most cake mixes can be baked in the Thermatronic II with good results and some time savings. Instructions are included in this section for many of the popular cake mixes. However some mixes may react differently than predicted due to formulation changes by the manufacturer. Glass baking dishes are used for most cake mixes, except when otherwise indicated, as in Angel Food cakes. Glass and ceramic 10-cup Bundt dishes were used for Bundt and Streusel dessert cakes. If this type of dish is not available, these cakes may be prepared in a 3-quart oblong baking dish or baked conventionally in a metal Bundt pan.

Angel Roll

Microwave Power:	Low	Off
Oven Selector:	Bake	Bake
Oven Temperature:	375°F, preheated	375°F
Shelf Position:	2	2

1/2 pkg. (14-1/2-oz.) 2-step angel food
   cake mix

Powdered sugar

Filling:

1 to 2 cups sliced fresh fruit (strawberries,
   peaches, apricots, bananas, raspberries, etc.)
1/2 cup reserved whole or large pieces
   of fruit for garnish
1 cup (1/2 pt.) whipping cream

1 teaspoon vanilla
Dash salt
2 tablespoons powdered sugar
2 tablespoons sliced nuts

Line a 15-1/2" x 10-1/2" METAL jelly roll pan with waxed paper. Allow paper to extend about 1-1/2" at ends. Generously grease waxed paper with butter or shortening. Prepare two-step angel food cake mix as directed on the package, using only 1/2 of the ingredients. Turn batter into prepared pan. Spread evenly, being sure corners are filled with batter. Place in oven crosswise. Bake at 375° with Microwave on Low, 1-1/2 minutes. Rotate pan 1/4 turn. Continue to Bake at 375° with Microwave on Low, 1-1/2 minutes longer. Turn Microwave Off. Continue to Bake at 375° 5 to 7 minutes, or until golden brown. While cake is baking, sift powdered sugar onto a clean tea towel in 15" x 10" rectangle. When cake is done, immediately invert onto sugared area. Gently peel off waxed paper. Starting with narrow edge, loosely roll cake in towel. Place seam side down on wire cooling rack. Cool. Gently unroll cake; remove towel. Spread with fruit and cream filling or other desired filling.

Filling:

Prepare fruit and chill. Combine cream, vanilla and salt. Beat until frothy; gradually add sugar and beat until stiff. Spread 3/4 of whipped cream over cake roll, spreading to within an inch of the edge. Sprinkle with fruit.

Reroll cake. Decorate with the rest of the cream and reserved fruit. Sprinkle with sliced nuts. Place seam side down on serving plate. Chill at least 1 hour. Makes 8 to 10 servings.

Angel Food Cake Mix *(One Step)*

Microwave Power:	Off	Low	Off
Oven Selector:	Bake	Bake	Bake
Oven Temperature:	375°F, preheated	375°F	400°F
Shelf Position:	1	1	1

1 pkg. (16-oz.) 1-step angel food cake mix

Prepare 1-step angle food cake mix as directed on package, using an ungreased 10-inch METAL tube pan. Bake at 375°, 22 minutes. Continue to Bake at 375° with Microwave on Low, 4-1/2 to 5 minutes. If extra browning is necessary turn Microwave Off and Bake at 400°, 3 to 5 minutes.

Angel Food Cake Mix *(Two Step)*

Microwave Power:	Low	Off
Oven Selector:	Bake	Bake
Oven Temperature:	400°F, preheated	400°F
Shelf Position:	2	2

1 pkg. (14-1/2-oz.) 2-step angel food cake mix

Prepare 2-step angel food cake mix as directed on package, using an ungreased 10-inch METAL tube pan. Bake at 400° with Microwave on Low, 3 minutes. Rotate pan 1/2 turn. Continue to Bake at 400° with Microwave on Low for an additional 3 minutes. Turn Microwave Off. Continue to Bake, 8 to 10 minutes or until top crust is golden brown. Place cake pan upside down and cool completely before removing from pan.

Quick Pineapple Upside Down Cake

Microwave Power:	High	Off	Medium
Oven Selector:	Off	Bake	Bake
Oven Temperature:	Off	375°F, preheated	375°F
Shelf Position:	2	2	2

1/3 cup butter
1/2 cup brown sugar, firmly packed
1 can (20-oz.) crushed pineapple

6 to 10 Maraschino cherries
1 pkg. (9-oz.) single layer yellow cake mix

In a 1-1/2-quart round cake dish melt butter with Microwave on High about 1 minute. Preheat oven. Stir brown sugar into butter and spread evenly in dish. Drain pineapple, reserving liquid and 1/4 cup of pineapple. Pour remaining pineapple over butter-brown sugar mixture, arrange cherries over pineapple. Prepare cake mix according to package directions, substituting pineapple liquid for water. Stir reserved crushed pineapple into batter and pour into dish. Bake at 375°, 15 minutes. Then continue to Bake at 375° with Microwave on Medium, 3 to 6 minutes or until cake tests done. Cool 10 minutes, loosen edges, invert on serving plate. Makes 6 to 8 servings.

Cake from a Mix

Microwave Power:	Off	Medium
Oven Selector:	Bake	Bake
Oven Temperature:	375°F, preheated	375°F
Shelf Position:	2	2

1 pkg. (18-1/2-oz.) cake mix

Grease a 3-quart oblong baking dish or two 1-1/2-quart round cake dishes. Cut waxed paper to fit bottoms of round cake dishes. Prepare mix as package directs, do not overmix. Pour batter into prepared baking dish or dishes. Place oblong baking dish on oven shelf with handles positioned right to left or stagger two-layer dishes in back and front of oven, leaving at least one inch of space between the two dishes and sides of oven. Bake at 375°, 15 minutes; then add Microwave on Medium and continue to Bake at 375°, 1 to 3 minures or until cake tests done. Cool 10 minutes on wire rack before removing from dish.

Chocolate Upside Down Cake

Microwave Power:	Off	Medium
Oven Selector:	Bake	Bake
Oven Temperature:	400°F, preheated	400°F
Shelf Position:	2	2

1 cup light brown sugar, firmly packed
1/2 cup cocoa
2 cups water
12 marshmallows, quartered

1 pkg. (18-1/2-oz.) devil's food cake mix
1 cup chopped nuts
Whipped cream

In an ungreased 3-quart oblong baking dish mix brown sugar and cocoa. Stir in water. Add marshmallows. Prepare cake mix following package directions. Spoon batter over the mixture in the dish, covering completely. Top with nuts. Bake at 400°, 10 minutes; then add Microwave on Medium and continue to Bake at 400°, 7 to 9 minutes or until cake tests done. Give dish a 1/4 turn after 5 minutes. When serving, turn cake pieces over so fudge-like mixture becomes a topping. Serve with whipped cream. Makes 12 to 15 servings.

Single Layer Cake from a Mix

Microwave Power:	Off	Medium
Oven Selector:	Bake	Bake
Oven Temperature:	375°F, preheated	375°F
Shelf Position:	2	2

1 pkg. (9-oz.) cake mix

Prepare mix according to package directions. Pour batter into prepared 1-1/2-quart round cake dish. Bake at 375°, 12 minutes. Continue to Bake at 375° with Microwave on Medium, 1 to 2 minutes or until cake tests done.

Classic White Cake

Microwave Power:	Off	Medium
Oven Selector:	Bake	Bake
Oven Temperature:	375°F, preheated	375°F
Shelf Position:	2	2

1/4 cup soft butter	3/4 teaspoon salt
1/4 cup soft shortening	1 cup milk
1-1/2 cups sugar	1 teaspoon vanilla
2-1/2 cups sifted flour	4 egg whites, stiffly beaten
2-1/2 teaspoons baking powder	

In large bowl of electric mixer, cream together butter, shortening and sugar until fluffy. Sift together flour, baking powder and salt. Add flour mixture and milk alternately to creamed mixture, beating well after each addition. Add vanilla and thoroughly fold in egg whites. Pour into 2 prepared 1-1/2-quart round cake dishes. Bake at 375°, 18 minutes. Continue to Bake at 375° with Microwave on Medium, 1 to 3 minutes or until cake tests done. Cool before frosting. Makes two 8-inch layers.

"Easy Do" Sour Cream Cake

Microwave Power:	Medium
Oven Selector:	Bake
Oven Temperature:	400°F, preheated
Shelf Position:	2

4 eggs	3/4 cup cooking oil
1 box (2-layer size) yellow cake mix	1/2 cup sugar
1 cup (1/2 pt.) dairy sour cream	

Place eggs in large glass mixer bowl, beat 1 minute with electric mixer at medium speed. Add remaining ingredients, beat 4 minutes at medium speed. Pour into greased 3-quart oblong glass baking dish. Place dish with handles front to back. Bake at 400° with Microwave on Medium, 10 to 11 minutes, or until cake tests done.

Golden Cake

Microwave Power:	Off	Medium
Oven Selector:	Bake	Bake
Oven Temperature:	375°F, preheated	375°F
Shelf Position:	2	2

1/2 cup soft shortening	3/4 teaspoon salt
1-1/2 cups sugar	1 cup milk
2-1/4 cups sifted cake flour	1 teaspoon vanilla
3 teaspoons baking powder	2 eggs

In a large bowl of electric mixer, cream together shortening and sugar until light and fluffy. Sift together flour, baking powder and salt. Add flour mixture alternately with milk to creamed mixture; beat 2 minutes. Add vanilla and eggs; beat 2 minutes more. Pour into 2 prepared 1-1/2 quart-round cake dishes or a 3-quart oblong baking dish. Bake at 375°, 18 minutes for layer cakes, or 20 minutes for oblong baking dish. Then Bake at 375° with Microwave on Medium, 1 to 3 minutes or until cake tests done. Makes two 8-inch layers or one 13" x 9".

Variations:

Nutmeg Cake
Sift 2 teaspoons nutmeg with flour, baking powder and salt.

Butterscotch Cake
Substitute brown sugar for granulated sugar and use 1/4 cup shortening and 1/4 cup butter in place of 1/2 cup shortening in basic recipe.

Basic Bundt Cake Mix

Microwave Power:	Off	Medium
Oven Selector:	Bake	Bake
Oven Temperature:	375°F, preheated	375°F
Shelf Position:	2	2

1 pkg. (18-1/4-oz.) Basic Bundt Cake Mix

Prepare mix according to package directions. Pour batter into a well greased glass tube dish or 3-quart oblong baking dish. Bake at 375°, 20 minutes in glass tube dish, or 15 minutes in 3-quart oblong dish. Continue to Bake at 375° with Microwave on Medium, 2 to 5 minutes or until cake tests done. Cool according to package directions.

One Bowl Vanilla Cake

Microwave Power:	Off	Medium
Oven Selector:	Bake	Bake
Oven Temperature:	375°F, preheated	375°F
Shelf Position:	2	2

2-1/4 cups sifted cake flour
1-1/2 cups sugar
3-1/2 teaspoons baking powder
3/4 teaspoon salt

1/2 cup soft shortening
1 cup milk
1-1/2 teaspoons vanilla
4 egg whites

In large bowl of an electric mixer, sift together flour, sugar, baking powder and salt. Add shortening and 2/3 cup of milk; beat two minutes, scraping sides of bowl often. Add remaining 1/3 cup milk, vanilla and egg whites; beat two minutes. Pour batter into 2 prepared 1-1/2-quart round cake dishes. Bake at 375°, 18 minutes. Then continue to Bake at 375° with Microwave on Medium, 1 to 3 minutes or until cake tests done. Cool before frosting. Makes two 8-inch layers.

Spice Cake

Microwave Power:	Off	Medium
Oven Selector:	Bake	Bake
Oven Temperature:	375°F, preheated	375°F
Shelf Position:	2	2

1/2 cup soft shortening
1-1/2 cups sugar
2-1/4 cups sifted cake flour
3 teaspoons baking powder
1-1/2 teaspoons cinnamon
3/4 teaspoon salt

1/2 teaspoon allspice
1/2 teaspoon cloves
1/2 teaspoon nutmeg
1 cup milk
1 teaspoon vanilla
2 eggs

In large bowl of electric mixer, cream together shortening and sugar until light and fluffy. Sift together flour, baking powder, cinnamon, salt, allspice, cloves and nutmeg. Add flour mixture alternately with milk to creamed mixture; beat 2 minutes. Add vanilla and eggs; beat 2 minutes more. Pour into 2 prepared 1-1/2-quart round cake dishes or a 3-quart oblong baking dish. Bake at 375°, 18 minutes for layer cakes, or 20 minutes for oblong baking dish. Then continue to Bake at 375° with Microwave on Medium, 1 to 3 minutes or until cake tests done. Makes two 8-inch layers or one 13" x 9".

Nana's Dark Chocolate Cake

Microwave Power:	High	Off	Medium
Oven Selector:	Off	Bake	Bake
Oven Temperature:	Off	400°F, preheated	400°F
Shelf Position:	2	2	2

1/3 cup shortening
5 tablespoons cocoa
1 cup sugar
1 egg

1-1/2 cups sifted flour
2 teaspoons baking soda
1 cup sweet milk

Frosting:

1/4 cup cocoa
1-1/2 cups powdered sugar

1/4 cup half and half
1 teaspoon vanilla

In large glass bowl of electric mixer melt shortening and cocoa with Microwave on High, 2-1/2 to 3 minutes. Add sugar; cream thoroughly. Mix in egg, beating until fluffy. Sift flour and baking soda together; add to creamed mixture alternately with sweet milk. Pour batter into greased 8-inch square cake dish. Bake at 400°, 10 minutes; then add Microwave on Medium, 4 to 5 minutes, or until cake tests done. Immediately frost hot cake with the frosting. Makes one 8-inch square cake.

Frosting:
Place all ingredients in small glass bowl of electric mixer and combine thoroughly. Spread over hot cake.

Streusel Swirl Dessert Cake Mix

Microwave Power:	Off	Medium
Oven Selector:	Bake	Bake
Oven Temperature:	375°F, preheated	375°F
Shelf Position:	2	2

1 pkg. (27-1/4-oz.) Streusel Swirl Dessert Cake Mix

Prepare mix according to package directions. Assemble batter and streusel mixture as directed on the package. Pour into a well greased glass tube dish or 3-quart oblong baking dish. Bake at 375°, 20 minutes in a glass tube dish, or 15 minutes in 3-quart oblong dish. Continue to Bake at 375° with Microwave on Medium, 2 to 5 minutes or until cake tests done. Cool according to package directions.

Pearl's Mocha Date Cake

Microwave Power:	High	Off	Medium
Oven Selector:	Off	Bake	Bake
Oven Temperature:	Off	400°F, preheated	400°F
Shelf Position:	2	2	2

1 cup hot coffee
3/4 cup (1/2 lb.) dates, cut up
1 teaspoon baking soda
1/2 cup (1 stick) butter
1 cup sugar
2 eggs

1 teaspoon vanilla
1-3/4 cups sifted flour
2 tablespoons cocoa
1/8 teaspoon salt
1 pkg. (6-oz.) semi-sweet chocolate pieces
1/2 cup chopped nuts

Bring coffee to a boil in a 4-cup liquid measure with Microwave on High, 1-1/2 to 2 minutes. Add dates and soda; stir and cool. Preheat oven. With a mixer cream butter, sugar, eggs and vanilla. Sift together flour, cocoa and salt. Alternately add date mixture and flour mixture to cream mixture. Pour into a greased 2-quart oblong baking dish. Sprinkle top with chocolate pieces and nuts. Bake at 400°, 10 minutes; then add Microwave on Medium and continue to Bake at 400°, 6 to 9 minutes or until cake tests done with a toothpick. Makes 15 to 18 servings.

German Chocolate Cake

Microwave Power:	High	Off	Medium
Oven Selector:	Off	Bake	Bake
Oven Temperature:	Off	400°F, preheated	400°F
Shelf Position:	2	2	2

1 bar (4-oz.) sweet cooking chocolate
1/3 cup water
1/2 cup (1 stick) butter
1 cup sugar
3 eggs

1 teaspoon vanilla
1-3/4 cups sifted flour
1 teaspoon soda
1/2 teaspoon salt
2/3 cup buttermilk

Combine chocolate and water in a 2-cup liquid measure. Melt with Microwave on High, 2 to 2-1/2 minutes, stirring twice; cool. Cream butter and sugar until fluffy; gradually beat in eggs one at a time. Blend in chocolate mixture and vanilla. Sift together dry ingredients and add to creamed mixture alternately with buttermilk. Pour batter into two greased and waxed paper lined 1-1/2-quart round cake dishes. Bake at 400°, 10 minutes. Then add Microwave on Medium and continue to Bake at 400°, 3-1/2 to 5 minutes or until toothpick tests clean. Cool 10 minutes. Turn onto a cooling rack and cool. Frost with German Pecan Frosting. Makes 12 servings.

Applesauce Raisin Cake

Microwave Power:	Off	Medium
Oven Selector:	Bake	Bake
Oven Temperature:	375°F, preheated	375°F
Shelf Position:	2	2

1/2 cup shortening
1 cup brown sugar, firmly packed
2 eggs, beaten
2 cups sifted cake flour
1 teaspoon baking soda
1 teaspoon cinnamon
1/2 teaspoon salt

1/2 teaspoon cloves
1/2 teaspoon nutmeg
1/4 teaspoon baking powder
2/3 cup chopped raisins
2/3 cup chopped nuts
1-1/2 cups applesauce

Cream shortening and sugar until fluffy, add eggs and beat thoroughly. Sift dry ingredients together. Stir raisins and nuts into flour mixture. Add alternately with applesauce to creamed mixture, beating well after each addition. Pour batter into a greased 2-quart oblong baking dish. Bake at 375°, 20 minutes. Then continue to Bake at 375° with Microwave on Medium, 3 to 6 minutes or until cake tests done. Makes 1 loaf.

Two-Step Bundt Cake Mix

Microwave Power:	Off	Medium
Oven Selector:	Bake	Bake
Oven Temperature:	375°F, preheated	375°F
Shelf Position:	2	2

1 pkg. (23-1/2 to 27-1/4-oz.) Two-Step Bundt Cake Mix*

Prepare mix according to package directions. Assemble batters as directed on the package in a well greased glass tube dish. Bake at 375°, 25 minutes. Continue to Bake at 375° with Microwave on Medium, 3 to 6 minutes or until cake tests done. Cool according to package directions.
*Results may vary according to flavor, because each mix is formulated differently.

Favorite Pineapple-Carrot Cake

Microwave Power:	High	Off	Medium
Oven Selector:	Off	Bake	Bake
Oven Temperature:	Off	400°F, preheated	400°F
Shelf Position:	2	2	2

Buttermilk Syrup:

3/4 cup sugar
1/4 teaspoon baking soda
1/3 cup buttermilk

1/3 cup (2/3 stick) butter
2 teaspoons light corn syrup
1 teaspoon vanilla

Cake:

3 eggs
1/2 cup salad oil
3/4 cup buttermilk
2 teaspoons vanilla
2-1/4 cups sifted flour
1-1/2 cups sugar
2 tablespoons wheat germ (optional)
1 teaspoon baking soda

2 teaspoons cinnamon
1/2 teaspoon salt
1 can (8-oz.) crushed pineapple,
   well drained
2 cups finely grated carrots
1 cup chopped pecans
1 cup flaked coconut

Buttermilk Syrup:

Combine sugar, soda, buttermilk, butter and corn syrup in a 2-quart casserole. Cook with Microwave on High, 5 to 6 minutes, stirring every 2 minutes. Syrup will boil and turn light golden. Stir in vanilla and set aside. Preheat oven.

Cake:

Beat eggs with oil, buttermilk and vanilla. Stir in all remaining cake ingredients and pour into a greased 3-quart oblong baking dish. Bake at 400°, 10 minutes; then add Microwave on Medium and continue to Bake at 400°, 8 to 11 minutes or until toothpick tests clean. Remove cake from oven and lightly prick surface with a meat fork. Slowly pour hot buttermilk syrup over cake. If necessary, reheat syrup with Microwave on High, 1 to 1-1/2 minutes. Makes 15 servings.

Our Best Fruit Cake

Microwave Power:	Off	Low
Oven Selector:	Bake	Bake
Oven Temperature:	350°F, preheated	350°F
Shelf Position:	2	2

1-1/2 cups broken assorted nuts
3/4 cup candied cherries
1/2 cup diced citron
1/2 cup diced candied pineapple
1/2 cup raisins
1/4 cup candied diced lemon peel
1/4 cup candied diced orange peel
1/4 cup dry currants
3/4 cup brandy, sherry, pineapple, orange or apple juice
1-1/2 cups sifted all purpose flour

1-1/2 teaspoons salt
1 teaspoon cinnamon
1 teaspoon allspice
1/2 teaspoon baking powder
1/2 teaspoon cloves
1/2 teaspoon nutmeg
3/4 cup brown sugar, firmly packed
1/2 cup oil
2 eggs

Combine nuts, fruits and 1/2 cup brandy, sherry or fruit juice. Soak at least 24 hours, stirring occasionally. Stir 3/4 cup flour into fruit mixture, toss well to coat all fruit. Sift remaining 3/4 cup flour with salt, baking powder and spices. Beat sugar and oil together; add eggs and beat two minutes. Add sifted dry ingredients alternately with remaining brandy, sherry or fruit juice, beating well after each addition. Pour batter over fruit mixture and blend thoroughly. Pour into a greased 1-1/2-quart loaf dish. Bake at 350°, 20 minutes. Continue to Bake at 350° with Microwave on Low, 10 to 15 minutes or until cake tests done. Turn oven Off. Allow cake to stand in warm oven 5 to 10 minutes or until nicely browned. Cool. Wrap cake in cheesecloth that has been soaked in brandy or sherry. Place in plastic bag and let stand at least one week. Makes 1 loaf.

Gingerbread from a Mix

Microwave Power:	Off	Medium
Oven Selector:	Bake	Bake
Oven Temperature:	400°F, preheated	400°F
Shelf Position:	2	2

1 pkg. (14-oz.) Gingerbread Mix

Prepare Gingerbread Mix according to package directions. Pour into a greased 2-quart square baking dish. Bake at 400°, 10 minutes, then add Microwave on Medium and continue to Bake at 400°, 2 to 4 minutes or until gingerbread tests done.

Orange Sponge Cake

Microwave Power:	Low
Oven Selector:	Bake
Oven Temperature:	375°F, preheated
Shelf Position:	1

6 eggs at room temperature, separated
1-2/3 cups sugar
1 to 1-1/2 tablespoons grated orange peel
2/3 cup orange juice

1-3/4 cups sifted flour
3/4 teaspoon baking powder
1/8 teaspoon cream of tartar

Beat egg yolks until thick and lemon colored. Gradually beat in sugar, orange peel and orange juice. Sift together flour and baking powder, and beat into egg yolk mixture. Wash and dry beaters. Beat egg whites and cream of tartar until stiff but not dry. Fold into yolk mixture and pour into an ungreased 10-inch METAL tube pan. Bake at 375° with Microwave on Low, 15 to 19 minutes or until toothpick tests clean. Cool upright on a cooling rack. Makes 1 cake.

Almond Chiffon Cake

Microwave Power:	Low	Off
Oven Selector:	Bake	Bake
Oven Temperature:	375°F, preheated	375°F
Shelf Position:	2	2

7 egg whites
1/2 teaspoon cream of tartar
2-1/4 cups sifted cake flour
1-1/2 cups sugar
3 teaspoons baking powder
1 teaspoon salt
1/2 cup milk

1/2 cup oil
1/4 cup water
5 egg yolks
1-1/2 teaspoons almond extract
Powdered sugar
1/4 cup chopped almonds, toasted

Beat egg whites and cream of tartar until stiff, but not dry. In a large bowl of electric mixer, sift together flour, sugar, baking powder and salt. Make a depression in the center and add the milk, oil, water, egg yolks and almond extract. Beat 1 minute, scraping sides of bowl often. Gradually fold beaten egg whites into batter a little at a time. Blend well after each addition to thoroughly combine ingredients. Pour into ungreased 10-inch METAL tube pan. Bake at 375° with Microwave on Low, 12 minutes. Turn Microwave Off. Continue to Bake at 375°, 4 to 8 minutes or until cake tests done and is nicely browned. Invert pan or funnel and cool completely. Remove from pan, dust with powered sugar and sprinkle toasted almonds over top. Makes 1 cake.

Velvet Pound Cake

Microwave Power:	Off	Low
Oven Selector:	Bake	Bake
Oven Temperature:	350°F, preheated	350°F
Shelf Position:	2	2

1 cup (2 sticks) butter, softened	2 cups sifted cake flour
1 cup sugar	1/4 teaspoon salt
4 egg yolks, beaten	1/4 teaspoon baking powder
1 teaspoon grated lemon peel	1/4 teaspoon nutmeg
1 teaspoon lemon extract	4 egg white, stiffly beaten

In large bowl of electric mixer, cream butter; add sugar and beat until light and fluffy. Add beaten egg yolks and beat 5 minutes. Add lemon peel and lemon extract. Sift together flour, salt, baking powder and nutmeg and add slowly to creamed mixture, combining thoroughly. Fold in beaten egg whites, a little at a time, until completely blended. Pour into greased 2-quart loaf dish. Bake at 350°, 30 minutes. Continue to Bake at 350° with Microwave on Low, 3 to 6 minutes or until cake tests done. Turn oven Off, let cake stand in warm oven 5 minutes. Cool 10 minutes, remove from dish and continue to cool on rack. Makes 1 loaf.

Pound Cake from a Mix

Microwave Power:	Off	Low
Oven Selector:	Bake	Bake
Oven Temperature:	350°F, preheated	350°F
Shelf Position:	2	2

1 pkg. (17-oz.) Pound Cake Mix

Prepare mix according to package directions. Pour into a greased 2-quart loaf dish. Bake at 350°, 25 minutes. Then add Microwave on Low and continue to Bake at 350°, 4 to 6 minutes or until cake tests done. Cool 15 minutes in dish. Then remove from dish and continue to cool on a wire rack.

Cherry-Orange Jubilee Cake

Microwave Power:	High	Off	Medium
Oven Selector:	Off	Bake	Bake
Oven Temperature:	Off	375°F, preheated	375°F
Shelf Position:	2	2	2

Topping:

1 can (16-oz.) dark sweet Bing cherries

3 tablespoons sugar

1-1/2 tablespoons cornstarch

1/4 cup orange juice

1/2 teaspoon grated orange peel

3 tablespoons brandy or Kirsch

Cake:

1/2 cup (1 stick) butter

1/2 cup sugar

1 egg

1/4 cup orange juice

1/2 teaspoon grated orange peel

1-3/4 cups sifted cake flour

1-1/2 teaspoons baking powder

1/2 teaspoon salt

1/4 cup milk

Topping:

Drain cherries, reserving liquid. Mix together sugar and cornstarch. Combine 1/2 cup cherry liquid, orange juice, and orange peel and stir into cornstarch-sugar mixture, until smooth. Cook, stirring often, with Microwave on High, 2 to 3 minutes or until mixture is thickened and clear. Stir in brandy and cherries, pour into a greased 1-1/2-quart round cake dish. Prepare cake batter.

Cake:

Cream together butter and sugar until fluffy. Add egg, orange juice and orange peel, beating well. Sift together flour, baking powder and salt; add alternately with milk to creamed mixture, beating until smooth. Pour batter evenly over cherries. Bake at 375°, 18 minutes. Then continue to Bake at 375° with Microwave on Medium, 3 to 5 minutes or until cake tests done. Cool 10 minutes; invert on serving platter. Makes one 8-inch layer.

"Snackin Cake" from a Mix

Microwave Power:	Off	Medium
Oven Selector:	Bake	Bake
Oven Temperature:	400°F, preheated	400°F
Shelf Position:	2	2

1 pkg. (14-1/2-oz.) "Snackin Cake" Mix

Prepare batter in 2-quart square cake dish according to package directions, making sure all mix is thoroughly moistened. Bake at 400°, 10 minutes; then add Microwave on Medium and continue to Bake at 400°, 2 to 3 minutes or until cake tests done.

Pudding Cake from a Mix

Microwave Power:	Off	Low
Oven Selector:	Bake	Bake
Oven Temperature:	400°F, preheated	400°F
Shelf Position:	2	2

1 pkg. (11-oz.) Pudding Cake Mix

Prepare mix according to package directions using a 2-quart square baking dish. Bake at 400°, 10 minutes, then add Microwave on Low and continue to Bake at 400°, 3 to 6 minutes, or until cake on top tests done. Cool 10 minutes.

Flaming Orange Babas

Microwave Power:	High
Oven Selector:	Off
Oven Temperature:	Off
Shelf Position:	2

4 slices pound cake (3/4-inch thick)
1/2 cup sugar
1-1/2 teaspoons cornstarch
2 teaspoons grated orange peel
1/2 cup orange juice

1/4 cup water
1/4 cup rum or brandy
1 cup (1/2 pt.) whipping cream
3 tablespoons chopped almonds

Arrange pound cake slices on serving platter; pierce each piece with a fork several times. In a 4-cup liquid measure, mix together sugar and cornstarch; add orange peel, orange juice and water. Cook with Microwave on High, 3 to 4 minutes, until mixture boils and is thickened and clear. Stir twice. Pour hot syrup over cake. Heat rum or brandy in a 1-cup liquid measure with Microwave on High, 15 seconds. Pour over cake; touch a flame to the surface immediately. After flame goes out, top with whipped cream and sprinkle with almonds. Makes 4 servings.

Cupcakes

Microwave Power:	Off	Medium
Oven Selector:	Bake	Bake
Oven Temperature:	400°F, preheated	400°F
Shelf Position:	2	2

Prepare mix or favorite cake recipe. Use 6-count METAL muffin pans only. Fill two 6-count greased or paper baking cup lined muffin pans, 2/3 full of batter. Bake at 400°, 5 minutes. Continue to Bake at 400° with Microwave on Medium, 2 to 3 minutes or until cupcakes test done.

Frostings, Fillings, Glazes

This section contains tempting cooked frosting and filling recipes, cooked with microwaves only. Use them on cakes from this book or your own favorites. Follow recipes carefully. Cook and stir ingredients thoroughly, but avoid overcooking. Beat recommended length of time to make frosting smooth and a good spreading consistency. Try Yummy Fudge Glaze over angel food cake for beautiful and delicious results.

Vanilla Frosting & Filling

Microwave Power:	High
Oven Selector:	Off
Oven Temperature:	Off
Shelf Position:	2

3/4 cup milk
5 tablespoons sifted cake flour
3/4 cup granulated sugar
3/4 cup shortening

1/4 teaspoon salt
1-1/2 teaspoons vanilla
1/2 cup chopped nuts
1 cup sifted powdered sugar

In a 4-cup liquid measure, combine milk and flour. Stir with wire whisk to thoroughly blend. Cook mixture with Microwave on High, 3 to 4 minutes until smooth and thick. Stir every 45 seconds. Let cool. Mix sugar, shortening and salt together with electric mixer until fluffy. Add cooled flour mixture and vanilla to sugar and shortening. Blend thoroughly until fluffy. Reserve 1/3 of icing for filling and add the 1/2 cup of nuts to it. Sift powdered sugar, add to remaining mixture and blend together. Makes enough filling and frosting for 8 or 9-inch two-layer cake.

Orange Frosting

Microwave Power:	High
Oven Selector:	Off
Oven Temperature:	Off
Shelf Position:	2

1/2 cup granulated sugar
2 tablespoons cornstarch
1/8 teaspoon salt
1 tablespoon fresh grated orange peel

2 tablespoons orange marmalade
1/3 cup orange juice
6 tablespoons butter
3 to 3-1/2 cups powdered sugar

In a 1-1/2-quart glass casserole mix together granulated sugar, cornstarch, salt and grated orange peel. Gradually blend in orange juice and marmalade. Cook with Microwave on High, 1-1/4 minutes; stir. Cook 1 minute and stir. Cook 1 to 2 minutes longer or until thick and clear. Add butter and stir well. Cool. Gradually blend in powdered sugar until frosting is thick enough to spread. Frosts two 8-inch layers.

German Pecan Frosting

Microwave Power:	High
Oven Selector:	Off
Oven Temperature:	Off
Shelf Position:	2

3 eggs
1 cup evaporated milk
1 cup sugar
1 teaspoon vanilla

1/3 cup (2/3 stick) butter
1-1/3 cups flaked coconut
1 cup chopped pecans

Slightly beat eggs in a deep 2-quart glass bowl. Stir in milk, sugar and vanilla; add butter. Cook with Microwave on High, 10 to 13 minutes, stirring often until mixture boils and thickens. Mixture will curd. Cool; beat until smooth and thick. Stir in coconut and pecans. Spread between layers and on top of cake. Frosts two 8-inch layers.

Burnt Sugar Frosting

Microwave Power:	High
Oven Selector:	Off
Oven Temperature:	Off
Shelf Position:	2

1/2 cup (1 stick) butter
1 cup light brown sugar, firmly packed
1/3 cup light cream or evaporated milk

1 teaspoon vanilla
2-1/2 to 3 cups powdered sugar

Place the butter and brown sugar in a 4-cup liquid measure. Cook with Microwave on High, 3 to 4 minutes until mixture reaches a full boil, stirring once. Add cream or evaporated milk. Allow to come to a boil again with Microwave on High, about 45 seconds. Cool to lukewarm. Add vanilla. Gradually beat in sugar until frosting is thick enough to spread. Frosts two 8-inch layers.

Mocha Fudge Frosting

Microwave Power:	High
Oven Selector:	Off
Oven Temperature:	Off
Shelf Position:	2

2/3 cup milk
2 cups sugar
1/2 cup (1 stick) butter
3 squares (1-oz. each) unsweetened chocolate

1/4 teaspoon salt
2 tablespoons instant coffee powder
1/2 teaspoon vanilla
3/4 to 1 cup powdered sugar

In 1-1/2-quart glass mixer bowl combine first 5 ingredients. Cook with Microwave on High, 6 minutes, stirring once. Allow mixture to reach a rolling boil, boil 1-1/2 minutes. Stir in instant coffee and vanilla. Cool. Beat thoroughly with electric mixer, 5 minutes. Gradually beat in powdered sugar until frosting is thick enough to spread. Frosts two 8-inch layers.

Rocky Road Frosting

Microwave Power:	High
Oven Selector:	Off
Oven Temperature	Off
Shelf Position:	2

2 squares (1-oz. each) unsweetened chocolate
1/3 cup evaporated milk
1/3 cup (2/3 stick) butter
2 cups miniature marshmallows

1 teaspoon vanilla
2-1/2 cups sifted powdered sugar
1/2 cup chopped nuts

In large glass mixer bowl, combine chocolate, milk and butter. Cook with Microwave on High, 1-1/2 minutes. Stir well; add 1 cup marshmallows. Cook with Microwave on High, 1 to 1-1/2 minutes or until marshmallows melt. Add vanilla. Beat with electric mixer to blend. Add sugar gradually until smooth and thick enough to spread. Fold in nuts and remaining marshmallows. Frosts two 8-inch layers or one 13 x 9-inch cake.

Yummy Fudge Glaze

Microwave Power:	High
Oven Selector:	Off
Oven Temperature:	Off
Shelf Position:	2

1/2 cup (1 stick) butter
2 squares (1-oz. each) unsweetened chocolate
2 cups sugar
1/4 cup light corn syrup

1/2 cup milk
1 teaspoon vanilla
2 pkgs. (3-oz. each) cream cheese, softened

Place butter and chocolate in large glass mixer bowl. Melt butter and chocolate with Microwave on High, 2 to 3 minutes. Add sugar, corn syrup and milk to chocolate mixture. Mix well. Cook with Microwave on High, 5 minutes, stirring twice. Continue cooking with Microwave on High, 1-1/2 to 2 minutes more, without stirring, allowing mixture to boil rapidly. Beat with electric mixer until lukewarm. Add the vanilla and cream cheese. Beat with electric mixer 4 minutes at medium speed. Allow to cool slightly. Pour over top of cake allowing it to run down sides. Glazes one 10-inch tube cake.

Pineapple Glaze

Microwave Power:	High
Oven Selector:	Off
Oven Temperature:	Off
Shelf Position:	2

1 tablespoon cornstarch
1/4 cup sugar
Dash salt
1 can (8-oz.) crushed pineapple, undrained

1/2 teaspoon lemon juice
1/2 teaspoon vanilla
2 to 3 drops yellow food coloring

Combine cornstarch, sugar and salt in a 4-cup liquid measure. Stir in undrained pineapple. Cook with Microwave on High, 3 minutes; stir. Continue cooking with Microwave on High, 1 to 2 minutes more or until clear and thickened. Stir in remaining ingredients. Chill until set. Makes enough to glaze the top of angel food cake or a cheese cake.

Creamy Lemon Glaze

Microwave Power:	High
Oven Selector:	Off
Oven Temperature:	Off
Shelf Position:	2

2 cups sifted powdered sugar
2 teaspoons grated fresh lemon peel

2 tablespoons lemon juice
1/4 cup butter

In large glass bowl stir together sugar, lemon peel and juice. Add butter. Heat with Microwave on High, 1 to 2 minutes or until butter is melted. Beat with electric mixer until creamy and smooth. Pour immediately over top of cake. Allow glaze to drizzle down sides. Use with angel food, sponge or pound cake.

"Easy Do" Chocolate Glaze

Microwave Power:	High
Oven Selector:	Off
Oven Temperature:	Off
Shelf Position:	2

1-1/2 cups sugar
6 tablespoons butter
6 tablespoons milk

1/2 cup semi-sweet chocolate pieces
1/2 teaspoon vanilla

In a 2-quart glass mixer bowl, bring sugar, butter and milk to a boil with Microwave on High, 4 to 5 minutes. Then boil 30 seconds. Add the chocolate pieces and vanilla; mix with an electric mixer. Pour warm over brownies.

Creamy Peach Filling

Microwave Power:	High
Oven Selector:	Off
Oven Temperature:	Off
Shelf Position:	2

1 can (16-oz.) peach halves or slices
1/2 cup sugar
2 teaspoons cornstarch
1/2 teaspoon salt
1 cup (1/2 pt.) half and half

1 pkg. (3-oz.) cream cheese, cubed
1 teaspoon vanilla
1/2 teaspoon almond extract
2 tablespoons brandy (optional)
    or brandy flavoring

Drain peaches reserving syrup and cubing fruit. Chill peaches. In a 1-1/2-quart glass casserole, mix together sugar, cornstarch and salt. Stir in half and half and up to 1/3 cup reserved syrup. Cook with Microwave on High, 3 minutes. Stir; continue cooking with Microwave on High, 1 to 2 minutes, bringing to a boil and boil for 1 minute. Beat in cream cheese cubes, vanilla and almond extract, using rubber scraper. Cover surface with waxed paper and chill. Save some peaches for garnish. Fold rest of peaches and brandy or brandy flavoring into cooked filling. Use as filling for angel roll.

Jubilee Cherry Topping

Microwave Power:	High
Oven Selector:	Off
Oven Temperature:	Off
Shelf Position:	2

1 can (1-lb.) pitted Bing cherries, drain,
    reserving syrup
1/4 cup cherry syrup
1-1/4 cups Burgundy or rose
1 pkg. (4-3/4-oz.) raspberry-currant or strawberry
    Danish Dessert mix

1/8 teaspoon cinnamon
1/8 teaspoon nutmeg
1/2 teaspoon almond extract

Drain cherries, reserving syrup. Combine cherry syrup, wine and Danish Dessert mix in a 1-1/2-quart casserole. Bring to a boil with Microwave on High, 4 to 4-1/2 minutes, stirring occasionally. Boil 45 seconds. Stir in remaining ingredients; cover surface with a film of waxed paper or plastic wrap. Chill. Use as a topping for cheese pie.

Variation:
Substitute sour cherries for a great flavor contrast. Follow the recipe above, but use cherry water instead of syrup and add 1/4 cup sugar with Danish Dessert mix before cooking sauce.

Candy

Some candies simply require melting or short cooking of ingredients which are then stirred with nuts, cereal or other ingredients. Follow recipes carefully, stir often and be careful not to overcook. Many recipes of this type can be easily converted for use in the Thermatronic II. Although High power is used for most candies, when converting recipes, Medium and Low powers may also be used to cook delicate candy ingredients, such as melting carmels. Other candy recipes layer ingredients which are then set with microwaves only or microwaves and heat.

Longer cooking candies, such as fudge and pralines, are made with a sugar syrup that must be boiled rapidly to a specific temperature. A full rolling boil can be achieved and maintained with microwaves, with little chance of scorching. Use a very large (4 to 5 quart) glass-ceramic dish to help avoid boil-overs, and that will withstand high cooking temperatures. For best results use a candy thermometer, but not in the oven when microwave power is on. Cook the syrup the minimum time specified in the recipe, then measure the temperature of the mixture with the candy thermometer. If the syrup is not up to temperature, remove the thermometer and continue cooking. Check carefully with candy thermometer every 1 to 2 minutes, since during the last few minutes of cooking, the temperature will rise very quickly. After cooking, the mixture should be allowed to cool to lukewarm, without being disturbed, before beating. For a smooth, creamy candy, beating should not be interrupted after it has begun. Try one of these recipes, following instructions carefully, before attempting to prepare other favorite candy recipes.

Old Fashioned Fudge

Microwave Power:	High
Oven Selector:	Off
Oven Temperature:	Off
Shelf Position:	2

4 sq. (1 oz. each) unsweetened chocolate
1-1/4 cups milk
3 cups sugar
1/4 teaspoon salt

1 tablespoon light corn syrup
3 tablespoons butter or margarine
1-1/2 teaspoons vanilla
3/4 cup chopped walnuts

Combine chocolate and milk in a 4-quart casserole. Cook, uncovered with Microwave on High, 3 to 4 minutes or until milk is hot and chocolate begins to melt. Stir until chocolate melts completely. Add sugar, salt and corn syrup. Cook uncovered with Microwave on High, 5 to 7 minutes or until mixture comes to a full boil, stirring twice. Continue to cook uncovered with Microwave on High, 8 to 10 minutes, without stirring, or until syrup reaches 236°F on a thermometer. Check temperature about every 2 to 3 minutes, then every minute until 236°F is reached. Temperature rises quickly near the end. Add butter and vanilla. Cool without stirring, until mixture is lukewarm (110°F). DO NOT beat mixture until it has cooled. Beat with electric mixer until mixture loses its gloss and is thick. Stir in nuts, spread into a buttered 8-inch square pan. Cool. Cut into squares. Makes about 2 pounds.

Pecan Pralines

Microwave Power:	High
Oven Selector:	Off
Oven Temperature:	Off
Shelf Position:	2

1 cup granulated sugar
2 cups brown sugar, firmly packed
1-1/4 cups milk
1/4 cup light corn syrup

1/8 teaspoon salt
1 teaspoon vanilla
1-1/2 cups pecan halves

In a 4-quart casserole combine all ingredients, except vanilla and pecans. Stir to blend well. Cook uncovered with Microwave on High, 5 minutes, stirring twice. Continue to cook with Microwave on High, 15 to 20 minutes or until syrup registers 238°F on a candy thermometer. Cool to lukewarm (110°F). Beat with an electric mixer until mixture thickens. Stir in vanilla and pecans. Spoon into cupcake papers to form patties. Makes about 2 dozen.

Toffee Crunch

Microwave Power:	High
Oven Selector:	Off
Oven Temperature:	Off
Shelf Position:	2

3/4 cup (1-1/2 sticks) butter
3/4 cup plus 2 tablespoons sugar
2 tablespoons plus 2 teaspoons
   light corn syrup

3/4 cup semi-sweet chocolate pieces
1/3 cup shredded toasted coconut
   or chopped, toasted almonds

Partially melt butter in 2-quart casserole with Microwave on High, 1 to 1-1/2 minutes. Do not overcook or let separate. Mix in sugar and cook with Microwave on High, 2-1/2 to 3 minutes; stirring every 30 seconds until sugar is completely dissolved. Stir in corn syrup. Cook with Microwave on High, 5 to 6 minutes, until syrup is light brown in color and a small amount of mixture is brittle when dropped in cold water. Stir lightly to blend. Do not overmix. Immediately pour into lightly buttered 2-quart oblong baking dish. Sprinkle chocolate pieces over surface of toffee. Allow chocolate to melt, then spread lightly and evenly over toffee. Sprinkle with coconut or almonds and lightly press into chocolate. Cool completely and break into irregular pieces. Makes about 1 pound.

Chinese Chews

Microwave Power:	High
Oven Selector:	Off
Oven Temperature:	Off
Shelf Position:	2

1 pkg. (6-oz.) semi-sweet chocolate pieces
1 pkg. (6-oz.) butterscotch pieces
1 can (3-oz.) chow mein noodles

1 can (6-1/2-oz.) cocktail peanuts
2/3 cup raisins (optional)

Place chocolate and butterscotch pieces in a 2-quart casserole. Melt with Microwave on High, 3 minutes. Stir. Continue to melt with Microwave on High, 1/2 to 1-1/2 minutes; stir until smooth. Add remaining ingredients; stir to coat well. Drop by teaspoons onto waxed paper lined trays. Refrigerate until firm. Makes 4 dozen.

Variation:
For a more chocolate flavor, use another 6-ounce package of semi-sweet chocolate pieces in place of the butterscotch pieces.

Seven Layer Squares

Microwave Power:	High	Low
Oven Selector:	Off	Bake
Oven Temperature:	Off	400°F, preheated
Shelf Position:	2	2

3/4 cup (1-1/2 sticks) butter
1-1/2 cups graham cracker crumbs
1 cup (6-oz. pkg.) semi-sweet chocolate pieces
1 cup (6-oz. pkg.) butterscotch pieces

1 cup chopped walnuts or pecans
1 cup shredded coconut
1 can (13-oz.) sweetened condensed milk

In a 3-quart oblong baking dish, melt butter with Microwave on High, 3/4 to 1 minute. Preheat oven. Spread melted butter to coat bottom and sides of baking dish. Sprinkle graham cracker crumbs evenly over bottom, followed by a layer of chocolate pieces, butterscotch pieces and nuts. Top with the coconut and drizzle sweetened condensed milk evenly over all. Bake at 400° with Microwave on Low, 10 to 12 minutes. Immediately loosen edge with a knife, then allow to cool before cutting into squares. Makes about 3 dozen squares.

S'Mores

Microwave Power:	High
Oven Selector:	Off
Oven Temperature:	Off
Shelf Position:	2

1 milk chocolate candy bar (1.2-oz.)
6 graham cracker squares

3 large marshmallows

Place 1/3 of chocolate bar on each of 3 graham crackers on plate. Top each with a marshmallow. Heat with Microwave on High, 40 to 45 seconds, or until marshmallows puff. Top each with another graham cracker square. Makes 3 servings.

Variation:
Spread peanut butter on first 3 graham cracker squares, then proceed with other ingredients as directed in recipe.

Coconut Almond Clusters

Microwave Power:	High
Oven Selector:	Off
Oven Temperature:	Off
Shelf Position:	2

3 tablespoons butter
3 tablespoons milk
1 pkg. (15.4-oz.) creamy white frosting mix
1 can (3-1/2-oz.) flaked coconut

1 teaspoon almond extract
1/2 cup coarsley chopped almonds
Red food coloring

In a 2-quart bowl, heat butter and milk with Microwave on High, 1 to 2 minutes or until butter melts. Stir in dry frosting mix. Cook with Microwave on High, 2 to 3 minutes, until bubbly. Stir each minute. Mixture will be smooth and glossy. Be careful not to overcook. Stir in coconut, almond extract, almonds and a few drops of food coloring. Drop by teaspoon onto waxed paper. Makes about 4 dozen candies.

Coconut Toffee Bars

Microwave Power:	High	Low
Oven Selector:	Off	Off
Oven Temperature:	Off	Off
Shelf Position:	2	2

1 tablespoon butter
11 graham cracker squares
1/2 cup (1 stick) butter
3/4 cup brown sugar, firmly packed

1/4 cup chopped almonds
1 pkg. (6-oz.) semi-sweet chocolate pieces
1/2 cup flaked coconut

Melt 1 tablespoon butter in 2-quart oblong baking dish with Microwave on High, 45 seconds to 1 minute. Spread evenly over bottom of dish. Place graham crackers in dish. Set aside. Combine 1/2 cup butter and brown sugar in 4-cup liquid measure. Cook with Microwave on High, 2 to 3 minutes, until butter is melted; stir once. Stir in almonds. Pour syrup over graham crackers. Cook with Microwave on Low, 5 to 6 minutes or until bubbly. Sprinkle with chocolate pieces and cook with Microwave on Low, 1-1/2 to 2 minutes or until chocolate is softened. Spread chocolate evenly over top and sprinkle with coconut. Chill at least 1 hour. Cut into bars. Makes about 24 bars.

Candied Orange Peel

Microwave Power:	High
Oven Selector:	Off
Oven Temperature:	Off
Shelf Position:	2

4 large Navel oranges   3 cups sugar
Hot tap water

With sharp knife, remove peel from orange in quarters; scrape out any pulp. Cut into 1/4-inch wide strips. Place peel in a 1-1/2-quart covered glass casserole, pour 2 cups hot tap water over peel. Cover; cook with Microwave on High, 6 minutes. Drain. Pour 2 additional cups hot tap water over peel. Stir; cover and continue cooking with Microwave on High, 6 minutes. Stir; cover and let stand in the hot water for 30 minutes. Peel should be tender. In 4-cup liquid measure place 2 cups sugar and 1/2 cup water; stir. Cook sugar and water with Microwave on High, 4 minutes; stir. Return to boiling; cook with Microwave on High, 1 to 2 minutes or until sugar is dissolved. Drain orange peel and pour hot sugar syrup over all. Cover and bring to a boil. Cook with Microwave on High, 5 minutes. Stir and cook uncovered with Microwave on High, 10 minutes longer or until translucent. Stir after 5 minutes. Drain peel. While still hot, roll in remaining sugar, coating all sides. Cool on wire rack. Allow to dry 24 hours.

Cereal & Pasta

Included here are instructions for preparing a selection of popular cooked cereals. In most recipes, water, cereal and salt are combined in a deep bowl or large liquid measure and cooked with microwave on High. When preparing instant and quick cream of wheat, however, the best method is to bring water to boil on High, then add cereal and cook. Try a type of oatmeal, cream of wheat or grits, before experimenting with your own favorite hot cereal. Add a teaspoon of butter or margarine to cereals if boiling over is a problem.

Generally, we do not recommend cooking rice and pasta in the Thermatronic II oven, since there is no time saved. Cook rice and pasta on the cooktop and leave the microwave oven free for other cooking operations. A few recipes in other sections of the cookbook combine uncooked rice or noodles with other ingredients which are then cooked together. This method does save some time, since total cooking time for all the foods is shortened.

A hint:
Cook a large batch of rice or noodles on the cooktop, then freeze portions for use in casseroles. Rice and noodles defrost and heat nicely on Medium power.

Noodle Kuechl

Microwave Power:	Medium
Oven Selector:	Bake
Oven Temperature:	400°F, preheated
Shelf Position:	2

1 pkg. (8-oz.) noodles, cooked and drained
1 cup (1/2 pt.) cottage cheese
1 cup (1/2 pt.) dairy sour cream

2 eggs
1/4 cup butter, melted
1/2 teaspoon salt

Cook noodles on cooktop according to package directions. Place noodles in a 2-quart casserole. In separate mixing bowl combine remaining ingredients and mix thoroughly. Pour over noodles stirring well to combine. Bake at 400° with Microwave on Medium, 12 to 14 minutes. Makes 4 servings.

Noodles Romanoff

Microwave Power:	Medium
Oven Selector:	Bake
Oven Temperature:	400°F, preheated
Shelf Position:	2

1 pkg. (8-oz.) noodles, cooked and drained
3 tablespoons butter, melted
1 cup (1/2 pt.) dairy sour cream
1 cup (1/2 pt.) cottage cheese
1/4 cup minced green onion

1/2 teaspoon Worcestershire sauce
1/2 teaspoon salt
1/8 teaspoon white pepper
Dash Tabasco sauce or cayenne pepper
1 cup grated sharp Cheddar cheese

Cook noodles on cooktop according to package directions. Place noodles in a 2-quart casserole. In separate mixing bowl combine remaining ingredients, except grated cheese. Stir well to blend. Pour mixture over noodles, stirring well to combine. Bake at 400° with Microwave on Medium, 8 minutes. Sprinkle grated cheese over top. Continue to Bake at 400° with Microwave on Medium, 3-1/2 to 4 minutes until casserole is hot and bubbly and cheese is melted. Makes 4 servings.

Granola

Microwave Power:	Medium
Oven Selector:	Bake
Oven Temperature:	325°F, not preheated
Shelf Position:	2

1 cup old fashioned oats
2/3 cup toasted wheat or oat flakes
1/3 cup wheat germ
1/3 cup flaked coconut
1/3 cup chopped almonds
3 tablespoons sesame seeds

1/4 cup oil
1/4 cup honey
1/2 teaspoon vanilla
1/4 teaspoon salt
1/3 cup snipped dried fruits
   (apples, apricots, dates, raisins, etc.)

Mix oats, wheat or oat flakes, wheat germ, coconut, almonds and sesame seeds in a 3-quart oblong baking dish. Drizzle oil and honey over dry ingredients, add vanilla and salt and mix well. Bake at 325° with Microwave on Medium, 10 to 12 minutes or until lightly browned and crisp. Mix in dried fruits. Cool. Serve with milk. Makes about 3 cups.

Old Fashioned Oatmeal

Microwave Power:	High
Oven Selector:	Off
Oven Temperature:	Off
Shelf Position:	2

1 cup water
1/3 cup regular oats

1/4 teaspoon salt

Combine water and oats in large cereal bowl. Heat to boiling with Microwave on High, 2 to 3 minutes. Cook 2 to 3 minutes, until thickened, stirring after 1 minute. Stir in salt. Cover with plastic wrap and let stand 5 minutes. Makes 1 serving.

Instant Cream of Wheat *(One Serving)*

Microwave Power: High
Oven Selector: Off
Oven Temperature: Off
Shelf Position: 2

3/4 cup water   1/8 teaspoon salt
3 tablespoons instant cream of wheat

Heat water to boiling in a 4-cup liquid measure or deep bowl with Microwave on High, 2-1/2 to 3 minutes. Stir in cereal; cook until boiling with Microwave on High, 45 seconds to 1 minute. Stir in salt. Cover with plastic wrap and let stand 2 to 3 minutes. Makes 1 serving.

Quick Cream of Wheat *(One Serving)*

Microwave Power: High
Oven Selector: Off
Oven Temperature: Off
Shelf Position: 2

1 cup water   1/8 teaspoon salt
3 tablespoons quick cream of wheat

Heat water to boiling in a 4-cup liquid measure or deep bowl with Microwave on High, 3 to 4 minutes. Stir in cereal; cook 1-1/2 minutes, stirring every 30 seconds. Stir in salt. Cover with plastic wrap and let stand 5 minutes, stir once. Makes 1 serving.

Regular Cream of Wheat *(One Serving)*

Microwave Power:	High
Oven Selector:	Off
Oven Temperature:	Off
Shelf Position:	2

1-1/4 cups water   1/8 teaspoon salt
3 tablespoons regular cream of wheat

Combine water, cereal and salt in a 1-1/2-quart uncovered casserole. Bring to a boil with Microwave on High, 3 to 4 minutes; stir. Continue cooking with Microwave on High, 3 to 4 minutes, stirring twice. Cover; let stand 5 minutes before serving. Makes 1 serving.

Regular Cream of Wheat *(Four Servings)*

Microwave Power	High
Oven Selector:	Off
Oven Temperature:	Off
Shelf Position:	2

3-3/4 cups water   1/2 teaspoon salt
2/3 cup regular cream of wheat

Combine water, cereal and salt in 3-quart uncovered casserole. Bring to a boil with Microwave on High, 6 to 7 minutes; stir. Continue cooking with Microwave on High, 2 to 3 minutes, stirring twice. Cover; let stand 5 minutes before serving. Makes 4 servings.

Quick Cooking Oatmeal *(One Serving)*

Microwave Power:	High
Oven Selector:	Off
Oven Temperature:	Off
Shelf Position:	2

3/4 cup water   1/4 teaspoon salt
1/3 cup quick cooking oats

Heat water to boiling in a 4-cup liquid measure or deep bowl with Microwave on High, 2-1/2 to 3 minutes. Stir in oats; cook until boiling with Microwave on High, 30 to 45 seconds. Continue to boil 30 seconds. Stir in salt. Cover with plastic wrap and let stand 2 to 3 minutes. Makes 1 serving.

Quick Cooking Oatmeal *(Four Servings)*

Microwave Power:	High
Oven Selector:	Off
Oven Temperature:	Off
Shelf Position:	2

3 cups water   1/2 teaspoon salt
1-1/3 cups quick cooking oats

Heat water to boiling in 2-1/2-quart covered casserole with Microwave on High, 8 to 9 minutes. Stir in oats; cook until boiling with Microwave on High, 1 to 2 minutes. Continue to boil 1 minute. Stir in salt. Cover and let stand 2 to 3 minutes. Makes 4 servings.

Grits *(One Serving)*

Microwave Power:	High
Oven Selector:	Off
Oven Temperature:	Off
Shelf Position:	2

1 cup water   1/8 teaspoon salt
1/4 cup quick grits

Combine water, grits and salt in a 4-cup liquid measure. Cook with Microwave on High, 8 to 9 minutes, or until desired doneness. Cover and let stand a few minutes if a softer texture is desired. Makes 1 serving.

Grits *(Four Servings)*

Microwave Power:	High
Oven Selector:	Off
Oven Temperature:	Off
Shelf Position:	2

4 cups water   1/2 teaspoon salt
1 cup quick grits

Combine water, grits and salt in a 2-1/2-quart casserole. Cook with Microwave on High, 14 to 16 minutes, or until desired doneness. Cover and let stand a few minutes if a softer texture is desired. Makes 4 servings.

Marshmallow Krispies

Microwave Power:	High
Oven Selector:	Off
Oven Temperature:	Off
Shelf Position:	2

1/4 cup butter

40 large marshmallows

4 cups toasted rice cereal

Butter a 2-quart oblong baking dish. Place butter and marshmallows in a 3-quart casserole. Melt with Microwave on High, 1-1/2 minutes. Stir; continue cooking with Microwave on High, 1 to 2 minutes, until butter and marshmallows are melted, stirring every 30 seconds. Mix in cereal until well coated. Press mixture into prepared dish with a buttered spatula. Allow to cool before cutting. Makes about 24 pieces.

Variations:

Add 1/4 cup crunchy peanut butter and cook with butter and marshmallows.

With the cereal add 1 cup of any of the following: raisins, peanuts, semi-sweet chocolate pieces, or butterscotch pieces.

Cookies

Most of the cookies in this book, like the Chocolate Chip Cookie Bars, are baked in square or oblong glass baking dishes then cut into bar cookies. In testing, it was found that this method saved a great deal of time over conventional baking methods. Bar cookies baked with a combination of heat and microwave power are moist and chewy. Occasionally, a recipe uses a metal pan to achieve best results.

High, Medium and Low powers are used with baking heat, depending on the individual recipe. Oven temperatures are often higher than conventional recipes to achieve good browning in the shortened bake times. After trying some recipes, lower oven temperatures 25°F if you prefer a light brown cookie. If a darker cookie is desired, turn oven off and let baking dish remain in hot oven until sufficiently browned.

Combination heat and microwave baking is not recommended for sliced and drop cookies. Since only one oven shelf is used with microwave energy, most drop cookies can be baked as fast or faster on two metal cookie sheets on two oven racks with conventional baking heat. Some of these recipes cook and combine ingredients which are formed into individual cookies without further baking, for a type of drop cookie.

Golden Apricot Bars

Microwave Power:	High	Low
Oven Selector:	Off	Bake
Oven Temperature:	Off	425°F, preheated
Shelf Position:	2	2

Filling:

2 cups dried apricots,	1 cup pitted dates,
snipped into small pieces	snipped into small pieces
1 cup hot water	1/2 cup brown sugar, firmly packed

Crust:

3/4 cup butter, softened	1/2 teaspoon salt
1 teaspoon vanilla	1 teaspoon soda
1 cup brown sugar, firmly packed	1-3/4 cups quick cooking oats
1-3/4 cups sifted flour	

Place apricots and hot water in a 1-1/2-quart glass casserole. Cover and cook with Microwave on High, 6 minutes, stirring once. Mix in dates and sugar; cover and cook with Microwave on High, 4 to 5 minutes, until thick. Cool.

Crust:

Preheat oven. Blend together butter, vanilla and sugar. Add remaining ingredients to make a crumb-like mixture. Firmly press 2-1/4 cups of crumb mixture into bottom of a greased 2-quart oblong baking dish.

Evenly spread filling over crumb mixture. Top with remaining crumbs and gently press into surface of filling. Bake at 425° with Microwave on Low, 3 minutes. Rotate dish 1/4 turn. Continue to Bake at 425° with Microwave on Low, 3 minutes more. Turn Microwave Off. Continue to Bake, 2 to 5 minutes, or until lightly browned. Cool completely. Cut into 2 x 2 inch squares. Makes 32 bars.

Date Bar Mix

Microwave Power:	Low	Off
Oven Selector:	Bake	Bake
Oven Temperature:	400°F, preheated	400°F
Shelf Position:	2	2

1 pkg. (14-oz.) Date Bar Mix

Prepare mix according to package directions. Bake at 400° with Microwave on Low, 6 minutes. Turn Microwave Off and continue to Bake at 400°, 5 to 8 minutes or until browned. Cool. Cut into 16 or 20 bars.

"Easy Do" Brownies

Microwave Power:	Low
Oven Selector:	Bake
Oven Temperature:	425°F, preheated
Shelf Position:	2

1/2 cup (1 stick) butter
1 cup sugar
4 eggs

1 can (1 lb.) chocolate syrup
1 cup sifted flour
1 cup chopped nuts (optional)

Cream butter and sugar together. Add eggs one at a time and mix in thoroughly. Blend in the syrup. Stir in flour and nuts, just until flour disappears. Pour into greased 3-quart oblong glass baking dish. Bake at 425° with Microwave on Low, 5 minutes. Rotate dish 1/4 turn. Continue to Bake at 425° with Microwave on Low, 5 to 7 minutes or until brownies test done. Cool and frost with "Easy-Do" Chocolate Glaze. Makes 2 to 3 dozen brownies.

Dream Bars

Microwave Power:	Low
Oven Selector:	Bake
Oven Temperature:	450°F, preheated
Shelf Position:	2

Crust:
1/2 cup (1 stick) butter
1/2 cup brown sugar, firmly packed

1 cup sifted flour

Topping:
2 eggs
1 cup brown sugar, firmly packed
1 teaspoon vanilla
2 tablespoons sifted flour

1/2 teaspoon salt
1/2 teaspoon baking powder
1-1/3 cups (3-1/2-oz. can) flaked coconut
3/4 cup chopped nuts

Crust:
Using a pastry blender, cut butter into brown sugar and flour. Pat into 2-quart oblong baking dish. Bake at 450° with Microwave on Low, 3 minutes. Rotate dish 1/4 turn. Continue to Bake with Microwave on Low, 2 to 3 minutes or until crust is light golden brown.

Topping:
Beat eggs with brown sugar and vanilla. Set aside. Combine flour with salt and baking powder. Toss together with coconut and nuts. Stir in egg mixture. Pour over cooked crust. Bake at 450° with Microwave on Low, 3 minutes. Rotate dish 1/4 turn. Continue to Bake at 450° with Microwave on Low, 1-1/2 to 2-1/2 minutes or until golden brown. Makes 24 bars.

Traci's Fudge Cookies

Microwave Power:	High
Oven Selector:	Off
Oven Temperature:	Off
Shelf Position:	2

1/2 cup (1 stick) butter

2 cups sugar

1/4 cup milk

2 tablespoons cocoa

1/4 teaspoon salt

1/2 cup crunchy peanut butter

2 cups quick cooking oatmeal

1 teaspoon vanilla

1/2 chopped nuts

Combine butter, sugar, milk, cocoa and salt in a 2-1/2-quart casserole. Cook with Microwave on High, 2 minutes. Stir until butter is melted and rest of ingredients are thoroughly mixed. Cook with Microwave on High, 2 to 4 minutes. Mixture should come to a rolling boil and boil for 1 minute. Add the remaining ingredients in order listed. Stir until mixture starts to thicken. Drop quickly by teaspoons onto a pan lined with waxed paper. If mixture is crumbly, it is overcooked. Makes about 4 dozen cookies.

Honey & Apricot Balls

Microwave Power:	High
Oven Selector:	Off
Oven Temperature:	Off
Shelf Position:	2

1/2 cup (1 stick) butter

3/4 cup brown sugar, firmly packed

1 teaspoon cinnamon

1/3 cup honey

1-1/3 cups quick cooking oatmeal

1/2 cup wheat germ

1/3 cup sesame seeds

1-1/4 cups chopped walnuts, almonds or pecans

1 cup flaked coconut

2/3 cup dried apricots, snipped

Place butter in 8-inch square baking dish. Melt with Microwave on High, 1-1/2 to 2 minutes. Blend in brown sugar, cinnamon and honey. Add remaining ingredients and mix well. Cook with Microwave on High, 7 to 8 minutes, stirring every 2 minutes. Mixture should gently bubble. Spread onto a piece of waxed paper. When cool enough to handle, roll into 1-inch balls. Makes about 90 balls.

Honey & Apricot Balls, Dream Bars, Traci's Fudge Cookies, Chocolate Chip Cookie Bars

Chocolate Chip Cookie Bars

Microwave Power:	Low	Off
Oven Selector:	Bake	Bake
Oven Temperature:	375°F, preheated	375°F
Shelf Position:	2	2

1 cup (2 sticks) butter, softened
3/4 cup sugar
3/4 cup brown sugar, firmly packed
2 eggs
1-1/2 teaspoons vanilla
2-1/4 cups sifted flour

1 teaspoon baking soda
1/2 teaspoon baking powder
3/4 teaspoon salt
2 cups (12-oz. pkg.) semi-sweet
  chocolate pieces
3/4 cup chopped nuts (optional)

In a large mixing bowl beat together butter and sugars until creamy. Beat in eggs and vanilla. Sift together flour, baking soda, baking powder and salt; stir into creamed mixture. Add chocolate pieces and nuts, if desired. Spread dough evenly into a greased 3-quart oblong baking dish. Bake at 375° with Microwave on Low, 4 minutes. Rotate dish 1/4 turn. Continue to Bake at 375° with Microwave on Low, 4 minutes longer. Turn Microwave Off, continue to Bake at 375°, 2 to 6 minutes or until brown and cookies test done. Cool on a rack 30 minutes before cutting into bars. Makes 2 to 3 dozen bars.

Brownie Mix

Microwave Power:	Off	Medium
Oven Selector:	Bake	Bake
Oven Temperature:	375°F, preheated	375°F
Shelf Position:	2	2

1 pkg. (22-1/2-oz.) brownie mix

Prepare mix according to package directions. Pour batter into a greased 3-quart oblong baking dish. Bake at 375°, 10 minutes; then add Microwave on Medium, 3-1/2 to 4 minutes, or until brownies test done. Rotate dish 1/2 turn after 2 minutes. Makes 2 to 3 dozen brownies.

Variation:
For 17-1/4 ounce package, use a greased 8-inch square baking dish. Bake at 375°, 10 minutes, then add Microwave on Medium, 3 to 3-1/2 minutes, or until brownies test done. Rotate dish 1/4 turn after 2 minutes. Makes about 16 brownies.

Desserts

This section contains recipes for a variety of fruit, pudding, gelatin and cake type desserts. They range from easy and quick, like Butterscotch Rum Fondue, to extra elegant, like Perfect Cream Cheese Pie with Jubilee Cherry Topping.

Fruit desserts, such as Brandied Fruit Compote and Chunky Spiced Apples are cooked with microwave energy only. Fruit-with-crust type desserts use microwave energy to cook the fruit quickly and baking heat to brown the crust or topping. In Rhubarb Cobbler the rhubarb is cooked as the oven preheats then baked with a biscuit mix topping. Try this recipe substituting any favorite fresh fruit.

In testing it was found that best results with Cheese Pie were achieved by baking it in a metal pie pan. This helps keep the outside edge of the filling from cooking too quickly. We suggest baking all cheese cakes and cheese pies in metal pie pans following the directions in the Perfect Cream Cheese Pie recipe.

In baking custard type desserts, including Old Fashioned Bread Pudding, a combination of heat and low microwave power is used to set the custard and brown the surface. Puddings and related desserts are cooked with microwave power only and stirred often after half of cooking to insure a smooth mixture.

Microwave power is very useful for dissolving gelatin, softening cream cheese and defrosting frozen fruits for many gelatin and cold soufflé desserts. Try several dessert recipes in this book then experiment with your own favorite ingredients and our methods.

Apple Crisp

Microwave Power:	Medium
Oven Selector:	Bake
Oven Temperature:	400°F, preheated
Shelf Position:	2

2 lbs. tart cooking apples, sliced
1/3 cup sugar

1/2 teaspoon cinnamon

Topping:
3/4 cup brown sugar, firmly packed
1/2 cup sifted flour
1/2 cup rolled oats
1/2 teaspoon cloves

3/4 teaspoon cinnamon
3/4 teaspoon nutmeg
1/3 cup butter, softened

Pare and slice apples. Mix with sugar and cinnamon. Place in lightly greased 8-1/4-inch round glass baking dish.

Topping:

With pastry blender mix topping ingredients together, until mixture is crumbly. Sprinkle over apples. Bake at 400° with Microwave on Medium, 13 to 15 minutes, or until apples test done 1 inch from center. Makes 6 to 8 servings.

Apple Pastry

Microwave Power:	Medium
Oven Selector:	Bake
Oven Temperature:	400°F, preheated
Shelf Position:	2

1 egg, beaten
6 tablespoons granulated sugar
6 tablespoons brown sugar, firmly packed
1/2 cup sifted flour
1 teaspoon baking powder

Pinch salt
1/2 teaspoon vanilla
1 cup chopped walnuts
1-1/2 cups grated apple
Ice cream or whipped cream

In 1-1/2-quart bowl, beat egg and combine with other ingredients in order listed. Mix thoroughly. Spread batter in lightly greased 9-inch pie plate. Bake at 400° with Microwave on Medium, 6 to 8 minutes. Serve hot or cold with ice cream or whipped cream. Makes 6 to 8 servings.

Swedish Apple Cake

Microwave Power:	High	Medium
Oven Selector:	Off	Bake
Oven Temperature:	Off	400°F, preheated
Shelf Position:	2	2

1-1/2 cups sifted flour
6 tablespoons quick cooking oats
6 tablespoons brown sugar,
   firmly packed
3/4 cup butter, softened
3 tablespoons chopped walnuts

3 cups sliced apples (about 1 lb.)
2 teaspoons lemon juice
6 tablespoons granulated sugar
2-1/4 teaspoons cornstarch
1/4 teaspoon cinnamon
6 tablespoons water

Combine flour, oats and brown sugar. Add butter and mix together with a pastry blender to resemble crumbs. Reserve 1 cup of this mixture for the top. Press the remainder into the bottom of a well greased 1-1/2-quart round cake dish. Sprinkle with walnuts. Pour lemon juice over apples; mix thoroughly. Mix granulated sugar, cornstarch and cinnamon together in a 1-quart casserole; add water and combine. Cook cornstarch mixture with Microwave on High, 4 to 5 minutes or until mixture is thickened and clear. Stir after 2 minutes and at the end of cooking. Stir in apples. Preheat oven. Place apple mixture on top of pastry. Sprinkle reserved crumb mixture over top. Bake at 400° with Microwave on Medium, 10 to 12 minutes or until apples are done. Cool. Serve with vanilla ice cream. Makes 8 servings.

Country Applesauce

Microwave Power:	High
Oven Selector:	Off
Oven Temperature:	Off
Shelf Position:	2

4 tart cooking apples, peeled and sliced
   (about 4 cups)
1/2 cup water

1 tablespoon fresh lemon juice
1/3 to 2/3 cup sugar

Place apples, water and lemon juice in a 1-1/2-quart covered casserole. Cook with Microwave on High, 8 to 12 minutes until apples are tender, stirring once. Stir in sugar, cover. Let stand a few minutes to dissolve sugar. Mash or put through a blender. Makes approximately 2 cups.

Variation:
For flavor variation substitute apple juice, cranberry juice, orange juice or white wine for water. For sugar, substitute honey, brown sugar or maple sugar.

Sour Cream Applesauce

Microwave Power:	High
Oven Selector:	Off
Oven Temperature:	Off
Shelf Position:	2

4 tart cooking apples, peeled and sliced (about 4 cups)
1/2 cup water
1 tablespoon fresh lemon juice

1/3 cup sugar
1/4 cup dairy sour cream
1/2 tablespoon flour
1/4 cup toasted slivered almonds

Place apples, water and lemon juice in a 1-1/2-quart covered casserole. Cook with Microwave on High, 8 to 12 minutes until apples are tender, stirring once. Stir in sugar; cover. Let stand a few minutes to dissolve sugar. Mash apples. Combine sour cream and flour; stir into mashed cooked apples. Cook with Microwave on High, 4 to 5 minutes to bring just to a boil, stirring once. Add almonds. Makes approximately 2 cups.

Chunky Spiced Apples

Microwave Power:	High
Oven Selector:	Off
Oven Temperature:	Off
Shelf Position:	2

4 tart cooking apples, peeled and sliced (about 4 cups)
1/4 cup orange juice
1/3 cup sugar

1 teaspoon grated orange peel
1/4 teaspoon cinnamon
1/8 teaspoon nutmeg

Place apples and orange juice in a 1-1/2-quart covered casserole. Cook with Microwave on High, 8 to 12 minutes until apples are tender, stirring once. Mix remaining ingredients together and stir into apples; cover. Let stand a few minutes to dissolve sugar. Makes approximately 2 cups.

Golden Apricot Dessert

Microwave Power:	High	Low
Oven Selector:	Off	Bake
Oven Temperature:	Off	375°F, not preheated
Shelf Position:	2	2

1 cup (2 sticks) butter, slightly softened
1 pkg. (18-1/2-oz.) yellow cake mix
1 can (1-lb., 14-oz.) apricot halves and syrup

1/2 cup sugar
1/3 to 2/3 cup chopped nuts
Whipped cream or ice cream (optional)

With a pastry blender, cut butter into cake mix until mixture resembles crumbs. Set aside. Drain syrup from apricots into a 2-quart oblong baking dish. Add sugar and cook with Microwave on High, 5 minutes, stirring once. Add apricots and any remaining syrup, distributing evenly in dish. Spread cake mix crumbs evenly over fruit mixture and sprinkle with nuts. Bake at 375° with Microwave on Low, 25 to 28 minutes, or until top is cooked and golden brown. Serve warm or cold. Top with whipped cream or ice cream, if desired. Makes 8 to 12 servings.

Favorite Pie Filling Dessert

Microwave Power:	Low
Oven Selector:	Bake
Oven Temperature:	375°F, not preheated
Shelf Position:	2

1 cup (2 sticks) butter, slightly softened
1 pkg. (18-1/2- oz.) yellow cake mix

2 cans (21-oz.) cherry pie filling,
  or your favorite
1/2 to 1 cup chopped nuts

With a pastry blender, cut butter into cake mix until mixture resembles crumbs. Set aside. Spread pie filling over entire bottom of a 3-quart oblong baking dish. Distribute cake mix crumbs evenly over pie filling and sprinkle with nuts. Bake at 375° with Microwave on Low, 26 to 30 minutes, or until top is cooked and golden brown. Makes 12 to 16 servings.

Old Fashioned Strawberry Shortcake

Microwave Power:	High	Low	Off
Oven Selector:	Off	Bake	Bake
Oven Temperature:	Off	425°F, preheated	425°F
Shelf Position:	2	2	2

2 tablespoons butter
2-1/2 cups biscuit mix
1/4 cup sugar
1 egg
1/2 cup half and half
4 cups (3 baskets, 12-oz. each) strawberries,
  stemmed and sliced

8 to 10 whole strawberries for garnish
1/4 cup sugar
1 cup (1/2 pt.) whipping cream, whipped
2 tablespoons sugar

Melt butter with Microwave on High, 30 to 45 seconds. Preheat oven. Combine biscuit mix and sugar. Add egg, half and half and melted butter; stir until biscuit mix is completely moistened. Spread evenly into a greased 1-1/2-quart round baking dish. Bake at 425° with Microwave on Low, 3 minutes. Rotate dish a half turn; continue to Bake at 425° with Microwave on Low, 3 minutes. Turn Microwave Off and continue to Bake at 425°, 2 to 4 minutes or until nicely browned. Cool. Remove from dish, split in half horizontally. Sweeten strawberries with 1/4 cup sugar. Whip cream with 2 tablespoons sugar. Spread half of whipped cream on bottom layer of shortcake. Top with about 3 cups of berries. Add second layer of shortcake. Spread remaining whipped cream over shortcake. Heap remaining berries in center of whipped cream and garnish edges with reserved whole berries. Cut in wedges. Makes 6 to 8 servings.

Georgia Peach Dessert

Microwave Power:	Low
Oven Selector:	Bake
Oven Temperature:	400°F, preheated
Shelf Position:	2

1 recipe Oatmeal Cookie Crust
2/3 cup (1-1/3 sticks) butter
1 cup sugar
1 cup brown sugar, firmly packed
2 eggs

1-1/2 cups sifted flour
5 to 5-1/2 cups fresh peach slices
  (about 2 lbs.)
Cinnamon (optional)

Prepare Oatmeal Cookie Crust as directed, but press into bottom of 3-quart oblong baking dish. Cream together butter and sugars; beat in eggs one at a time and stir in flour. Arrange peach slices over crust and spread creamed mixture over peaches. Sprinkle with cinnamon, if desired. Bake at 400° with Microwave on Low, 18 to 24 minutes or until golden brown and tests done with a toothpick. Makes 12 to 15 servings.

Rhubarb Cobbler

Microwave Power:	High	Low	Off
Oven Selector:	Bake	Bake	Bake
Oven Temperature:	400°F, not preheated	400°F	400°F
Shelf Position:	2	2	2

5 cups (about 2 lbs.) fresh rhubarb,
  sliced 1/2-inch thick
1 cup sugar
1/4 cup unsifted flour
1/2 teaspoon cinnamon
1/2 cup water

2 cups biscuit mix
1/4 cup sugar
2 tablespoons butter, melted
1/2 cup milk
Whipped cream or ice cream

Place rhubarb in a 2-quart square baking dish. Combine sugar, flour and cinnamon; add to rhubarb. Stir to mix well. Pour water over all. Bake at 400° with Microwave on High, 6 to 7 minutes until rhubarb is tender, stirring twice. While rhubarb is cooking, combine biscuit mix, sugar, melted butter and milk. Stir with a fork until moistened. Drop batter by spoonfuls over hot rhubarb and spread evenly. Bake at 400° with Microwave on Low, 5 minutes. Turn Microwave Off and continue to Bake at 400°, 4 to 7 minutes, until nicely browned. Serve warm with whipped cream or ice cream. Makes 6 servings.

Brandied Fruit Compote

Microwave Power:	High
Oven Selector:	Off
Oven Temperature:	Off
Shelf Position:	2

1 can (1-lb.) pear halves, in heavy syrup
1 can (1-lb.) peach halves, in heavy syrup
1 can (1-lb.) apricot halves, in heavy syrup
1 can (8-1/4-oz.) pineapple slices,
  in heavy syrup
1 can (1-lb.) dark sweet cherries, drained

2 teaspoons cornstarch
1/2 teaspoon ground cloves
1/4 cup brown sugar, firmly packed
1/4 cup butter
1/4 to 1/2 cup brandy

Drain pears, peaches, apricots and pineapple and combine syrups. Layer all fruit including cherries, in a 3-quart glass bowl. Measure 1-1/2 cups of syrup into a 4-cup liquid measure. Mix together cornstarch, cloves and brown sugar; stir into syrups and add butter. Cook with Microwave on High, 5 to 7 minutes or until mixture thickens and boils; stir twice. Pour over fruit; stir gently. Cook with Microwave on High, 5 to 7 minutes, until fruit is hot. Measure brandy in a 1-cup liquid measure. Heat with Microwave on High, 1/2 minute. Pour brandy over fruit and quickly ignite with a match. Makes 6 to 8 servings.

Peach Soufflé

Microwave Power:	High	Medium	Low
Oven Selector:	Off	Off	Off
Oven Temperature:	Off	Off	Off
Shelf Position:	2	2	2

2 cups hot water
1 pkg. (3-oz.) orange flavored gelatin
1 pkg. (3-oz.) peach flavored gelatin
2 pkg. (10 to 12-oz. each) frozen peaches
1-1/4 cups syrup drained from peaches
  (adding water if necessary)

1 pkg. (8-oz.) cream cheese
2 cups (1 pt.) whipping cream, whipped,
  reserve 1 cup whipped cream

Bring hot water to a boil in a 2-1/2-quart casserole with Microwave on High, 4 to 5 minutes. Add gelatins stirring to dissolve; refrigerate. Remove frozen peaches from containers, or snip plastic pouches and place in a glass bowl. Defrost with Microwave on Medium, 4-1/2 to 5-1/2 minutes or until peaches can be broken apart. Stir once while defrosting. Drain syrup and reserve; chop peaches and reserve. Remove cream cheese from foil wrapper and place in small mixing bowl. Soften with Microwave on Low, 1 to 2 minutes. Beat with an electric mixer and gradually blend in peach syrup. Stir into gelatin mixture. Refrigerate until gelatin mounds, about 2 hours. Fold in peaches and 3-cups whipped cream. Pour into six individual soufflés with 1/2-inch collars or one 5 to 6-cup soufflé with a 2-inch collar. Garnish with reserved whipped cream. Makes 6 servings.

Cherries Jubilee

Microwave Power:	High	Medium
Oven Selector:	Off	Off
Oven Temperature:	Off	Off
Shelf Position:	2	2

1 can (16-oz.) dark sweet Bing cherries
2 tablespoons sugar
2 teaspoons cornstarch

1 teaspoon grated orange peel (optional)
1/4 to 1/3 cup Kirsch or brandy
Vanilla ice cream

Thoroughly drain cherries, reserving liquid. Combine sugar and cornstarch in a serving bowl. Stir in reserved cherry liquid and orange peel. Cook with Microwave on High, 2 to 4 minutes, stirring often, until mixture is thickened and clear. Stir in cherries, cook with Microwave on High, 1 to 2 minutes or until cherries are hot. In a 1-cup liquid measure, heat Kirsch or brandy with Microwave on Medium, 1/2 minute. Pour over cherries and ignite. Spoon flaming cherry sauce over ice cream. Serve immediately. Makes 6 servings.

Lemon Creme

Microwave Power:	Low
Oven Selector:	Off
Oven Temperature:	Off
Shelf Position:	2

1 pkg. (3-oz.) lemon gelatin
3 tablespoons fresh lemon juice
3 eggs
1/2 cup sugar

1/8 teaspoon salt
1 tablespoon grated lemon peel
1 cup (1/2 pt.) whipping cream

Pour gelatin into a 1-quart casserole. Stir in lemon juice and let sit until softened. Cook with Microwave on Low, 3 to 4 minutes or until gelatin is completely dissolved. Beat eggs until foamy. Add sugar, salt and lemon peel, beating until thick and creamy. Beat in gelatin mixture. Whip cream until stiff and fold into lemon mixture. Spoon into individual dessert dishes. Chill. Makes 8 servings.

Perfect Cream Cheese Pie

Microwave Power:	Medium	Low		Off	Low
Oven Selector:	Off	Bake		Bake	Off
Oven Temperature:	Off	350°F, preheated		350°F	Off
Shelf Position:	2	2		2	2

Filling:

4 pkg. (3-oz. each) cream cheese

3/4 cup sugar

2 eggs

Dash salt

2 teaspoons vanilla

1 teaspoon grated lemon peel

1-1/2 teaspoons lemon juice

1 (9-inch) crumb crust in metal pie pan

Topping:

1 cup (1/2 pt.) dairy sour cream,
   room temperature

1/4 cup sugar

1 teaspoon vanilla

Pineapple Glaze or Jubilee Cherry
   Topping (optional)

Filling:

Place cream cheese in large mixer bowl. Soften with Microwave on Medium, 1-1/2 to 2 minutes. Preheat oven. Add sugar to cream cheese, beat with electric mixer until smooth. Beat in eggs, one at a time. Add remaining ingredients and beat until well blended. Pour into baked crust in a METAL pie pan. Bake at 350° with Microwave on Low, 3-1/2 minutes. Rotate 1/2 turn. Continue to Bake at 350° with Microwave on Low, 3-1/2 minutes more. Turn Microwave Off, continue to Bake at 350°, 7 to 11 minutes, or until center of pie is no longer wet. The filling may crack around edge, but it should not brown. Remove from oven and let cool for 10 minutes. Turn oven Off.

Topping:

Blend ingredients and spread evenly over surface of pie. Return to oven with Microwave on Low, 1-1/2 minutes. Oven will still be warm. Cool to room temperature and refrigerate at least 5 hours before serving. Top with a Pineapple Glaze or Jubilee Cherry Topping, cool if desired. Makes 8 to 10 servings.

Rich & Good Stirred Custard Pudding

Microwave Power:	High
Oven Selector:	Off
Oven Temperature:	Off
Shelf Position:	2

2 cups milk or half & half
4 egg yolks
1/4 to 1/3 cup sugar*
1 tablespoon cornstarch

1/4 teaspoon nutmeg
1 teaspoon vanilla
4 egg whites (optional)
1 to 4 teaspoons sugar (optional)*

Heat milk or half & half in a 2-cup liquid measure with Microwave on High, 2 to 3 minutes. In a 2-quart casserole, beat egg yolks with a wire whip; blend in hot milk. Combine sugar, cornstarch and nutmeg; blend into egg-milk mixture. Cook with Microwave on High, 1-1/2 minutes; stir. Continue to cook with Microwave on High an additional 1 to 2-1/2 minutes, stirring every 20 to 30 seconds until desired thickness. Stir in vanilla. Let cool to room temperature. If desired, beat egg whites, with sugar, until stiff. Fold into custard and spoon into custard cups. Makes 4 to 6 servings.

* Vary sugar to desired sweetness.

Baked Custard

Microwave Power:	High	Low	Off
Oven Selector:	Off	Bake	Bake
Oven Temperature:	Off	375° F, preheated	375° F
Shelf Position:	3	3	3

2 cups milk
3 eggs
1/4 cup sugar

1/4 teaspoon salt
Nutmeg

In a 2-cup liquid measure, scald milk with Microwave on High, 3 to 4 minutes. Preheat oven. In a 1-quart bowl, beat eggs with a wire whisk. Stir in sugar, salt and hot milk. Pour into six 6-ounce glass custard cups and sprinkle with nutmeg. Place custard cups in the bottom of the Thermador two-piece METAL broil pan. Place in the oven with handles right to left. Pour 3 cups of very hot tap water into the broil pan around the custards. Bake at 375° with Microwave on Low, 8 minutes. Turn Microwave Off. Continue to Bake at 375°, 8 to 9 minutes, or until a knife inserted near the center comes out clean. Makes six 6-ounce servings.

Pudding and Pie Filling Mix

Microwave Power:	High
Oven Selector:	Off
Oven Temperature:	Off
Shelf Position:	2

1 pkg. (3-1/8 to 3-3/4-oz.) pudding mix

Prepare as package directs using a 4-cup liquid measure. Cook with Microwave on High, 6 to 7 minutes, or until mixture boils. Stirring occasionally after 3 minutes. Makes 4 servings.

For 6 servings:
For 4-1/2 to 5-1/4-ounce pudding mix, use 2-1/2-quart casserole. Prepare as package directs. Cook with Microwave on High, 8 to 11 minutes, or until mixture boils, stirring occasionally after 4 minutes. Makes 6 servings.

Minute Tapioca Pudding

Microwave Power:	High
Oven Selector:	Off
Oven Temperature:	Off
Shelf Position:	2

2 cups milk
3 tablespoons minute tapioca
3 tablespoons sugar
1/8 teaspoon salt

1 egg yolk
1/2 teaspoon vanilla
1 egg white
2 tablespoons sugar

In a 2-cup liquid measure, heat milk with Microwave on High, 1 minute or to room temperature. Mix tapioca, 3 tablespoons sugar, salt, milk and egg yolk, in a 2-quart casserole. Let stand 10 minutes. Cook tapioca mixture with Microwave on High, 6 to 9 minutes, stirring often, or until mixture comes to a full boil. Stir in vanilla. Beat egg white until foamy, gradually adding 2 tablespoons sugar, whipping to soft peaks. Fold into hot mixture; pour into 6 dessert dishes. Chill. Makes 6 servings.

Variation:
Add 1 teaspoon maple flavoring before cooking.

Old Fashioned Bread Pudding

Microwave Power:	High	Low
Oven Selector:	Off	Bake
Oven Temperature:	Off	325°F, preheated
Shelf Position:	2	2

8 slices soft bread (about 4 cups)
2 cups milk
2 tablespoons butter
3 eggs
1/2 cup sugar

1/2 to 1 teaspoon cinnamon
1/4 teaspoon salt
1 teaspoon vanilla
1/2 cup raisins

Trim crusts from bread; cut into 1-inch squares. Place bread in 1-1/2-quart oblong baking dish. In a 4-cup liquid measure, heat milk and butter with Microwave on High, 5 to 6 minutes or until butter melts. Preheat oven. Beat eggs, blend in sugar and cinnamon. Gradually add hot milk to eggs, stirring until well blended. Stir in salt, vanilla and raisins. Pour egg mixture over bread. Let stand 10 minutes. Bake at 325° with Microwave on Low, 14 to 16 minutes or until knife inserted near center comes out clean. Makes 6 to 8 servings.

Butterscotch Rum Fondue or Sauce

Microwave Power:	Medium
Oven Selector:	Off
Oven Temperature:	Off
Shelf Position:	2

1-1/2 cups brown sugar, firmly packed
3 tablespoons butter
1/2 cup whipping cream

2 to 3 tablespoons light rum
Dessert Dips: Fresh fruit, angel
   or pound cake

Combine brown sugar, butter and cream in a 2-quart casserole. Blend well. Cook with Microwave on Medium, 4 to 5 minutes or until mixture boils, stirring often. Boil with Microwave on Medium, 2 minutes. Stir in rum. Cool slightly, serve hot as a dip for chunks of cake and fresh fruit. Or serve cold as a sauce for ice cream. Makes about 1-1/4 cups.

Main Dishes

Main dishes include a wide variety of casseroles combining meats, pasta, sauces, cheese and vegetables. We have tried to include a sampling of and variations on favorite recipes, such as Special Baked Beans and Deep Dish Chicken Pie. Some have a south-of-the-border influence with chiles and spices, like Baked Chicken-Cheese Tacos.

Low and Medium power settings allow many casseroles to heat evenly, without being stirred. The addition of baking heat gives casseroles a browned, crusty flavor and appearance.

Rice or noodles for casseroles are usually cooked on the cooktop first then added to other ingredients, with the exception of Turkey and Wild Rice Casserole.

Cheese casseroles are usually baked with Low power so the cheese will not toughen and become stringy or curdle. Some dishes are stirred during cooking, then topped with cheese or other toppings and then baked until bubbly and browned.

Some main dishes are prepared with a sauce that is first cooked on High, then combined with other ingredients and baked with heat and Low power. Very liquid main dishes, such as Italian Spaghetti Sauce and Quick Chili & Beans are cooked on High.

After trying several main dishes from this cookbook, it should be easy to convert your family's favorite entrée for cooking in the Thermatronic II oven.

Italian Macaroni & Cheese

Microwave Power:	High	Low
Oven Selector:	Off	Bake
Oven Temperature:	Off	400°F, not preheated
Shelf Position:	2	2

2 cups (8-oz.) mostaccioli, cooked and drained
3 tablespoons butter
3/4 cup chopped onion
3/4 cup chopped celery
1 to 2 cloves garlic, minced
2 cans (6-oz. each) tomato paste
2 cups water

1 teaspoon basil, crushed
1 teaspoon oregano, crushed
2 teaspoons salt
1/2 teaspoon sugar
1/2 teaspoon pepper
2/3 cup grated Parmesan cheese
2 cups (1 lb.) ricotta cheese

On cooktop cook mostaccioli according to package directions. Combine butter, onion, celery and garlic in a 1-1/2-quart casserole. Cook, stirring occasionally, with Microwave on High, 4 to 5 minutes. Add tomato paste, water seasonings and sugar. Cover and bring to a boil with Microwave on High, about 10 minutes. Uncover and cook with Microwave on High for an additional 5 minutes. In a 2-quart oblong utility dish, spread a thin layer of sauce over the bottom. Sprinkle with one-third of Parmesan cheese. Layer with half each of mostaccioli, ricotta, sauce and half of remaining Parmesan cheese. Repeat layers with remaining ingredients. Bake at 400° with Microwave on Low, 18 to 22 minutes or until hot, bubbly and golden brown. Makes 6 servings.

Combine butter, onion, celery and garlic; sauté with Microwave on High until transparent. Add remaining sauce ingredients and simmer to blend flavors.

Italian Macaroni & Cheese

Parmesan & Cheddar Macaroni Bake

Microwave Power:	High	Low
Oven Selector:	Off	Bake
Oven Temperature:	Off	425°F, not preheated
Shelf Position:	2	2

2 cups (8-oz.) elbow macaroni,
   cooked and drained
1/4 cup (1/2 stick) butter
1 small onion, finely chopped
1/4 cup flour
2 cups milk

1/2 teaspoon salt
1/8 teaspoon pepper
Two dashes cayenne pepper
1 teaspoon Worcestershire sauce
3/4 to 1-1/2 cups grated sharp Cheddar cheese
1/2 cup grated Parmesan cheese

Topping:
1 tablespoon butter, melted
1 cup bread crumbs

1/4 cup grated Parmesan cheese

On cooktop cook macaroni according to package directions. Place butter and onion in a 1-1/2-quart casserole. Cook with Microwave on High, 3 minutes, stirring once. Stir in flour and cook with Microwave on High, 1 minute. Blend in milk and cook with Microwave on High, 5 minutes. Stir. Continue to cook with Microwave on High, 1-1/2 to 2-1/2 minutes until thick and bubbly, stirring once. Blend in all remaining casserole ingredients. Heat with Microwave on High, 1 to 2 minutes to melt cheese. Pour into a buttered 2-1/2-quart glass casserole.

Topping:

Melt 1 tablespoon butter in a small glass bowl with Microwave on High, about 45 seconds. Toss with bread crumbs and Parmesan cheese. Sprinkle over top of casserole. Bake at 425° with Microwave on Low, 17 to 20 minutes until hot, bubbly and golden brown. Makes 4 to 6 servings.

Variation:

Sunday Special Macaroni and Cheese—Create your own "special." Add leftover bite-sized cooked meats, poultry, fish, cooked eggs, vegetables and other non-liquid ingredients.

Onion-Cheese Enchiladas

Microwave Power:	High	Low	Low
Oven Selector:	Off	Bake	Broil
Oven Temperature:	Off	400°F, preheated	High Broil
Shelf Position:	2	2	2

1 medium onion, chopped
2 tablespoons oil
1 recipe Red Chili Sauce or
  2-1/2 cups favorite enchilada sauce

1/4 cup oil
8 corn tortillas
3 cups grated Cheddar cheese

Combine onion and 2 tablespoons oil in a 1-1/2-quart casserole. Cover; cook with Microwave on High, 3 to 5 minutes or until onions are tender-crisp. Pour 1/2 cup sauce into bottom of a 2-quart oblong baking dish. In a 1-1/2-quart round cake dish heat 1/4 cup oil with Microwave on High, 2 minutes or until hot. Heat tortillas with Microwave on High, 1 minute. Dip each tortilla into hot oil, then in sauce. Place about 1 tablespoon onions and 2 tablespoons Cheddar cheese in center; roll tortilla to enclose filling and place seam-side down in baking dish. Pour remaining sauce over tortillas. Bake at 400° with Microwave on Low, 8 to 12 minutes or until sauce is bubbly. Sprinkle remaining cheese evenly over enchiladas; set oven at High Broil and continue to cook with Microwave on Low, 3 to 5 minutes or until cheese is melted and bubbly. Makes 4 servings.

Special Baked Beans

Microwave Power:	High	Low
Oven Selector:	Bake	Bake
Oven Temperature:	350°F, not preheated	350°F
Shelf Position:	2	2

2 cans (1-lb. each) pork and beans
2 tablespoons molasses
2 tablespoons catsup
2 teaspoons instant minced onions

2 teaspoons prepared mustard
2 teaspoons cider vinegar
1 cup (8-oz.) crushed pineapple, drained
4 slices cooked bacon, crumbled

Combine all ingredients in a shallow 2-quart casserole with lid. Cover; Bake at 350° with Microwave on High, 6 minutes. Remove lid; stir beans. Continue to Bake uncovered at 350° with Microwave on Low, 15 to 20 minutes. Makes 6 servings.

Quick Chili & Beans

Microwave Power:	High
Oven Selector:	Off
Oven Temperature:	Off
Shelf Position:	2

1 lb. ground beef
1 can (15-oz.) tomato sauce with tomato pieces
1 can (7-oz.) green chile salsa
1 tablespoon instant minced onions

1/2 to 1 teaspoon chili powder
1/2 teaspoon oregano leaves, crushed
1 to 2 cans (15-oz.) kidney beans, drained

Crumble beef in a 3-quart glass casserole. Cook with Microwave on High, 2 minutes. Stir; cook with Microwave on High for an additional 2 to 3 minutes or until done. Stir in tomato sauce, salsa, onion, chili powder and oregano. Cook with Microwave on High, 5 minutes. Add beans, heat with Microwave on High, 5 to 8 minutes or until thoroughly heated. Makes 4 to 5 servings.

Chili Ranchero

Microwave Power:	High	Low
Oven Selector:	Off	Off
Oven Temperature:	Off	Off
Shelf Position:	2	2

3 strips bacon, diced
3/4 cup chopped onion
3/4 cup chopped green pepper
1/2 teaspoon garlic powder
1-1/2 lbs. lean ground beef
1 can (1-lb.) tomato puree
1 to 2 cans (1-lb. each) kidney beans, drained

1 tomato, chopped and seeded
1 to 2 tablespoons chili powder
2 teaspoons sugar
1 teaspoon salt
1/8 teaspoon pepper
1/8 teaspoon cayenne pepper

Place bacon in a 3-quart casserole. Cook, uncovered, with Microwave on High, 5 to 6 minutes or until crisp, stirring twice. Remove bacon; drain and reserve. Add onion, green pepper and garlic powder to bacon fat in casserole. Cover and cook with Microwave on High, 3 to 4 minutes or until onions are soft. Add beef and cook uncovered with Microwave on High, 5 to 6 minutes, stirring twice. Add all remaining ingredients except reserved bacon. Cover and cook with Microwave on High, 10 to 12 minutes, until hot and bubbly. If a thicker sauce is desired, uncover and cook with Microwave on Low for an additional 5 to 10 minutes to evaporate some of liquid. Garnish with bacon. Makes 6 to 8 servings.

Enchilada Casserole

Microwave Power:	High	Low
Oven Selector:	Off	Bake
Oven Temperature:	Off	400°F, not preheated
Shelf Position:	2	2

1 lb. lean ground beef	2 tablespoons diced green chiles
1 medium onion, chopped	1 can (8-oz.) tomato sauce
1 clove garlic, minced	2/3 cup water
1 teaspoon salt	6 tortillas
1 teaspoon oregano, crushed	1/2 lb. (2 cups) grated Cheddar cheese,
1/2 teaspoon pepper	reserve 1/2 cup for top of casserole
1 tablespoon chili powder	

Crumble beef in a 1-1/2-quart casserole; add onion and garlic. Cook with Microwave on High, 5 to 6 minutes or until all pink is gone from meat, stirring once. In a 4-cup liquid measure, combine salt, oregano, pepper, chili powder, green chiles, tomato sauce and water. Bring to a boil with Microwave on High, 5 to 6 minutes. Pour a small amount of the sauce in the bottom of a 1-1/2 quart casserole, alternate layers of tortillas, meat sauce and cheese. Top with remaining 1/2 cup of cheese. Bake at 400° with Microwave on Low, 15 to 16 minutes or until bubbly and hot. Makes 4 servings.

Cabbage Bundles

Microwave Power:	High	Low
Oven Selector:	Off	Bake
Oven Temperature:	Off	400°F, not preheated
Shelf Position:	2	2

1 large head cabbage	1 teaspoon Worcestershire sauce
1/3 cup water	1/8 teaspoon pepper
1 lb. lean ground beef	1/4 teaspoon garlic powder
1 cup cooked rice	1 can (28-oz.) whole tomatoes
1/2 cup finely chopped onion	2 teaspoons soy sauce
1 egg, beaten	2 tablespoons brown sugar
1 teaspoon soy sauce	2 teaspoons cornstarch

Wash cabbage, remove core. Peel off 10 large outer leaves; cut in half, removing thick center rib. Place leaves in a flat 2-quart casserole; add water. Cover. Cook with Microwave on High, 3 to 5 minutes or until limp. Let stand, covered, until ready to stuff. Combine ground beef, rice, onion, egg, 1 teaspoon soy sauce, Worcestershire sauce, pepper, garlic powder and 1/4 cup juice from tomatoes. Place about 1/4 cup of meat mixture on each piece of cabbage; roll up and tuck in edges to form bundles. Place seam side down in a 2-quart oblong utility dish, forming two rows. Cut up tomatoes with kitchen shears. Combine tomatoes, 2 teaspoons soy sauce, brown sugar and cornstarch in a 4-cup liquid measure. Cook with Microwave on High, 3 to 4 minutes or until mixture begins to thicken. Pour over cabbage bundles. Bake, uncovered, at 400° with Microwave on Low, 20 to 25 minutes, or until meat is cooked. Makes 4 to 6 servings.

Stuffed Green Peppers

Microwave Power:	High	Medium
Oven Selector:	Off	Bake
Oven Temperature:	Off	375°F, preheated
Shelf Position:	2	2

4 medium green peppers	1/2 teaspoon oregano, crushed
1/2 cup finely chopped onion	1/4 teaspoon garlic powder
1 lb. lean ground beef	1/8 teaspoon pepper
1-1/2 cups cooked rice	1 can (15-oz.) tomato sauce, reserve 1/4 cup
1 teaspoon salt	Grated Parmesan cheese

Cut tops off peppers about 1 inch from top of stem. Remove stems and seeds and chop remaining tops of peppers to make 1/2 cup. Remove seeds and membranes from inside peppers; place peppers open-side up in a glass utility dish or round glass cake dish. Cover loosely with plastic wrap. Cook with Microwave on High, 5 to 6 minutes or until tender. Let stand, covered, 5 minutes; remove from dish and turn upside down on paper towel to drain. Combine chopped green pepper, onion and crumbled beef in a 2-quart casserole. Cook with Microwave on High, 5 to 6 minutes or until vegetables are tender and all pink is gone from meat. Stir twice while cooking. Drain fat if necessary. Preheat oven. To meat mixture add rice, salt, oregano, garlic, pepper and tomato sauce. Stuff peppers with meat-rice mixture, mound high on tops. Place in the utility or cake dish used for cooking peppers. Carefully spoon reserved tomato sauce over top of each pepper. Bake uncovered at 375° with Microwave on Medium, 8 to 10 minutes or until very hot. Sprinkle with Parmesan cheese. Makes 4 servings.

Spanish Stuffed Onions

Microwave Power:	High	High
Oven Selector:	Off	Bake
Oven Temperature:	Off	400°F, not preheated
Shelf Position:	2	2

4 large onions, peeled (about 1-1/2 lbs.)
1/4 cup water
1/2 lb. lean ground beef
1 can (8-oz.) tomato sauce
1 cup cooked rice

1 teaspoon chili powder
1/2 teaspoon salt
Dash pepper
1/2 cup shredded Cheddar cheese

Place onions and water in a 2-quart casserole. Cover; cook with Microwave on High, 9 to 12 minutes or until onions are just about tender. Drain. Scoop out centers of onions, leaving walls about 1/3-inch thick. Chop enough onion pulp to make 1/2 cup. Combine with ground beef in a 1-quart casserole. Cover; cook with Microwave on High, 4 to 5 minutes. Drain off fat. Stir in half the tomato sauce and all remaining ingredients, except cheese. Stuff onions with beef-rice mixture mounding high on top. Spoon any remaining mixture in dish around onions. Pour remaining tomato sauce over all. Sprinkle with cheese. Bake at 400° with Microwave on High, 8 to 10 minutes. Makes 4 servings.

Cook onions in covered dish until just tender. Scoop out centers. Mound meat and onion mixture high in onion shells, top with tomato sauce and cheese.

Beef Enchiladas

Microwave Power:	High	Low	Low
Oven Selector:	Off	Bake	Broil
Oven Temperature:	Off	400°F, not preheated	High Broil
Shelf Position:	2	2	2

1 lb. lean ground beef
1/2 medium onion, chopped
1 teaspoon chili powder
1/2 teaspoon salt
1/2 teaspoon cumin
1/4 teaspoon pepper

1/8 teaspoon garlic powder
1 recipe Red Chili Sauce or
   2-1/2 cups favorite enchilada sauce
1/4 cup oil
8 corn tortillas
1-1/2 cups grated Cheddar cheese

Combine ground beef and onion in a 1-1/2 quart casserole. Cover with a paper towel. Cook with Microwave on High, 4 to 6 minutes or until all pink is gone from meat. Drain fat, if necessary. Stir in chili powder, salt, cumin, pepper and garlic powder. Pour 1/2 cup sauce into bottom of a 2-quart oblong baking dish. In a 1-1/2-quart round cake dish, heat oil with Microwave on High, 2 minutes or until hot. Heat tortillas with Microwave on High, 1 minute. Dip each tortilla in oil, then in sauce. Place about 1/4 cup meat mixture in center, roll tortilla to enclose filling and place seam-side down in baking dish. Pour remaining sauce over tortillas. Bake at 400° with Microwave on Low, 8 to 12 minutes or until sauce is bubbly. Sprinkle cheese evenly over enchiladas, set oven at High Broil and continue to cook with Microwave on Low, 3 to 5 minutes or until cheese is melted and bubbly. Makes 4 servings.

Beef & Noodle Casserole

Microwave Power:	High	Low
Oven Selector:	Off	Bake
Oven Temperature:	Off	400°F, not preheated
Shelf Position:	2	2

1 pkg. (8-oz.) egg noodles	1 can (4-oz.) sliced mushrooms, drained
1 lb. lean ground beef	2 cans (8-oz. each) tomato sauce
1 onion, chopped	1 teaspoon salt
1 green pepper, chopped	1/8 teaspoon pepper
1 can (12-oz.) whole corn, drained	1 cup grated Cheddar cheese

On cooktop cook noodles according to package directions; drain. Combine ground beef, onion and green pepper in a 2-quart oblong baking dish. Cook with Microwave on High, 4-1/2 to 5 minutes or until meat is cooked and vegetables are limp; stir twice. Drain off fat, if necessary. Combine all ingredients except grated cheese and pour into a greased 3-quart casserole. Bake at 400° with Microwave on Low, 10 minutes. Stir. Top with cheese and continue to Bake at 400° with Microwave on Low, 10 to 13 minutes or until heated through, bubbly around the edges and golden on top. Makes 6 to 8 servings.

Variation:

For a Mexican flavor, add 1 to 2 tablespoons of Mexican seasoning to casserole mixture before cooking.

Turkey Tetrazzini

Microwave Power:	High	Low
Oven Selector:	Off	Bake
Oven Temperature:	Off	400°F, not preheated
Shelf Position:	2	2

6-oz. spaghetti, or vermicelli, broken in pieces, cooked and drained	1/2 teaspoon salt
	Dash each thyme, marjoram and white pepper
1/2 lb. fresh mushrooms, sliced	1/4 cup sherry
6 tablespoons butter	1/2 cup grated Parmesan cheese
6 tablespoons flour	4 cups cooked, diced turkey
1-1/4 cups half and half	2 tablespoons grated Parmesan cheese
1-1/2 cups chicken broth	1 tablespoon snipped fresh parsley (optional)

On cooktop cook spaghetti or vermicelli according to package directions. Combine mushrooms and butter in a 2-1/2-quart casserole. Cover; cook with Microwave on High, 5 minutes, stirring once. Gradually blend in flour to make a paste and stir in half and half until blended; then stir in chicken broth. Cook with Microwave on High, 5 to 6 minutes until thickened, stirring twice. Stir in seasonings, sherry and 1/2 cup Parmesan cheese. Stir in cooked spaghetti and turkey. Bake at 400° with Microwave on Low, 6 minutes. Stir. Sprinkle top with 2 tablespoons Parmesan cheese. Continue to Bake at 400° with Microwave on Low, 6 to 8 minutes or until top is bubbly and lightly browned. Sprinkle with parsley. Makes 6 servings.

Chicken-Noodle Casserole

Microwave Power:	Low	Low
Oven Selector:	Bake	Broil
Oven Temperature:	400°F, not preheated	Medium Broil
Shelf Position:	2	2

4 oz. noodles, cooked and drained
1 can (10-3/4-oz.) cream of mushroom soup
3/4 cup milk
1/4 lb. (1 cup) grated mild Cheddar cheese
1/3 cup chopped green pepper

2 tablespoons chopped pimiento
1/2 teaspoon salt
1/4 teaspoon pepper
2 cups diced cooked chicken
3/4 cup crushed potato chips

Cook noodles on cooktop according to package directions. Combine noodles and remaining ingredients, except potato chips, in a 2-1/2-quart casserole and mix well. Bake at 400° with Microwave on Low, 10 minutes. Stir; sprinkle with potato chips and Broil at Medium Broil with Microwave on Low, 5 to 6 minutes until top is browned. Makes 6 servings.

Partially cook casserole, then stir, bringing center portion to the outer edges. After stirring, add topping and finish cooking.

Deep Dish Chicken Pie

Microwave Power:	High	Low
Oven Selector:	Off	Bake
Oven Temperature:	Off	450°F, preheated
Shelf Position:	2	2

Filling:

1/2 cup diced celery

1/2 cup diced carrots

1-1/2 cups diced potatoes

1/2 cup chopped onion

1/2 teaspoon tarragon, crushed

1/4 cup butter

5 tablespoons flour

1/2 teaspoon seasoned salt

1/4 teaspoon white pepper

1-1/2 cups chicken broth (or 1-1/2 cups water and 2 chicken bouillon cubes)

2 cups diced cooked chicken

3/4 cup frozen peas, defrosted

1/2 cup light cream

Crust:

2 cups biscuit mix

3/4 cup light cream

1 egg yolk

1 tablespoon water

Combine celery, carrots, potatoes, onion, tarragon and butter in a 10-inch glass-ceramic skillet. Cover; cook with Microwave on High, 12 to 15 minutes or until vegetables are tender. Stir in flour, seasoned salt and pepper, then stir in chicken broth until smooth; add chicken and peas. Cook with Microwave on High, 4 to 5 minutes until mixture begins to thicken, stirring twice. Stir in cream, cook with Microwave on High, 2 to 3 minutes. Preheat oven. Prepare crust according to directions.

Crust:

Combine biscuit mix and cream, blend with a fork. Turn onto a lightly floured board. Knead quickly about ten times. Roll out to about 1/4 inch thick. Lay dough gently over filling mixture, bringing dough up over edge of casserole dish, trim overhang to 1 inch, turn under and flute against edge of casserole. Beat egg yolk with water and brush over top of crust. Make six small slits in crust. Bake at 450° with Microwave on Low, 7 to 9 minutes, or until crust is nicely browned. Let stand 5 minutes before serving. Makes 6 servings.

Baked Chicken-Cheese Tacos

Microwave Power:	High	Low
Oven Selector:	Off	Bake
Oven Temperature:	Off	400°F, not preheated
Shelf Position:	2	2

1/2 lb. Cheddar cheese, grated
1/2 lb. Monterey Jack cheese, grated
12 corn tortillas, in package
1 to 1-1/2 cups diced cooked chicken or turkey
1 can (7-oz.) chopped green chiles, not drained
1 tablespoon oil
1 small onion, chopped

1 clove garlic, minced
1 can (28-oz.) whole tomatoes, snipped into small pieces, undrained
1 can (8-oz.) tomato sauce
1 teaspoon oregano, crushed
1 teaspoon salt
1 pt. (2 cups) dairy sour cream

Toss together grated cheeses to mix; reserve 1 cup for topping. Heat tortillas in package with Microwave on High, 1 to 1-1/2 minutes or until softened. Divide filling ingredients evenly between tortillas using cheeses, chicken or turkey and 1 tablespoon chiles per tortilla. Roll tortillas and place seam side down in a lightly greased 3-quart oblong utility dish. Place oil, onion and garlic in a 2-1/2-quart casserole; cover. Cook with Microwave on High, 3 minutes. Stir in tomatoes, tomato liquid, tomato sauce, oregano and salt. Cover and cook with Microwave on High, 10 minutes. Remove cover and continue to cook with Microwave on High, 5 to 7 minutes to thicken. Pour over tortillas, carefully covering all surfaces. Bake at 400° with Microwave on Low, 10 minutes. Sprinkle surface with reserved cheese. Continue to Bake at 400° with Microwave on Low for an additional 5 to 8 minutes or until hot, bubbly and heated through. Garnish with dollops of sour cream. Makes 6 servings.

Turkey & Wild Rice Casserole

Microwave Power:	High	Medium	High	Medium
Oven Selector:	Off	Off	Off	Bake
Oven Temperature:	Off	Off	Off	400°F, preheated
Shelf Position:	2	2	2	2

2-1/2 cups water
1 tablespoon butter
1 pkg. (6-oz.) Long Grain and Wild Rice Mix
1/2 lb. ground pork sausage
1 jar (4-1/2-oz.) sliced mushrooms, undrained

1 can (10-1/2-oz.) cream of mushroom soup
2 tablespoons dry vermouth
4 cups cooked, diced turkey
1/3 cup sliced almonds

Place water and butter in a 2-1/2-quart covered glass casserole. Bring to a boil with Microwave on High, 5 to 7 minutes. Add rice and seasonings; cover. Continue cooking with Microwave on Medium, 18 to 20 minutes or until rice tests done. Let stand 5 minutes. If all the water has not been absorbed, do not drain. Crumble sausage in a 1-quart glass dish. Cook with Microwave on High, 2 minutes. Stir; continue to cook with Microwave on High, 1 to 2 minutes longer or until sausage is cooked. Drain. Preheat oven. In a separate bowl combine mushrooms, mushroom liquid, condensed soup and vermouth. In a 2-1/2-quart buttered casserole, layer half each of cooked rice, sausage, turkey and soup mixture. Repeat layers. Sprinkle with almonds. Cover. Bake at 400° with Microwave on Medium, 10 minutes. Uncover and continue to Bake at 400° with Microwave on Medium, 8 to 10 minutes or until bubbly. Makes 4 to 6 servings.

Ham-Yam Towers

Microwave Power:	High	Medium
Oven Selector:	Off	Bake
Oven Temperature:	Off	375°F, not preheated
Shelf Position:	2	2

2 tablespoons butter
1 can (29-oz.) yams, drained and mashed
1/4 teaspoon salt
1/4 cup chopped pecans
1 lb. cooked ham, ground (2 cups) or
　blender flaked (2-1/2 cups)

2 to 3 eggs
16 slices bacon (about 1 lb.)
1 can (20-oz.) pineapple slices
8 stuffed olives

Melt butter in a 1-cup liquid measure with Microwave on High, 30 to 45 seconds. Whip together butter, yams, salt and pecans; shape into 8 patties. Combine ham with eggs. Flaked ham will require more egg. Shape into 8 patties. Arrange 2 slices of bacon crisscrossed on broil pan; top with pineapple slice, yam pattie and ham pattie. Wrap bacon slices over top and anchor each with a toothpick. Place on wire rack in glass-ceramic open roaster. Bake at 375° with Microwave on Medium, 15 to 18 minutes or until bacon is cooked. Garnish with olives. Makes 8 servings.

Variation:

If desired, 16 slices of pineapple may be used. Prepare as above, but top each stack with an additional pineapple slice before folding up bacon. Baking instructions remain the same.

Italian Sausage with Peppers & Zucchini

Microwave Power:	High
Oven Selector:	Off
Oven Temperature:	Off
Shelf Position:	2

1 lb. sweet Italian sausage, cut in chunks
1 medium onion, thinly sliced
1 small clove garlic, crushed and minced
2 medium green peppers, cut in 1-inch cubes
1 can (28-oz.) whole tomatoes,
   partially drained and cut up

1 lb. zucchini, sliced
1/2 lb. mushrooms, cut in quarters
1 teaspoon salt
1 teaspoon oregano, crushed
1/2 teaspoon pepper

Combine sausage, onion and garlic in a 4-quart casserole. Cook with Microwave on High, 4 minutes. Add peppers; continue to cook with Microwave on High, 3 to 4 minutes or until sausage is no longer a pink color. Drain excess fat. Add remaining ingredients, cook with Microwave on High, 10 to 15 minutes or until zucchini and peppers are tender-crisp, stirring twice during cooking. Do not overcook or allow vegetables to get soggy. Makes 6 to 8 servings.

Italian Spaghetti Sauce

Microwave Power:	High
Oven Selector:	Off
Oven Temperature	Off
Shelf Position:	2

1 lb. Italian sausage, skin removed
1 onion, finely chopped
1 clove garlic, minced or
   1/4 teaspoon garlic powder
3 tablespoons fresh minced parsley
1/2 cup finely chopped celery
1 teaspoon oregano, crushed
1/2 teaspoon basil, crushed
1/2 teaspoon marjoram, crushed
1/4 teaspoon mint leaves, crushed

1 can (1 lb. 12 oz.) whole tomatoes, cut-up
1 can (6 oz.) tomato paste
1-1/2 teaspoons salt
1/8 teaspoon pepper
1 whole bay leaf
1 cup water
1/2 cup Burgundy or water or liquid
   drained from mushrooms
1 can (4 oz.) mushrooms, drained
Parmesan cheese

Crumble sausage into 3-quart casserole. Cover with a paper towel; cook with Microwave on High, 5 minutes or until all pink has disappeared, stirring after 2-1/2 minutes. Drain off most of the fat. Add onion, garlic, parsley, celery, oregano, basil, marjoram and mint leaves and stir well. Cover; cook with Microwave on High, 7 to 8 minutes or until onion and celery are tender, stirring once or twice. Stir in remaining ingredients. Cover; cook with Microwave on High, 25 to 30 minutes, stirring occasionally. Remove lid last 10 minutes to thicken sauce. Serve over cooked spaghetti and sprinkle with Parmesan cheese. Makes 4 to 6 servings.

Eggs

Microwave cooking is excellent for scrambling and poaching eggs. Scrambled eggs are soft and fluffy, but will toughen if overcooked. Mixing eggs to combine the yolk and white, plus the addition of other ingredients help eggs cook evenly. When not mixed, the yolk will usually cook faster than the white. Poaching eggs in water helps to equalize the temperature. Cook a poached egg until the yolk is just set, then let stand in water 1 or 2 minutes until white is set.

Combination heat and microwaves produce excellent results with egg casseroles, including soufflés. Try our Cheese Soufflé, then one of your favorites. Egg casseroles, are usually cooked with Low microwave power, with the exception of quiche. In testing, the best results with quiche were with High microwave power and oven heat, which quickly sets the egg-cheese filling. Then allow the quiche to stand in a hot oven to completely set the center without overcooking the edges.

Do not attempt to cook eggs in the shell in the microwave oven. Pressure can build-up within the egg causing it to burst.

Speedy Scrambled Eggs

Microwave Power: High
Oven Selector: Off
Oven Temperature: Off
Shelf Position: 2

Number of Eggs	Water or Milk	Glass Dish Size	Butter	Minutes*
1	1 tablespoon	6-oz. custard cup	1 teaspoon	1 to 1-1/2
2	2 tablespoons	6-oz. custard cup	2 teaspoons	1-1/2 to 2
3	3 tablespoons	9-inch pie plate	1 tablespoon	2 to 2-1/2
4	4 tablespoons	9-inch pie plate	4 teaspoons	2-1/2 to 3

Combine eggs and liquid with a fork. Season with salt and pepper, if desired. Melt butter with Microwave on High. Add eggs and cook with Microwave on High, according to above chart. Stir often with fork or rubber scraper. Butter may be omitted.

* Times are based on large eggs, at refrigerated temperature. For creamier scrambled eggs, reduce Microwave to Medium and cook. Cooking time will be approximately double.

Creamy Scrambled Eggs

Microwave Power:	High	Medium
Oven Selector:	Off	Off
Oven Temperature:	Off	Off
Shelf Position:	2	2

6 eggs
1/4 cup milk
1/4 teaspoon salt
Dash pepper

2 tablespoons butter
1 pkg. (3-oz.) cream cheese,
    cut into 1/2-inch cubes
Chopped chives or onion tops

Mix eggs with milk, salt and pepper. In a 1-1/2-quart casserole melt butter with Microwave on High, 45 seconds to 1 minute. Add egg mixture and cook with Microwave on Medium, 3 minutes. Stir. Cook with Microwave on Medium, stirring often until eggs are three quarters set, about 2 minutes. Blend in cream cheese. Cook with Microwave on Medium, stirring occasionally until set, 1-1/2 to 2-1/2 minutes depending upon temperature of cream cheese. Garnish with chives or onion tops. Makes 3 servings.

Savory Scrambled Eggs

Microwave Power:	High	Medium
Oven Selector:	Off	Off
Oven Temperature:	Off	Off
Shelf Position:	2	2

4 eggs	4 medium mushrooms, sliced (about 1/3 cup)
1/2 cup milk	1/2 cup avocado, diced
1/4 teaspoon salt	1/2 medium tomato, cut into eighths and seeded
Dash pepper	

Beat eggs, milk, salt and pepper until light and fluffy. Melt butter in an 8-inch round glass baking dish with Microwave on High, 45 seconds to 1 minute. Add eggs and mushrooms. Cook with Microwave on Medium, 1-1/2 minutes. Stir. Continue to cook with Microwave on Medium, stirring often until almost set, 3-1/2 to 4 minutes. Carefully fold in avocado and tomato. Continue cooking with Microwave on Medium, 30 seconds to 1 minute, to heat vegetables. Makes 2 to 4 servings.

Poached Eggs

Microwave Power:	High
Oven Selector:	Off
Oven Temperature:	Off
Shelf Position:	2

Quantity	Amount of Water	Cooking Container	Cooking Time for Eggs
1	1/4 cup	10-ounce custard cup	1/2 to 3/4 minute
2	1 cup	1-quart casserole	3/4 to 1-1/4 minutes
4	1-1/2 cups	2-quart casserole	1-1/2 to 1-3/4 minutes

Place specified amount of water in container indicated for desired quantity of eggs. Cover; bring water to a boil with Microwave on High. Break eggs one at a time, into saucer and slide into water; cover. Cook with Microwave on High according to chart.

Cheese Soufflé

Microwave Power:	Low	Off
Oven Selector:	Bake	Bake
Oven Temperature:	400°F, not preheated	400°F
Shelf Position:	2	2

1 cup thick White Sauce
1/4 teaspoon dry mustard
Dash cayenne pepper
1 cup grated sharp Cheddar cheese

3 eggs, separated
1/4 teaspoon cream of tartar
Grated Parmesan cheese

Make 1 cup thick White Sauce from recipe in sauce section. Add dry mustard and cayenne pepper when adding flour, salt and pepper in White Sauce recipe. Stir in Cheddar cheese. Let cheese melt. Beat egg yolks until lemony colored, add to cheese sauce. Beat egg whites and cream of tartar with electric mixer until stiff, but not dry. Fold egg whites into cheese sauce. Pour mixture into a 1-1/2-quart, straight sided glass casserole that has been buttered and dusted with grated Parmesan cheese. With a sharp knife, make a cut around casserole, about 2 inches from edge. Bake at 400° with Microwave on Low, 6 minutes. Turn Microwave Off and continue to Bake at 400°, 10 to 12 minutes. Makes 4 servings.

Eggs Benedict

Microwave Power:	High
Oven Selector:	Off
Oven Temperature:	Off
Shelf Position:	2

2 English muffins, split, toasted
2 tablespoons butter
4 thin slices ham

4 poached eggs
1/2 recipe Hollandaise Sauce

Arrange toasted muffin halves on a serving platter. In a round glass dish cook butter with Microwave on High, 2 minutes or until hot and bubbly. Lay ham in dish, turn to coat all sides with butter. Cook with Microwave on High, 2 to 3 minutes or until ham is hot. Place a slice of ham on each muffin half, top with a poached egg and pour hot Hollandaise Sauce over all. Serve immediately. Makes 2 servings.

Chile Relleno Bake

Microwave Power:	Low	Off
Oven Selector:	Bake	Bake
Oven Temperature:	350°F, preheated	350°F
Shelf Position:	2	2

6 eggs, separated
1 tablespoon flour
1/4 teaspoon salt
1/8 teaspoon white pepper

1 can (4-oz.) whole green chiles
1/4 lb. Cheddar cheese, sliced thin
1/4 lb. Monterey Jack cheese, sliced thin
1 recipe Red Chili Sauce

Beat egg whites until stiff, but not dry. Beat egg yolks until thick; stir in flour, salt and pepper. Fold into egg whites. Spread half of egg mixture into a greased 3-quart oblong baking dish. Slit chiles, open flat and remove any seeds. Lay chiles over egg mixture, layer cheeses over chiles and spread remaining egg mixture over all. Bake at 350° with Microwave on Low, 5 minutes. Turn Microwave Off and continue to Bake until light brown, 3 to 6 minutes. Cut in squares and serve immediately. Top with Red Chili Sauce. Makes 6 to 8 servings.

Classic Quiche Lorraine

Microwave Power:	High	High
Oven Selector:	Off	Bake
Oven Temperature:	Off	350°F, preheated
Shelf Position:	2	2

6 slices bacon
2 green onions, chopped
1 cup (1/2 pt.) whipping cream
1/2 cup milk
1/2 teaspoon salt

1/8 teaspoon white pepper
Dash nutmeg
4 eggs, beaten
2 cups shredded Swiss cheese
1 (9-inch) baked pie shell

Place bacon in a 2-quart oblong baking dish; cover with a paper towel. Cook with Microwave on High, 9 to 11 minutes or until bacon is crisp. Place 1 tablespoon bacon drippings in a 4-cup liquid measure; add green onions and cook with Microwave on High, 2 minutes. Stir in whipping cream, milk, salt, pepper and nutmeg. Cook with Microwave on High, 3 minutes, until hot but not boiling. Preheat oven. Pour cream mixture slowly into beaten eggs, stirring constantly. Stir in cheese. Crumble bacon into pie shell and pour milk-egg-cheese mixture over bacon. Bake at 350° with Microwave on High, 3 minutes. Rotate dish one half turn; continue to Bake at 350° with Microwave on High, 2 to 4 minutes or until filling is almost set in the center. Turn oven Off. Allow pie to stand in hot oven 15 minutes or until center is completely set. Cut in wedges and serve warm. Makes 6 to 8 servings.

Roasting Meats

Notes for Conventional Heat and Microwave

Roasting is done with a combination of Bake heat and Low microwave power. There are several factors to consider when roasting any cut of meat.

Size—Any weight roast can be roasted successfully, however, a small roast may not brown sufficiently in the suggested roasting time. So higher oven temperature may be required.

Shape—A long, thin roast will take less time to cook than a short, thick roast of the same weight. Symetrically shaped roasts will have more uniform cooking results than irregularly shaped roasts.

Temperature—A very cold roast from the refrigerator will take longer to cook than one which has warmed slightly. For best results, roasts that have been frozen should be thoroughly defrosted, unless following a freezer-to-table recipe.

Cut of Meat—Only tender cuts of meat are recommended for roasting with heat and microwave. Most lamb and pork roasts are considered tender cuts and give good results. Check recipes in the cookbook for techniques of cooking less tender cuts of meat that require moist heat for tenderizing.

Bone and Fat—The bone and fat content of a roast will have a definite effect on the way it cooks. A rib or standing roast may require a longer cooking time than a boneless roast of the same cut. Occasionally the interior meat directly adjacent to the bone will remain pink even though the meat thermometer registers a finished temperature. Longer cooking may dry the meat, however the roast can be sliced through to the bone in several places then returned to the oven to cook with microwave power and residual oven heat for a very short time (4 to 5 minutes on low power). Much fat within a roast can affect cooking and cause inaccurate readings on a meat thermometer.

Meat Thermometer—Most meat thermometers cannot be used when microwave power is present. However, a thermometer specifically designed for microwave use may be used when cooking with heat and microwave power, if it has a heat resistant cover. This oven has a built-in thermometer.

Dish for Roasting—Select a shallow glass or glass-ceramic baking dish for best results. Metal roasting pans are not recommended, except for large turkeys, (see pages 10 and 161).

Shielding—Occasionally some areas of a roast may cook more quickly than others. When this happens, small pieces of foil may be used to cover the meat at the fast cooking spots. Foil directs the microwave energy away from the covered areas.

Instructions for Conventional Heat and Microwave Energy

In a shallow glass or glass-ceramic baking dish place boneless roast fat side down, or bone-in roast, bone side down on a heat-proof trivet or directly in dish. Season as desired, but do not add salt until cooking is completed. Place baking dish in center of oven with shelf in #2 position. Set oven temperature and microwave power, as directed in meat roasting chart. Calculate approximate cooking time by multiplying weight of roast by minimum minutes per-pound listed on chart. For best results turn boneless roasts fat side up after half of cooking time. When roast has cooked minimum amount of time, remove from oven and insert a meat thermometer in thickest part of muscle and determine internal temperature. If necessary, remove thermometer and continue to cook, checking at about 5 minute intervals. When meat has reached desired internal temperature, cover loosely with foil and allow roast to stand specified time (meat will continue to cook and juices will set) before carving.

Roasting

Cut of Meat	Minutes per pound to cook	Internal Temperature at end of cooking °F	Approximate Standing Time	Special Instructions
BEEF Microwave Power: Low Oven Selector: Bake Oven Temperature: 325°F, not preheated Shelf Position: 2				

Rib Roast - Standing or Rolled
  Rare
  Medium
  Well
	
	8 to 11
	9 to 12
	10 to 14
		
		120° to 135°
		135° to 150°
		150° to 165°
			
			10 minutes
			15 minutes
			20 minutes
				Boneless roasts start cooking fat side down, then turn roast over after half of cooking time. Bone-in roasts cook with bone down, are not turned over.

Sirloin Roast -
  Rare
  Medium
  Well
	
	7 to 10
	9 to 11
	10 to 13
		
		120° to 135°
		135° to 150°
		150° to 165°
			
			10 minutes
			15 minutes
			20 minutes
				Salt after cooking.
				Shield fast cooking areas of roast with foil if necessary.

Rump - Rolled or Watermelon Cut -
  Rare
  Medium
  Well
	
	7 to 10
	9 to 11
	10 to 13
		
		120° to 135°
		135° to 150°
		150° to 165°
			
			10 minutes
			15 minutes
			20 minutes
				Small roasts (1-1/2 to 3 lbs.) use 350°F or 375°F oven temperature.

LAMB Microwave Power: Low Oven Selector: Bake Oven Temperature: 350°F, not preheated Shelf Position: 2				

Shoulder, Leg, Rib or Loin
  Medium
  Well
	
	8 to 11
	10 to 12
		
		150° to 170°
		170° to 180°
			
			15 minutes
				Start cooking boneless roasts fat side down, turn over after half of cooking. Cook bone-in roasts bone down, do not turn over, except legs.
				
				Shield narrow end of leg roasts after half of cooking, when turning over.
				
				Salt after cooking.

PORK Microwave Power: Low Oven Selector: Bake Oven Temperature: 350°F, not preheated Shelf Position: 2				
Pork Loin or Rib	10 to 13	175° to 180°	15 minutes	Bone in roasts cook bone down, do not turn over. Boneless roasts start fat side down, turn over after half of cooking. Shield ends of roast with foil toward end of cooking if very brown. Season to taste, but salt after cooking.

Roast Prime

138

Beef

Along with basic roasting information, we have included a variety of recipes for less tender cuts of beef, ground beef and others. Beef dishes can be cooked with bake or broil heat in combination with microwave energy; or when first browned on the cooktop, can be cooked with microwave only.

Ground beef is well suited to microwave and combination cooking. Included are some basic recipes, such as Basic Meat Loaf, to introduce you to beef cookery in the Thermatronic II oven. Try a few of these recipes, then incorporate the methods given here to your own special meat loaf. Check other sections, like appetizers and main dishes for more ground beef recipes.

Our testing indicated that best results were achieved with less tender cuts of meat when they were first browned on the cooktop. If a glass-ceramic casserole or skillet is used, the meat can be browned, then cooked in the oven in the same utensil.

Low microwave power and a bake heat are used to cook the meat for a short time, then a low bake heat (325°F) is used to slowly simmer the meat in liquid until it is tender. This method usually cuts total cooking time by about half compared with conventional cooking.

Freezer Pot Roast and Freezer Swiss Steak are recipes for cooking frozen less tender cuts of beef without thawing the meat. The meat is first cooked with Low microwave power only, then a 300°F bake heat is added to the last part of cooking to add browning. A tight fitting lid is important in this method. Be sure to allow meat to stand, covered, at least 10 minutes after cooking.

Freezer Pot Roast

Microwave Power:	Low	Low
Oven Selector:	Off	Bake
Oven Temperature:	Off	300° F, not preheated
Shelf Position:	2	2

3 lbs. boneless chuck roast, frozen
1 envelope (1-1/4 to 1-1/2-oz.) dry
   onion soup mix
1 lb. (4 small) new potatoes, peel and
   quartered

1 cup sliced celery, cut 1-inch thick
1 cup thinly sliced onion, separated
2 cups slivered carrots, cut 2-inches long

Place completely frozen meat in a 3-quart casserole and cover tightly. Cook with Microwave on Low, 30 minutes. Turn meat over and sprinkle with 1/2 package of onion soup mix, spreading evenly to edges of meat. Cover tightly. Cook with Microwave on Low, 30 minutes. Turn meat over, sprinkle with remaining soup mix and place vegetables over and around meat. Cover tightly. Bake at 300° with Microwave on Low, 20 to 30 minutes, until meat and vegetables are tender. Let stand covered 10 minutes before serving. Makes 4 to 6 servings.

Place frozen meat in cooking dish, cover tightly and cook. After approximately 2/3 of cooking time, turn roast over again, add remaining soup mix and vegetables, return to oven and finish cooking.

Freezer Swiss Steak

Microwave Power:	Low	Low
Oven Selector:	Off	Bake
Oven Temperature:	Off	300°F, not preheated
Shelf Position:	2	2

3 lbs. thick top round steak, frozen	1 teaspoon salt
1 can (8-oz.) tomato sauce	1 teaspoon oregano, crushed
1/4 cup dry red wine	Dash pepper
3 tablespoons instant minced onion	

Place completely frozen meat in a 3-quart casserole and cover tightly. Cook with Microwave on Low, 30 minutes. Turn meat over, pour on tomato sauce and wine; sprinkle with seasonings. Cover tightly and Bake at 300° with Microwave on Low, 30 to 40 minutes or until meat is tender. Let stand covered 10 minutes before serving. Makes 4 to 6 servings.

Chinese Pepper Steak

Microwave Power:	Low	Off	Low
Oven Selector:	Bake	Bake	Off
Oven Temperature:	325°F, not preheated	325°F	Off
Shelf Position:	2	2	2

2 lbs. top round steak, cut into 1/4-inch strips	1 teaspoon sugar
3 tablespoons oil	2 bay leaves
2 medium onions, thinly sliced	1/2 teaspoon leaf thyme, crushed
1 cup thinly sliced celery	2 large green peppers, cut into 1/2-inch strips
2 cups (1 lb.) canned tomatoes	2 teaspoons soy sauce
1-1/2 teaspoons salt	1/4 cup cold water
1/2 teaspoon pepper	2 tablespoons cornstarch

Have meat tenderized when purchased or pound with a meat mallet. On the cooktop heat oil in a 4-quart glass-ceramic saucepot. Brown meat strips quickly in hot oil. Add onions, celery, tomatoes, salt, pepper, sugar, bay leaves and thyme. Cover and Bake at 325° with Microwave on Low, 15 minutes. Turn Microwave Off and continue to Bake at 325°, 15 to 25 minutes or until meat is just about tender. Turn Oven Off. Add green peppers, cook with Microwave on Low, 10 to 12 minutes or until meat is tender and peppers are cooked. Remove bay leaves. Combine soy sauce, water and cornstarch. Stir into pepper steak; cook with Microwave on Low, 3 to 5 minutes, stirring twice. Serve over rice. Makes 6 to 8 servings.

Barbecue-Broiled Roast

Microwave Power:	Medium
Oven Selector:	Broil
Oven Temperature:	High Broil, not preheated
Shelf Position:	3

Marinade:

2 tablespoons instant minced onion

1/4 cup soy sauce

1/4 cup Worcestershire sauce

1/2 cup oil

1/2 cup catsup

3/4 cup wine vinegar

2 teaspoons rosemary, crushed

1 teaspoon dry mustard

1 round bone or chuck roast, 2 to 3 inches thick

Blend marinade ingredients together. Place roast in 3-quart oblong baking dish; cover with marinade. Cover dish; marinate in refrigerator 24 to 48 hours, turning meat occasionally. When ready to cook, place meat on Thermatronic II two-piece broil pan. Broil on High Broil with Microwave on Medium, 5 to 6 minutes per pound. Turn roast over every 10 minutes; baste generously with remaining marinade each time roast is turned. Cooking time will depend on thickness of roast and desired degree of doneness. This roast should not be cooked too well done in the center.

Perfect Beef Stroganoff

Microwave Power:	Medium
Oven Selector:	Off
Oven Temperature:	Off
Shelf Position:	2

3 tablespoons butter

1-1/2 lbs. beef sirloin,
  cut into 1/2 x 2-inch strips

1 cup chopped onion

3 tablespoons flour

1/2 teaspoon salt

1/8 teaspoon pepper

3/4 cup boiling water

1 beef bouillon cube

1 tablespoon catsup

1/4 lb. fresh mushrooms,
  sliced 1/4-inch thick

1 cup dairy sour cream

3 tablespoons dry white wine

On the cooktop heat 2 tablespoons butter in a 10-inch glass-ceramic skillet. Brown meat strips quickly on all sides. Remove beef as it browns; set aside. In remaining butter, sauté onions until just limp. Turn off heat. Add flour, salt and pepper, stirring until smooth. Mix boiling water and bouillon cube, stirring to dissolve; add catsup and combine. Gradually add bouillon to flour mixture. Add meat and mushrooms, stirring to blend. Cover, cook with Microwave on Medium, 8 to 10 minutes until sauce comes to a boil. Add sour cream and wine, stirring until well blended. Heat uncovered with Microwave on Medium, 4 to 5 minutes, to heat through. Serve over wild rice and white rice combined or over noodles. Makes 4 to 5 servings.

Meatballs & Rice

Microwave Power:	High
Oven Selector:	Off
Oven Temperature:	Off
Shelf Position:	2

1 lb. lean ground beef
1/4 cup uncooked long grain rice
1 teaspoon salt
1 tablespoon oil
1 can (28-oz.) tomatoes
1/2 cup chopped onion
2 cups thinly sliced carrots

1 cup thinly sliced celery
1 cup thinly sliced celery
1 teaspoon oregano, crushed
1 bay leaf
1 beef bouillon cube
1 cup water

Combine beef, rice and salt. Form into 16 balls. On cooktop heat oil in 4-quart glass-ceramic saucepot. Brown meatballs on all sides. Drain fat, if necessary. Add remaining ingredients. Cover; cook with Microwave on High, 20 to 25 minutes or until vegetables are done. Makes 4 servings.

Pizza Burgers

Microwave Power:	Low	High
Oven Selector:	Broil	Off
Oven Temperature:	High Broil, preheated	Off
Shelf Position:	4	2

2 lbs. lean ground beef
1/2 cup grated mozzarella cheese
2 tablespoons grated Parmesan cheese

1 teaspoon instant minced onion
1/2 teaspoon salt
1/4 cup chopped ripe olives

Sauce:
1 can (8-oz.) tomato sauce
1/2 teaspoon oregano, crushed

1/2 teaspoon garlic salt

Divide meat into 6 oval patties, 3-1/2 inches by 7 inches. Combine mozzarella cheese, Parmesan cheese, onion, salt and olives. Place equal amount of mixture on top of each patty. Fold patties in half; pinch to seal and shape into about 3-1/2-inch rounds. Place on two-piece broil pan. Preheat Broil on High for 2 minutes, then Broil on High Broil with Microwave on Low, 6 to 7-1/2 minutes. Slightly undercook to desired doneness. Meat will continue to cook after being removed from oven. Move rack to Shelf Position 2.

Sauce:
Combine tomato sauce, oregano and garlic salt in a 2-cup liquid measure. Heat with Microwave on High, 2 to 2-1/2 minutes, or until hot. Serve with burgers. Makes 6 servings.

Basic Meat Loaf

Microwave Power:	High	Medium
Oven Selector:	Off	Bake
Oven Temperature:	Off	425°F, preheated
Shelf Position:	2	2

1 medium onion, finely chopped
1/2 medium bell pepper, finely chopped
2 eggs
1 cup milk
2 cups corn flakes

1/2 teaspoon salt
1/4 teaspoon pepper
1 teaspoon Worcestershire sauce
1-1/2 lbs. lean ground beef

Place chopped onions and bell pepper in a 1-quart glass casserole; cover and cook until limp with Microwave on High, 4 to 5 minutes. Preheat oven. Beat eggs slightly in a 3-quart bowl. Stir in milk, corn flakes, salt, pepper and Worcestershire sauce. Combine cooked vegetables and meat with milk mixture. Place meat mixture in a 2-quart glass loaf dish. Bake at 425° with Microwave on Medium, 7 minutes. Rotate dish 1/4 turn. Continue to bake at 425° with Microwave on Medium, 6 to 9 minutes or until done. Let stand 10 minutes before removing to platter. Makes 4 to 6 servings.

Variation:
For an extra flavor treat, add 1/2 cup cooked and cubed ham, ham-type canned luncheon loaf, or cooked smokie links.

Meatzza Pizza

Microwave Power:	Low
Oven Selector:	Bake
Oven Temperature:	450°F, preheated
Shelf Position:	2

1 lb. lean ground beef
1/2 cup seasoned dry bread crumbs
1/2 teaspoon salt
1/8 teaspoon pepper
1/8 teaspoon garlic powder
1 egg, beaten
1 can (15-oz.) pizza sauce

1/2 teaspoon oregano, crushed
1 cup grated Cheddar cheese
1 cup grated mozzarella cheese
1 jar (4-oz.) sliced mushrooms, drained
Cooked sausage, salami, olives and green pepper slices (optional)

Mix together ground beef, bread crumbs, salt, pepper, garlic powder, egg and 1/4 cup pizza sauce. Press into a 10-inch glass pie plate to form a crust. Bake at 450° with Microwave on Low, 6 to 8 minutes or until cooked through and edges are brown. Drain excess fat from meat. Sprinkle crust with oregano and spread with remaining pizza sauce. Top pizza sauce with cheeses, mushrooms and any other desired toppings. Bake at 450° with Microwave on Low, 2 to 4 minutes or until cheese is melted and bubbly. Let stand 5 minutes. Cut into wedges. Makes 4 servings.

Swiss Steak

Microwave Power:	Low	Off
Oven Selector:	Bake	Bake
Oven Temperature:	325°F, not preheated	325°F
Shelf Position:	2	2

2 lbs. round steak, 1/2-inch thick
1/4 cup flour
1-1/2 teaspoons salt
1/8 teaspoon pepper
3 tablespoons shortening
1 onion, sliced
1/2 teaspoon oregano, crushed
1/4 teaspoon garlic powder

1/2 cup chopped celery
1/2 cup chopped green pepper
1 can (28-oz.) tomatoes, mashed,
    do not drain
1/4 cup water
1/4 pound mozzarella cheese,
    thinly sliced (optional)

Pound meat with meat mallet to tenderize. Dredge meat in mixture of flour, 1 teaspoon salt, and pepper. On cooktop, heat shortening in a 4-quart glass-ceramic casserole. Add meat and brown on both sides. Cook onions until transparent. Stir in remaining ingredients, except cheese, and remaining flour mixture. Be sure all the meat is covered with liquid. Cover and Bake at 325° with Microwave on Low, 15 minutes. Turn Microwave Off. Continue to Bake at 325°, 20 to 25 minutes or until meat is tender. Top meat with cheese slices. Makes 4 to 6 servings.

Veal

Included here is a sampling of veal recipes. Veal cutlets are tender and cook quickly with Low microwave power. A veal roast can be roasted like beef to well done (165°F internal temperature on a meat thermometer.) Most veal recipes will adapt well to the Thermatronic II oven.

Veal Scaloppine

Microwave Power:	Low
Oven Selector:	Off
Oven Temperature:	Off
Shelf Position:	2

1 lb. thin veal cutlets
1/4 cup flour
1/4 cup (1/2 stick) butter
1 clove garlic, minced
1 jar (2-1/2-oz.) sliced mushrooms

1/2 cup dry white wine
1 chicken bouillon cube
1/4 cup water
Salt and pepper to taste

Coat veal with flour, reserve remaining flour. On cooktop, melt butter in a 10-inch glass-ceramic skillet; add garlic. Brown veal quickly in garlic butter. Stir in remaining flour, then mushrooms, wine, bouillon cube and water. Cook with Microwave on Low, 8 to 12 minutes or until veal is tender. Do not overcook or meat will become tough. Season with salt and pepper. Makes 4 servings.

Mrs. Beardo's Veal Rolls

Microwave Power:	Low
Oven Selector:	Off
Oven Temperature:	Off
Shelf Position:	2

6 veal cutlets (about 1 lb.)
2 tablespoons olive oil
2 tablespoons bread crumbs
Salt
Pepper
6 slices prosciutto or 4 oz. chip beef, sliced thin
1 pkg. (6-oz.) sliced mozzarella cheese, cut into
    12 pieces

3 tablespoons butter
2 tablespoons flour
1 cup sherry
1 can (4-oz.) sliced mushrooms, drained
Snipped parsely for garnish

Flatten cutlets, if necessary, and shape into squares. Spread each with 1 teaspoon olive oil and sprinkle each with 1 teaspoon bread crumbs. Lightly season with salt and pepper. Top each with a slice of prosciutto or chip beef and two pieces of mozzarella. Fold over like an envelope, tuck edges inward to seal in cheese, and close with toothpicks. Melt butter in a 10-inch glass-ceramic skillet on cooktop. Brown rolls on all sides and remove to a platter. Add flour to butter drippings and mix well. Add sherry and mushrooms and cook a few minutes until bubbly and thickened. Roll veal in gravy to cover all surfaces and add collected juices from platter. Cover and cook with Microwave on Low, 8 to 12 minutes or until hot and tender. Remove toothpicks and garnish with snipped parsley. Makes 6 servings.

Lamb

Lamb is generally cooked like beef when roasted or broiled. Consult the meat roasting notes and chart for lamb roasting information. Ground lamb may be substituted in most recipes calling for ground beef, including broiled patties. Try combining ground lamb, beef and pork in the Basic Meat Loaf recipe in the Beef section. Low microwave power speeds broiling, as in Minted Lamb Chops.

Cooked lamb is excellent in casseroles, and preparation is usually very fast since meat is cooked ahead. Roasted lamb is generally used when cooked lamb is called for in a recipe.

Easy Lamb Stew

Microwave Power:	High
Oven Selector:	Off
Oven Temperature:	Off
Shelf Position:	2

3/4 to 1 lb. carrots, peeled and cut diagonally into 1-inch pieces
2 tablespoons water
2 cups cubed cooked lamb
2 cans (10-1/2-oz. each) mushroom gravy
1 can (16-oz.) extra small whole new potatoes, drained

1/2 pkg. (20-oz.) frozen whole onions, not defrosted
1/2 to 1 pkg. (10-oz.) frozen, peas, not defrosted

Place carrots and water in a 3-quart casserole. Cover and slightly undercook following cooking time under listed *Vegetables,* do not drain. Add all remaining ingredients and cover. Cook with Microwave on High, 14 to 18 minutes, or until stew is hot, bubbly and onions and peas are just cooked. Stir 2 or 3 times while heating. Makes 5 to 6 servings.

Variation:
Cooked beef or pork may be substituted for lamb.

Lamb Curry

Microwave Power:	High
Oven Selector:	Off
Oven Temperature:	Off
Shelf Position:	2

3/4 cup milk
1/2 cup coconut
3 tablespoons butter
1/4 medium onion, thinly sliced
1 small tart apple, chopped
1/2 to 1 tablespoon curry powder
1/4 teaspoon coriander or ginger
1 tablespoon flour

1 beef bouillon cube
3/4 cup water
2 cups cubed cooked lamb
1 teaspoon salt
1/8 teaspoon pepper
Condiments: Raisins, chopped nuts, coconut, chutney or chopped hard cooked egg

In a 2-cup liquid measure, heat milk with Microwave on High, 2 to 3 minutes or until hot, but not boiling. Add coconut, let stand 15 minutes. In a 2-quart casserole, melt butter with Microwave on High, 1 minute or until bubbling. Stir in onion, apple, curry powder and coriander or ginger. Cover. Cook with Microwave on High, 4 minutes. Stir in flour. Cook uncovered with Microwave on High, 1 minute. Crumble bouillon cube into water. Add milk, coconut, bouillon, and lamb to onion mixture; stir to blend. Cook, stirring often, with Microwave on High, 5 to 6 minutes or until hot and thickened. Season with salt and pepper. Serve over rice topped with desired condiments. Makes 4 servings.

Minted Lamb Chops

Microwave Power:	High	Low
Oven Selector:	Off	Broil
Oven Temperature:	Off	High Broil, not preheated
Shelf Position:	2	3

Marinade:

1/2 cup apple-mint jelly
1/2 cup white wine vinegar
2 tablespoons brown sugar

1/2 teaspoon dry mustard
1 teaspoon grated lemon peel
1 tablespoon lemon juice

6 loin lamb chops (about 2-1/4 lbs.)
2 teaspoons cornstarch

2 drops green food color
Salt and pepper

Marinade:

In a 4-cup liquid measure, combine jelly, vinegar, brown sugar, mustard, lemon peel and lemon juice. Melt jelly with Microwave on High, 2-1/2 to 3 minutes. Cool slightly; pour over lamb chops and marinate for several hours.

Drain marinade into a 4-cup liquid measure. Add cornstarch and food coloring; mix well. Cook with Microwave on High, until mixture boils and thickens, 2-1/2 to 3 minutes. Place lamb chops on Thermatronic II two-piece broil pan with thickest chops at ends of broil pan and tails turned toward center. Baste chops with sauce. Broil at High Broil with Microwave on Low, 6 minutes. Turn over and baste. Continue to Broil at High Broil with Microwave on Low, 4-1/2 to 7 minutes or until done. Sprinkle with salt and pepper and serve with sauce. Makes 3 servings.

Place thickest portion of chops toward outer edge, tails and thinner pieces towards the center.

Minted Lamb Chops

Pork

Pork cuts, including bacon, ham and wieners, are usually tender, so adapt well to microwave and combination cooking. Pork chops or ribs may be broiled or baked with microwave power to speed cooking. Consult roasting notes and chart for information on cooking pork roasts. Also check index for pork recipes in other sections of the cookbook. Small pieces of pork cook quickly, so combine well with tender, crisp vegetables in oriental style main dishes.

Bacon cooks on High microwave power without heat. We have suggested two methods of cooking, on paper towels to absorb grease or on a microwave safe rack in a dish, so that the fat will drip away from the bacon. Cooking time will vary based on thickness of bacon, amounts of fat and lean, temperature of bacon, size of slices and desired degree of crispness.

Precooked ham is cooked with Low microwave power to thoroughly heat it and a low (325°F) broil heat to brown the top and glaze, if used. During cooking, if the ham is browned sufficiently, but the center does not register 130°F internal temperature on a meat thermometer; turn off the broiler, but continue to cook the ham with Low microwave power.

Wieners are heated most evenly in a covered dish on Low power to thoroughly heat them without overcooking the ends. Also see Hot Dogs (wieners in buns) in the Sandwich section and Hot German Potato Salad with Knockwurst in the Salad section.

Curried Orange Pork Chops

Microwave Power:	Medium	High
Oven Selector:	Off	Off
Oven Temperature:	Off	Off
Shelf Position:	2	2

3 tablespoons flour	8 loin pork chops, 1/2-inch thick
1-1/2 teaspoons seasoned salt	(about 2 to 2-1/2 lbs.)
1-1/2 teaspoons curry powder	2 tablespoons oil
3/4 teaspoon paprika	3/4 teaspoon grated orange peel
1/4 teaspoon pepper	3/4 cup orange juice
1/8 teaspoon cloves	1 large orange, sliced in 8 thin slices

Combine flour and seasonings; reserve 1 tablespoon. Coat chops with flour mixture. On cooktop heat oil in 10-inch glass-ceramic skillet. Brown chops on both sides. Add orange peel and orange juice. Cover; cook with Microwave on Medium, 10 to 14 minutes, or until chops are tender; rearrange chops after 6 minutes. When chops are tender, drain liquid into a 2-cup liquid measure, add water to make 1 cup, if necessary. Combine reserved flour mixture with 1 tablespoon water. Mix into hot liquid until smooth. Cook with Microwave on High, 2 to 3 minutes until thickened, stirring twice. Place orange slices on chops and pour sauce over all. Makes 4 to 6 servings.

Savory Pork Chops

Microwave Power:	High	Low	Off
Oven Selector:	Off	Broil	Broil
Oven Temperature:	Off	325°F, not preheated	High Broil
Shelf Position:	2	2	2

6 (1-inch thick) loin pork chops (2-1/2 to 3 lbs.),	1/4 cup (1/2 stick) butter
with fat trimmed off	2 cups soft bread crumbs (4 to 5 slices of bread)
1 teaspoon salt	2 tablespoons finely chopped onion
1 teaspoon paprika	1/4 teaspoon salt
Dash of pepper	1/4 teaspoon thyme, crushed
1/2 cup milk	Dash pepper

Place chops, with thickest portion on outer edges, in a 2-quart oblong baking dish. Tails should face toward center of dish. Sprinkle with salt, paprika and pepper. Pour milk around chops. Melt butter in a 4-cup liquid measure with Microwave on High, 1/2 to 1 minute. Add remaining ingredients and toss lightly with a fork. Top each chop with an equal amount of stuffing mixture. Place dish in oven with handles right to left. Broil at 325° with Microwave on Low, 18 to 24 minutes or until center chops are done. Rotate dish 1/2 turn after half of cooking time. If a crunchier dressing is desired turn Microwave Off and Broil on High Broil a few additional minutes. Makes 4 to 6 servings.

Pork Hawaiian

Microwave Power:	Medium	High
Oven Selector:	Broil	Off
Oven Temperature:	High Broil	Off
Shelf Position:	2	2

2 lbs. pork shoulder or tenderloin, cut into cubes
1/3 cup brown sugar, firmly packed
2 tablespoons cornstarch
1/2 teaspoon ground ginger
1/4 teaspoon garlic powder
1/4 cup soy sauce
2 tablespoons catsup
1 can (20-oz.) pineapple chunks,
  packed in pineapple juice

Water
1/3 cup wine vinegar
1/4 cup soy sauce
1 tablespoon cornstarch
1 onion, cut into chunks
1 green pepper, cubed
1 can (8-oz.) water chestnuts, drained
1 jar (3-oz.) sliced mushrooms, drained

Place pork cubes in a 2-3/4-quart glass-ceramic baking dish. Combine brown sugar, cornstarch, ginger and garlic powder in a 2-cup liquid measure. Stir in soy sauce and catsup and pour over pork. Stir to coat all of pork. Broil on High Broil with Microwave on Medium, 8 to 10 minutes or until pork is cooked, stirring twice. Turn Broiler Off. Drain pineapple, reserving juice. To pineapple juice add water to make 1-1/4 cups of liquid, add vinegar and soy sauce; stir in cornstarch. Pour over cooked pork, add onion and green pepper. Cook with Microwave on High, 8 minutes, stirring once. Add water chestnuts, pineapple chunks and mushrooms. Continue to cook with Microwave on High, 2 to 3 minutes, until thickened. Serve over hot rice. Makes 6 to 8 servings.

Oriental Asparagus with Pork

Microwave Power:	High
Oven Selector:	Off
Oven Temperature:	Off
Shelf Position:	2

1 pkg. (10-oz.) frozen asparagus spears or cuts
2 teaspoons sugar
2-1/2 teaspoons cornstarch
1/4 cup soy sauce
1/4 cup water

2 cups cubed cooked pork
2 tablespoons oil
1 clove garlic, crushed
1/4 cup whole almonds

Place asparagus in a 1-quart glass casserole. Cover; cook with Microwave on High, 4-1/2 to 5-1/2 minutes or until just thawed and partially cooked. Do not cook completely. Slice spears in thirds after cooking. While asparagus is cooking, mix together sugar and cornstarch; stir in soy sauce and water. Pour over cooked pork, stirring to coat all of meat. Allow to stand 10 to 15 minutes. Combine oil and garlic in a 2-quart casserole. Cover; cook with Microwave on High, 3 minutes. Remove garlic. Add almonds, pork and asparagus. Cook with Microwave on High, 7 to 10 minutes or until mixture is thickened and hot, stirring twice. Serve over rice. Makes 4 servings.

Baked Pre-Cooked Ham

Microwave Power:	Low
Oven Selector:	Broil
Oven Temperature:	325°F, not preheated
Shelf Position:	2

1 (2 to 8 lb.) pre-cooked ham

Suggested ham glazes:

1 cup whole cranberry sauce or;
1 cup currant jelly and 1 tablespoon
   prepared mustard or;

1 cup brown sugar, 3/4 cup crushed pineapple,
   2 teaspoons prepared mustard, and
   1/8 teaspoon ground cloves mixed.

Place ham in a glass ceramic baking dish. Baste with juices or ham gelatin. Broil at 325° with Microwave on Low, 8 to 10 minutes per pound or until meat thermometer registers 130° when placed on center of slice. Baste ham occasionally with juices. Allow ham to stand, covered, 10 to 15 minutes before slicing.

To glaze:
Use favorite ham glaze or one of the suggestions. Spoon on top of ham during last half of cooking time. Continue to cook as directed.

Sugar Glazed Ham Slice

Microwave Power:	Low
Oven Selector:	Broil
Oven Temperature:	High Broil, not preheated
Shelf Position:	3

1 ham slice, 1-inch thick	1 tablespoon dry mustard
(1-1/2 to 2-1/2 lbs.)	1/4 teaspoon ground cloves
1/2 cup brown sugar, firmly packed	

Cut off excess fat and score remaining layer. Mix together brown sugar, dry mustard and cloves. Place ham on wire rack in glass-ceramic baking dish. Sprinkle half of the sugar mixture evenly over ham slice. Broil on High Broil with Microwave on Low, 5 to 6 minutes per pound. Turn over halfway through cooking time and sprinkle with remaining sugar mixture. Makes 6 to 8 servings.

American Chop Suey

Microwave Power:	High
Oven Selector:	Off
Oven Temperature:	Off
Shelf Position:	2

2 large onions, sliced	2 cans (10-3/4-oz. each) condensed
1-1/2 green peppers,	cream of mushroom soup
cut into 1-inch cubes	1 can (8-oz.) sliced mushrooms, drained
2 cups celery, cut diagonally	1 can (8-oz.) water chestnuts,
into 1-inch slices	drained and sliced
1 to 2 tablespoons oil	1/3 to 1/2 cup soy sauce
2 cups cubed cooked pork	1/3 cup sherry (optional)
3 cups (8-oz.) fresh bean sprouts	2 tablespoons cornstarch (optional)

Combine onions, green peppers and celery in a 3-quart casserole. Toss evenly with oil; cover. Cook with Microwave on High, 7 to 10 minutes or until vegetables are tender-crisp; stir 3 times. Stir in pork, bean sprouts, condensed soup, mushrooms and water chestnuts. Season with soy sauce. Cover. Cook with Microwave on High, 8 to 10 minutes or until hot; stir 3 times. If desired, combine sherry and cornstarch and stir into chop suey. Heat to thicken with Microwave on High. Serve with steamed rice. Makes 6 to 8 servings.

Chow Mein Variation:
Prepare recipe above but serve over fried noodles in place of steamed rice.

Pork

Bacon

Microwave Power: High
Oven Selector: Off
Oven Temperature: Off
Shelf Position: 2

Amount	Time**
5 slices	6 to 9 minutes
4 slices	5 to 8 minutes
3 slices	3 to 6 minutes
2 slices	2 to 5 minutes

Separate bacon,* arrange slices in a single layer on a microwave safe rack in a baking dish or on two layers of paper towels in a 2-quart oblong baking dish. Cover with a paper towel. Cook with Microwave on High according to the chart.

*TIP: To separate cold bacon, heat whole package with Microwave on High, 1 minute, remove as many slices as desired.

**Cooking time will vary based on thickness of bacon, amounts of fat and lean, temperature of bacon, size of slices, and desired degree of crispness.

Wieners

Microwave Power: Low
Oven Selector: Off
Oven Temperature: Off
Shelf Position: 2

Amount	Time
1	2 to 3 minutes
2	2-1/2 to 3-1/2 minutes
3	3-1/2 to 4-1/2 minutes, rotate dish 1/2 turn at 2 minutes
4	4-1/2 to 5-1/2 minutes, rotate dish 1/2 turn at 2-1/2 minutes.

Place wieners in dish and cover. Heat with Microwave on Low.

Roasting Poultry

Notes for Conventional Heat and Microwave

By combining Bake or Broil heat and Medium microwave power, poultry has a crisp exterior and moist interior. Turkey, chicken, and Cornish Game Hens are at their best in a fourth to a third the time of conventional roasting. There are some things to keep in mind when roasting poultry.

Temperature of the Bird—Poultry, especially turkey, should be completely defrosted before roasting. A very cold or partially frozen turkey will not be completely cooked inside the thigh or next to the bone when a meat thermometer registers done in the breast. Continued cooking may dry and overcook exterior areas.

Stuffing—Poultry can be successfully roasted either stuffed or unstuffed. A stuffed bird will require a slightly longer roasting time. See poultry roasting chart.

Oven Temperature—Large turkeys are roasted at the same oven temperature as conventional roasting (325°F), but smaller birds require higher oven temperatures to achieve a crisp brown skin in the shortened cooking time with microwave power. Consult roasting chart for suggested oven temperatures.

Testing for Doneness—Indications of doneness are an easily moveable drumstick and no pink tinged juice or pink flesh next to bone. Pop-up indicators can remain in poultry, but should not be used as an accurate indicator of doneness.

Meat Thermometer—Read section under meat roasting.

Shielding—Small pieces of aluminum foil may be used to cover leg ends, wing tips and neck opening if they cook too quickly.

Turn Over—It is recommended that poultry begin roasting with the breast down, then be turned over after half the cooking time, for the very best roasting results. To turn turkey over easily, grasp each end through a thick layer of paper towels and quickly flip over.

Instructions for Conventional Heat and Microwave Energy

Prepare poultry as for conventional roasting. If stuffed, close openings with string or metal skewers. Secure wings to body and tie legs together. Place poultry breast-side down on a rack in a glass or glass-ceramic oblong baking dish. Bird may also be placed on a non-metal trivet or directly in dish. For very large poultry place oven shelf on #1 position, otherwise use #2 shelf position. Set oven temperature and microwave power as directed in poultry roasting chart. Calculate approximate cooking time by multiplying weight of bird by minimum minutes-per-pound listed on chart. Roast half of time, turn poultry breast-side up. Shield any fast cooking areas, if necessary, and remove excess juices in dish. Continue to roast with heat and microwave power for minimum amount of time. Remove poultry from oven, insert a meat thermometer into thickest part of breast and determine internal temperature. If poultry is not done, remove meat thermometer and continue to cook, checking at about 5 to 10 minute intervals, depending on size of bird. When poultry has reached desired internal temperature, cover loosely with foil and allow to stand for time specified on chart.

Roasting Utensils—When roasting turkeys weighing 18 pounds or larger, use lower half of broil pan with a conventional roasting rack.

Poultry

Microwave Power: Medium
Oven Selector: See Chart
Oven Temperature: See Chart, not preheated
Shelf Position: 2, unless otherwise indicated

Type of Poultry	Oven Selector	Oven Temperature	Minutes per pound to cook	Internal Temperature at end of cooking °F	Approximate Standing Time	Special Instructions
Turkey 7 to 14 lbs. Stuffed	Bake	350°F	7 to 9	Breast 165° Stuffing 160°	20 minutes	Cook first half of time with breast down, turn over, cook breast up.*
Not Stuffed	Bake	350°F	5 to 8	Breast 165°	20 minutes	
15 to 22 lbs. Stuffed	Bake	325°F	6 to 8	Breast 165° Stuffing 160°	20 minutes	Shield leg and wing ends with foil if necessary. Use shelf position 1 for large birds.
Not Stuffed	Bake	325°F	5 to 7	Breast 165°	20 minutes	
Chicken (not stuffed) 2-1/2 to 5 lbs.	Bake	450°F	5 to 7	Breast 175°	10 minutes	Shield leg and wing ends with foil after half of cooking, if necessary.
Cornish Hens (not stuffed) 2 - about 1 lb. each	Broil	Medium Broil	Total Time: 20 to 25		5 minutes	Shield leg ends with foil at start of cooking. Salt after cooking.

*Turn turkey over easily by grasping each end through a thick layer of paper towels and quickly flip over.

Poultry

Combination bake and microwave or broil and microwave cooking produces excellent results with poultry and shortens cooking time by half or more. This section contains a wide variety of chicken, turkey, Cornish Hen and stuffing recipes, as well as poultry casseroles. Also consult the Main Dish and Appetizer sections for more recipes using poultry.

Medium microwave power is used to cook most poultry, except where it is desirable to have ingredients simmer together for a longer time as in Chicken in White Wine and Herbs. Bake and broil temperatures higher than conventional cooking are used to achieve browning in the shorter cooking times.

Poultry roasts and browns beautifully in the Thermatronic II oven, and the interior is moist and tender. Consult the poultry roasting notes and chart for specific roasting information. Try your favorite poultry stuffed with one of the delicious stuffings in this section.

The outside of poultry should not be salted until near the end or after cooking. Salt can cause food, especially poultry skin, to burn and dehydrate.

Start cooking breast-side-down. Cook halfway, then turn over by grasping ends through a double thickness of paper towels.

Easy Oven-Fried Chicken

Microwave Power:	Medium
Oven Selector:	Bake
Oven Temperature:	400°F, not preheated
Shelf Position:	2

1 frying chicken (about 2-1/2 lbs.), cup up

1/2 cup (1 stick) butter, melted

1-1/2 cups seasoned corn bread stuffing mix, crushed

Salt and pepper

Wash and dry chicken pieces. Dip each piece in butter, then crushed stuffing mix. Place skin side up in a 3-quart oblong baking dish. Bake at 400° with Microwave on Medium, 20 to 25 minutes. Sprinkle with salt and pepper. Makes 4 to 6 servings.

Broiled Chicken Halves

Microwave Power:	Medium
Oven Selector:	Broil
Oven Temperature:	High Broil, not preheated
Shelf Position:	2

1 chicken broiler, split in half

Unsalted butter (optional)

Prepare chicken and place skin side down in 10-inch glass-ceramic skillet. Place breasts towards outside of dish, backs together in center. Brush with melted butter, if desired. Broil at High Broil with Microwave on Medium, 7 to 8 minutes per pound. Turn skin side up half way through the cooking time; brush with melted butter and continue cooking until chicken tests done with fork. Makes 2 servings.

Chicken Cordon Bleu

Microwave Power:	High	Medium
Oven Selector:	Off	Broil
Oven Temperature:	Off	Medium Broil, preheated
Shelf Position:	2 or 4	4

2 whole chicken breasts, split and boned
4 slices Prosciutto or Westphalian ham

4 slices Muenster or Monterey Jack cheese
2 tablespoons butter

Lightly pound each piece of chicken until flattened. For each piece, wrap one piece of ham around one piece of cheese; place on one side of breast. Fold breast and skin over; pinch shut and skewer with toothpicks. Melt butter in a 2-3/4-quart glass-ceramic baking dish with Microwave on High, about 1/2 minute. Coat chicken in melted butter, place the thick side of breast toward outside of dish. Preheat Broiler on Medium Broil, 2 minutes. Broil on Medium Broil with Microwave on Medium, 5 to 7 minutes or until chicken tests done and is golden brown. Remove toothpicks and serve with Mushroom Cheese Sauce from Sauce section. Makes 3 to 4 servings.

Chicken Marengo

Microwave Power:	Medium
Oven Selector:	Off
Oven Temperature:	Off
Shelf Position:	2

1 pkg. (1-1/2-oz.) spaghetti sauce mix
1/2 cup fine dry bread crumbs
2-1/2 lbs. frying chicken, cut up
1/4 cup oil

2/3 to 3/4 cup dry white wine
3 tomatoes, quartered and cut in half
1/4 pound fresh mushrooms, sliced

Combine dry spaghetti sauce mix and bread crumbs. Roll chicken lightly in crumb mixture. Heat oil in a 4-quart glass-ceramic saucepot on cooktop; brown chicken and drain off excess fat. Add remaining crumb mixture and wine. Cover; cook with Microwave on Medium, 7 minutes. Add tomatoes and mushrooms. Cover; continue to cook with Microwave on Medium, 4 to 7 minutes or until chicken is tender and vegetables are cooked. Makes 4 servings.

Sweet & Sour Barbecued Chicken

Microwave Power:	Medium	High
Oven Selector:	Bake	Off
Oven Temperature:	400°F, not preheated	Off
Shelf Position:	2	2

1 chicken (3 to 3-1/2 lbs.), cut-up
1 pkg. (half of 2-3/4-oz. box)
   dry onion soup mix
1/2 cup apricot jam

1 bottle (8-oz.) Russian salad dressing
1/3 cup water
1 to 1-1/2 tablespoons instant flour

Place chicken in a 2-quart oblong baking dish with thickest pieces toward edge of dish. Combine soup mix and jam; blend in salad dressing and water. Pour sauce over chicken. If time permits, cover and marinate in refrigerator up to 24 hours. Bake at 400° with Microwave on Medium, 14 to 18 minutes or until chicken tests done. Turn Oven Off. Remove chicken from baking dish, skim off excess fat, if desired. Sprinkle sauce with flour and blend. Cook with Microwave on High, 1-1/2 to 2 minutes or until thickened, stirring once. Add chicken, turning in sauce to cover all surfaces. Makes 4 servings.

Chicken Almond

Microwave Power:	High
Oven Selector:	Off
Oven Temperature:	Off
Shelf Position:	2

1 pkg. (6-oz.) frozen Chinese pea pods
   with water chestnuts and bamboo shoots
2 cups thinly sliced celery
1/2 cup sliced fresh mushrooms
2 cups diced cooked chicken

3 tablespoons cornstarch
3 tablespoons soy sauce
2 cups hot water
2 chicken bouillon cubes
1/2 cup whole toasted almonds

Place frozen vegetables in 10-inch glass-ceramic skillet; cover. Cook with Microwave on High, 2 minutes or until easily broken apart. Add celery and cook with Microwave on High, 4 to 6 minutes until celery is tender. Add mushrooms and chicken. Cover and set aside. In 4-cup liquid measure mix cornstarch and soy sauce, gradually stir in water. Add bouillon cubes; stir to dissolve. Cook with Microwave on High, 7 to 10 minutes until mixture thickens and becomes clear; stir every 2 minutes. Pour over chicken mixture, stirring to coat. Heat, if necessary, with Microwave on High, 1 to 2 minutes. Stir; sprinkle with toasted almonds. Serve with hot rice. Makes 4 to 6 servings.

Chicken in White Wine & Herbs

Microwave Power:	High	Low	High
Oven Selector:	Bake	Bake	Bake
Oven Temperature:	325°F, not preheated	325°F	325°F
Shelf Position:	2	2	2

1 whole chicken (2-1/2 to 3 lbs.)
   rinsed, giblets removed
2 chicken bouillon cubes, crushed
1 bay leaf
1 teaspoon tarragon
1 teaspoon chopped dried parsley or
   1 tablespoon chopped fresh parsley
1/4 teaspoon thyme, crushed
1/8 teaspoon coarsely ground pepper
1/8 teaspoon ground sage

2 medium carrots, chopped
1 celery stalk with leaves, chopped
1 small onion, chopped
1-1/2 cups dry white wine
   (Chablis, Chenin Blanc or Rhine)
1/2 cup water
1/2 pound fresh mushrooms, sliced
2 tablespoons flour
1/2 cup water

Place chicken in a 4-quart casserole with a lid. Add bouillon, bay leaf, tarragon, parsley, thyme, pepper, sage, carrots, celery and onion around chicken. Pour wine and 1/2 cup water over all; vegetables should be covered with liquid. Cover; Bake at 325° with Microwave on High, 10 minutes. Baste chicken with liquid, but leave vegetables in bottom of casserole. Cover; Bake at 325° with Microwave on Low, 15 minutes. Baste chicken and add mushrooms; continue to Bake at 325° with Microwave on Low, 10 to 15 minutes or until chicken is tender. Stir flour into 1/2 cup water; then stir into chicken broth. Bake at 325° with Microwave on High, 5 minutes or until sauce is thickened. Baste chicken with sauce. Makes 4 to 6 servings.

Sherried Chicken Breasts

Microwave Power:	Medium
Oven Selector:	Broil
Oven Temperature:	Medium Broil, not preheated
Shelf Position:	2

3 whole chicken breasts (halved into 6 pieces)
1 can (10-3/4-oz.) cream of mushroom soup,
   undiluted

1/3 cup sherry
1 can (2-1/2-oz.) sliced mushrooms, drained
3/4 cup grated sharp Cheddar cheese

Place chicken breasts in a 2-3/4-quart oblong glass-ceramic baking dish, with thick side of breasts toward edge of dish. Combine soup, sherry and mushrooms; spoon over chicken covering all surfaces. Sprinkle with cheese. Broil on Medium Broil with Microwave on Medium, 18 to 22 minutes or until chicken tests done. Makes 6 servings.

Chicken Royal

Microwave Power:	High	Medium
Oven Selector:	Off	Broil
Oven Temperature:	Off	Medium Broil, not preheated
Shelf Position:	3	3

Stuffing:

1/4 cup (1/2 stick) butter
1/2 cup chopped celery
1/2 medium onion, chopped

1 envelope (1/2 of a 13-oz. box) seasoned
   bread stuffing mix
3/4 cup water

4 whole chicken breasts (about 2 lbs.),
   boned with all skin intact
1/4 cup flour
1/2 teaspoon salt
1/4 teaspoon paprika

Dash pepper
1/2 cup (1 stick) butter
1/2 cup hot water
1 chicken bouillon cube

Stuffing:

In a 1-1/2-quart casserole place 1/4 cup butter, celery and onion. Cover and cook with Microwave on High, 3 to 4 minutes. Stir in dressing and toss with water. Set aside.

Loosen skin from chicken breast and fold away, but do not detach completely. Lightly pound each side of breast to flatten. Combine flour, salt, paprika and pepper in a pie plate. Dredge chicken in flour mixture. Mound dressing on one side of breast, reserving some dressing. Fold skin over like a package and skewer with toothpicks. Place 1/2 cup butter in a pie plate and melt with Microwave on High, 1/2 to 1 minute. Lightly roll chicken in butter and place breast side down in the corners of a 2-3/4-quart oblong glass-ceramic baking dish. Heat water in a 1-cup liquid measure with Microwave on High, 1 to 2 minutes, until hot. Stir in bouillon cube to dissolve. Pour over remaining dressing; toss lightly to moisten and pile in center of baking dish. Broil on Medium Broil with Microwave on Medium, 5 minutes. Turn chicken, skin side up and drizzle with remaining butter. Lightly toss dressing. Continue to Broil on Medium Broil with Microwave on Medium, 3-1/2 to 8 minutes or until chicken tests done. Remove toothpicks and serve with Sour Cream Mushroom Sauce. Makes 4 servings.

Cornish Hens with Corn Bread Stuffing

Microwave Power: Medium
Oven Selector: Broil
Oven Temperature: Medium Broil, not preheated
Shelf Position: 2

2 Cornish hens, 15 to 18 oz. each   1/4 cup butter, melted
1 recipe Corn Bread-Sausage Stuffing

Rinse and dry hens. Stuff each with about half of the Corn Bread-Sausage Stuffing. Secure cavity opening with a toothpick. Place back side up on wire rack in glass-ceramic baking dish. Brush backs with butter. Cover end of each leg with a small piece of aluminum foil. Broil, back side up, on Medium Broil with Microwave on Medium, 10 minutes. Turn over; brush breast side with butter and continue to Broil on Medium Broil with Microwave on Medium, 10 to 15 minutes or until hens are done. Allow to stand 10 minutes. Makes 2 to 4 servings.

Corn Bread-Sausage Stuffing

Microwave Power: High
Oven Selector: Off
Oven Temperature: Off
Shelf Position: 2

1/4 lb. bulk sausage   1-1/2 cups packaged dry Corn Bread Stuffing
1/2 cup finely chopped apple   1/2 cup chicken broth
2 tablespoons butter   Dash ground sage
1/2 teaspoon instant minced onion

Place sausage in a 1-1/2-quart casserole, cover with a paper towel. Cook with Microwave on High, 2 to 3 minutes, or until sausage is no longer pink. Drain off fat. Combine apple, butter and onion in a 2-cup liquid measure. Cook with Microwave on High, 1 minute. Add all ingredients to sausage. Stir with fork to blend and moisten dry stuffing. Use to stuff two Cornish Game Hens or one roasting chicken.

Chinese Glazed Cornish Hens

Microwave Power:	Medium
Oven Selector:	Bake
Oven Temperature:	425°F, not preheated
Shelf Position:	2

2 Cornish hens, 15 to 18 oz. each
1 recipe Chinese Rice Stuffing

1 recipe Chinese Apricot Glaze (page 210)
1/4 cup butter, melted

Thoroughly defrost Cornish hens, remove giblets, rinse and dry. Stuff each hen with half of Chinese Rice Stuffing. Close mouth of cavity; secure with toothpicks. Tie legs of each hen together with string. Then cover ends of legs with a small piece of foil, one piece of foil covering both legs. Place hens breast side up in a glass-ceramic baking dish. Brush with butter. Bake at 425° with Microwave on Medium, 10 minutes, brushing again with butter after the first 5 minutes. Brush a generous coating of Chinese Apricot Glaze on each hen. Continue to Bake at 425° with Microwave on Medium, 10 to 15 minutes, brushing twice with glaze. Allow to stand 10 minutes. Makes 2 to 4 servings.

Chinese Rice Stuffing

Microwave Power:	High
Oven Selector:	Off
Oven Temperature:	Off
Shelf Position:	2

1/4 cup (1/2 stick) butter
2 tablespoons minced onion
4 medium mushrooms, chopped
1/4 cup chopped dried apricots

1 tablespoon chopped parsley
1/8 teaspoon ginger
1-1/2 teaspoons soy sauce
1-1/2 cups cooked white or brown rice

Combine butter, onion and mushrooms in a 1-quart casserole. Cover; cook with Microwave on High, 3 to 4 minutes or until vegetables are tender. Stir in remaining ingredients. Use to stuff two Cornish Game Hens or one chicken. Makes about 1-3/4 cups.

Stuffing Casserole

Microwave Power:	High	Medium
Oven Selector:	Off	Broil
Oven Temperature:	Off	High Broil, not preheated
Shelf Position:	2	2

1/3 cup butter
1 cup chopped celery
3/4 cup chopped onion
1/2 cup chopped dried apricots
5 cups dry bread cubes
1/2 cup chopped pecans

2 teaspoons dried parsley, crushed
1 teaspoon poultry seasoning
1/2 teaspoon salt
1/4 teaspoon pepper
1 to 1-1/4 cups chicken broth
2 tablespoons dry white wine (optional)

Combine butter, celery, onion and apricots in a 4-quart glass-ceramic saucepot. Cover; cook with Microwave on High, 7 to 9 minutes or until vegetables are limp. Stir once. Mix in remaining ingredients. Refrigerate until after turkey is cooked. While the oven is still hot from the turkey, cook the dressing in the glass-ceramic saucepot or a 10-inch glass-ceramic skillet. Cover; cook with Microwave on High, 4 to 6 minutes or until hot. Stir; uncover and brown with Broil at High Broil and Microwave on Medium, 6 to 8 minutes, until golden. Makes about 6 cups dressing.

Sausage Stuffing

Microwave Power:	High
Oven Selector:	Off
Oven Temperature:	Off
Shelf Position:	2

1 lb. Italian Sausage
1-1/2 cups finely chopped celery
  (stalks and leaves)
1 cup finely chopped onion
1/2 cup finely chopped green pepper
1 box (13-oz.) dry seasoned
  dressing mix, about 8 cups

1 tablespoon dried parsley, crushed
1-1/2 cups chicken stock or other liquid
1 egg, beaten
Other seasonings to taste, depending on
  seasoning in mix (sage, thyme,
  marjoram, or poultry seasoning)

In 4-1/2-quart casserole crumble sausage and cook with Microwave on High, 4 to 5 minutes or until all pink is gone. Stir once, do not drain. Add celery, onion and green pepper; cover. Cook with Microwave on High, 7 to 9 minutes, until vegetables are limp. Stir once. Add dressing mix and parsley, chicken stock and egg; toss lightly to mix. Add other seasonings, as desired. Makes stuffing for 10 to 12 pound bird.

Fish & Seafood

Fish may be cooked with microwaves only or in combination with Bake and Broil heat. Microwaves only are used to steam or poach whole fish or fillets in a variety of liquids.

Fish is broiled on the two-piece Thermatronic II broil pan or in a glass-ceramic dish with a heat-proof and microwave safe rack. Basting with butter helps the fish to brown, yet stay moist.

Generally, Low power and Broil are used for thick pieces (over 3/4 inch) of fish so that some browning will occur, but edges will not cook too quickly and dry out. These usually need to be turned over. Thinner pieces of fish may be broiled with Medium microwave power to cook very quickly and eliminate turning over. Be careful not to overcook fish or it will become dry and dehydrated.

Baked fish, especially when a crisp coating is desired, is baked uncovered with a high oven temperature and Low microwave power. This hastens cooking, yet allows time for the exterior to brown and crisp.

Whole fish or large thick sections of a whole fish are usually covered and poached or steamed, with microwave power only, with or without liquid. High power cooks large pieces of fish the most efficiently. Covering helps to equalize the temperature and keep in moisture. It is sometimes necessary to cut into a thick piece of fish to determine if the interior is completely cooked.

Shell fish, such as clams, oysters, shrimp and lobster cook quickly in the microwave oven in their shells. Most shellfish, cooked in the shell, are cooked on High power with microwave only. Microwave and broil can be combined to cook shelled or partially shelled seafood, such as Broiled Lobster Tail.

Fresh fish gives the best results when cooked with microwaves, but thawed frozen fish can be prepared successfully and some fish can be cooked from a frozen state. Frozen or thawed fish gives off more liquid when cooked than fresh fish, making frozen fish best for dishes with a broth or sauce.

Fish and seafood casseroles use different power levels and oven heats depending on the type of ingredients. Check methods used in different recipes. Note that some recipes use raw seafood cooked in combination with other ingredients, while others contain cooked ingredients that are simply heated together.

Shrimp Curry

Microwave Power:	High
Oven Selector:	Off
Oven Temperature:	Off
Shelf Position:	2

1 cup chopped celery
1/2 cup chopped onion
1/4 cup (1/2 stick) butter
5 tablespoons flour
1 teaspoon salt
1 teaspoon curry powder
1/2 teaspoon sugar
1/8 teaspoon ginger
2 chicken bouillon cubes

2 cups hot water
1 lb. cooked shrimp, drained
1/2 teaspoon lemon juice
2 tablespoons sherry
Cooked rice
Condiments: chopped peanuts, coconut, chopped hard cooked egg, crisp crumbled bacon, chutney, raisins

Combine celery, onion and butter in a 1-1/2-quart casserole. Cover; cook with Microwave on High, 7 to 8 minutes until vegetables are limp. Stir in flour, salt, curry powder, sugar and ginger. Cover; cook with Microwave on High, 1 minute. Mix bouillon cubes into water; stir to dissolve. Add bouillon to flour mixture gradually, stirring until smooth. Cook with Microwave on High, 8 to 10 minutes until thickened and smooth, stirring occasionally. Add shrimp and lemon juice. Cover; heat with Microwave on High, 3 to 4 minutes to heat shrimp. Stir in sherry. Serve over hot rice with condiments. Makes 4 to 6 servings.

Steamed Shrimp

Microwave Power:	High
Oven Selector:	Off
Oven Temperature:	Off
Shelf Position:	2

1/2 lb. fresh raw shrimp in shells
1/2 cup butter
2 tablespoons lemon juice

1/2 teaspoon salt
1/4 teaspoon caraway seeds (optional)

Thoroughly wash shrimp. Combine all ingredients in 2-quart casserole. Cover; cook with Microwave on High, 4 to 6 minutes or until shrimp is firm. Let stand covered 5 minutes. Shell and devein. Serve as desired.

Shrimp Curry

Shrimp Stuffed Sole Roll-ups

Microwave Power:	High	Medium	High
Oven Selector:	Off	Off	Off
Oven Temperature:	Off	Off	Off
Shelf Position:	2	2	2

Filling:

2 tablespoons butter

2 green onions, minced

2 to 3 cans (4-1/2-oz. each) small shrimp, rinsed and drained or 1 pkg. (7-oz.) frozen shrimp

3 tablespoons snipped parsley

1/2 cup dry bread crumbs

1/4 to 1/3 cup mayonnaise

1/4 to 1/3 cup dry vermouth

1 teaspoon Worcestershire sauce

1/8 teaspoon pepper

Few dashes cayenne

Seasoned salt

6 sole fillets (1-1/2 to 2 lbs.)

1/2 cup dry vermouth

2 teaspoons to 1 tablespoon instant flour

Snipped parsley

Filling:

Combine butter and onions in a 2-cup liquid measure. Melt butter and slightly wilt onions with Microwave on High, 2 minutes. Add half of shrimp and remaining filling ingredients. Blend well and increase seasoning, as desired.

Divide mixture evenly between fish fillets; roll up and place seam side down in 2-quart square baking dish. Pour vermouth around fish and cover. Cook with Microwave on Medium, 9 to 12 minutes or until fish flakes with a fork. If desired, spoon juices into a 2-cup measure. Sprinkle with instant flour (1 cup liquid, use 1 tablespoon flour) and cook with Microwave on High until hot and thickened. Pour over fish roll-ups, and garnish with remaining shrimp and parsley. Makes 6 servings.

Shrimp a la Créole

Microwave Power:	High
Oven Selector:	Off
Oven Temperature:	Off
Shelf Position:	2

1 cup chopped onion

2 green peppers, chopped

1 cup chopped celery

3 tablespoons butter

1 can (15-oz.) tomato sauce

1/2 cup dry red wine or water

1 bay leaf

1/2 teaspoon salt

1/2 teaspoon pepper

2 lbs. shrimp, uncooked

Combine onion, green pepper, celery and butter in 2-1/2-quart casserole. Cover; cook with Microwave on High, 7 to 9 minutes until onions are transparent, stirring once. Add tomato sauce, wine or water, bay leaf, salt and pepper. Cover and cook with Microwave on High, 5 minutes. Add shrimp; cover and cook with Microwave on High, 6 to 8 minutes or until shrimp are tender. Serve over rice. Makes 4 servings.

Broiled Lobster Tails

Microwave Power:	Low
Oven Selector:	Broil
Oven Temperature:	High Broil, not preheated
Shelf Position:	3

2 medium lobster tails (8 to 12 oz. each)
1/4 cup butter, melted

With scissors, snip membrane covering flesh lengthwise next to shell. Remove membrane. Bend tail backwards sharply to crack shell and prevent tail from curling. Place shell side down in a glass-ceramic baking dish. Brush with butter. Broil on High Broil with Microwave on Low, 9 to 15 minutes, depending on weight and desired doneness. Brush with butter twice while broiling. Makes 2 servings.

Lobster Newburg

Microwave Power:	High	Medium
Oven Selector:	Off	Off
Oven Temperature:	Off	Off
Shelf Position:	2	2

3 tablespoons butter
1 tablespoon flour
1/4 teaspoon salt
Dash cayenne
3 tablespoons sherry

3 egg yolks, well beaten
1 cup (1/2 pt.) whipping cream
2 cups cubed cooked lobster
Buttered toast
Paprika

In a 2-quart casserole, melt butter with Microwave on High, 1/2 to 1 minute. Stir in flour, salt and cayenne; blend well. Cook with Microwave on High, 1 minute. Add sherry; stir until evenly blended. Thoroughly mix egg yolks and cream; slowly stir into flour mixture. Cook with Microwave on High, 4 to 6 minutes, stirring each minute, until mixture is hot and thickened. Do not boil. Add lobster. Heat with Microwave on Medium, 2 to 3 minutes. Serve over hot, buttered toast, sprinkled with paprika. Makes 4 servings.

Broiled Sea Bass with Bacon-Almond Topping

Microwave Power:	High	Medium
Oven Selector:	Off	Broil
Oven Temperature:	Off	High Broil, not preheated
Shelf Position:	2	3

3 slices bacon
2 lbs. sea bass fillets
4 tablespoons dry sherry
1/3 cup melted butter
Grated peel of 1 lemon

Juice of 1 lemon
1/2 teaspoon salt
1/8 teaspoon pepper
1/3 cup slivered, toasted almonds
2 tablespoons chopped parsley

Cook bacon with Microwave on High, 5 to 6 minutes or until crisp. Cut sea bass into serving pieces. Marinate in sherry, 15 minutes. Drain. Arrange on Thermatronic II two-piece broil pan. Combine melted butter, lemon peel and lemon juice, salt and pepper. Baste fish with half lemon-butter mixture. Broil at High Broil with Microwave on Medium, 5 minutes. Baste with remaining lemon-butter mixture. Continue to cook on High Broil with Microwave on Medium, 3 to 6 minutes or until fish is browned and flakes easily with a fork. Do not overcook. Remove to a serving dish, top with toasted almonds and crumbled bacon, baste with a small amount of juices from bottom of broiler pan. Sprinkle with parsley. Makes 4 servings.

Whole Baked Fish

Microwave Power:	High
Oven Selector:	Off
Oven Temperature:	Off
Shelf Position:	2

3 to 6 lb. whole fish, cleaned
1 teaspoon seasoned salt
2 small stalks celery with leaves
4 thin slices onion
2 sprigs parsley
1 lemon, thinly sliced
1/2 teaspoon tarragon

4 whole cloves
1/4 teaspoon coarsely ground black pepper
1 bay leaf
2 tablespoons lemon juice
1/2 cup white wine and 1/2 cup water *or*
    3/4 cup clam broth and 1/4 cup water

Rinse and dry fish; place in a 2 or 3-quart oblong baking dish. Sprinkle inside cavity of fish with seasoned salt, then insert celery, onion, parsley and half of lemon slices. Place remaining lemon slices around fish with tarragon, cloves, pepper, bay leaf, lemon juice and wine and water or clam broth and water. Cover with plastic wrap. Cook with Microwave on High, 4 to 8 minutes per pound* or until fish flakes easily. Do not overcook. Let stand, covered 10 minutes.

*Cooking time per pound will depend on thickness and temperature of the fish.

Oven-Fried Fish Fillets

Microwave Power:	Low
Oven Selector:	Bake
Oven Temperature:	450°F, preheated
Shelf Position:	2

1-1/2 lbs. fish fillets
1 cup bread crumbs
2 tablespoons Parmesan cheese
1/2 teaspoon tarragon, crushed
1/2 teaspoon paprika
1 teaspoon seasoned salt

Dash pepper
1 egg, beaten
1/2 cup evaporated milk
2 tablespoons butter or margarine,
   melted

Rinse and dry fish fillets. Combine bread crumbs, Parmesan cheese, tarragon, paprika, seasoned salt and pepper. Mix together egg and milk in a shallow dish. Dip fish first in egg-milk mixture, then in crumb mixture, turning to coat all sides. Arrange fillets in a lightly buttered 3-quart oblong glass baking dish. Drizzle butter over fish. Bake, uncovered, at 450° with Microwave on Low, 10 to 14 minutes. Makes 3 to 4 servings.

Stuffed Baked Fish

Microwave Power:	Low
Oven Selector:	Bake
Oven Temperature:	400°F, preheated
Shelf Position:	2

1-1/2 cups seasoned stuffing mix
1/2 teaspoon tarragon, crushed
1/2 teaspoon freeze dried chives
1/2 teaspoon seasoned salt
Dash pepper

1/2 cup butter, melted
1-1/2 teaspoons lemon juice
1 lb. whole fish (2 trout or 1 perch,
   haddock or other fish)
   cleaned and scaled

Combine stuffing mix, tarragon, chives, seasoned salt and pepper. Toss lightly with 1/3 cup butter and lemon juice. Dry fish. Brush inside with butter; place in a 2-quart oblong baking dish. Fill inside of fish with stuffing, mound extra stuffing along base of fish. Brush remaining butter over fish surface. Bake, uncovered at 400° with Microwave on Low, 9 to 12 minutes, until fish is cooked and stuffing is hot. Makes 2 servings.

Broiled Salmon Steaks Béarnaise

Microwave Power:	Low
Oven Selector:	Broil
Oven Temperature:	High Broil, not preheated
Shelf Position:	3

4 salmon steaks, 3/4 to 1-inch thick
   (about 2 lbs.)
1/4 cup (1/2 stick) butter, melted

Chopped parsley (optional)
Bearnaise sauce (see sauces)

Arrange salmon steaks on two-piece broil pan, with narrow bottom pieces toward center. Brush with melted butter. Broil at High Broil with Microwave on Low, 6 to 8 minutes or until fish begins to brown and appear cooked on one side. Turn salmon steaks over; brush with butter. Continue broiling at High Broil, with Microwave on Low, 3 to 6 minutes until browned and cooked through. Do not overcook. Spread warm Béarnaise Sauce over broiled salmon steaks. Sprinkle with chopped parsley, if desired. Makes 4 servings.

Sea Bass in Creamy Wine Sauce

Microwave Power:	Medium	High
Oven Selector:	Off	Off
Oven Temperature:	Off	Off
Shelf Position:	2	2

2 tablespoons catsup
1 tablespoon Worcestershire sauce
1/2 cup dry white wine
2 lbs. white sea bass, rinsed and dried,
   cut into serving pieces
1/4 cup (1/2 stick) butter
1/3 cup chopped onion
1/2 cup chopped green pepper
1 can (4-oz.) mushroom slices, reserve liquid

1/4 cup flour
1/2 cup (approximately) whipping cream
1/4 to 1/2 teaspoon seasoned salt
Few dashes pepper
Dash cayenne
1 tomato, chopped and seeded
2 tablespoons snipped fresh parsley

In a 2-quart oblong utility dish, combine catsup, Worcestershire sauce and wine. Turn fish once in wine liquid; arrange in an even layer with thickest portions near the edges of the dish. Cover with plastic wrap and cook with Microwave on Medium, 9 to 12 minutes or until fish just flakes with a fork. Do not overcook. Recover with plastic wrap and place to one side. In a 1-1/2-quart glass casserole combine butter and onions; cover. Cook with Microwave on High, 2 minutes. Stir. Add green pepper and mushrooms; cover. Cook with Microwave on High, 3 minutes or until vegetables are limp. Stir in flour; cook, uncovered, with Microwave on High, 1 minute. Measure 1-1/2 cups liquid from fish. Discard any remaining wine liquid from fish. If extra liquid is needed, use reserved mushroom liquid. Add whipping cream to make 2 cups total. Slowly stir into butter mixture and cook with Microwave on High, about 6 to 8 minutes, stirring occasionally until thickened and bubbly. Season with salt, pepper and cayenne. Pour over fish and top with tomatoes. Heat to serve with Microwave on Medium, about 2 minutes. Sprinkle with parsley. Makes 6 to 8 servings.

Broiled Salmon Steaks with Béarnaise Sauce

Steamed Clams

Microwave Power:	High
Oven Selector:	Off
Oven Temperature:	Off
Shelf Position:	2

1 lb. fresh clams in shell
1/2 cup water

Thoroughly scrub and rinse clams. Combine clams and water in a 1-quart casserole. Cover; cook with Microwave on High, 4 to 6 minutes or until shells are partially opened Let stand, covered, 5 minutes. Serve with strained broth, melted butter and lemon juice. Makes 3 to 4 servings.

Old Fashioned Scalloped Oysters

Microwave Power:	Medium
Oven Selector:	Bake
Oven Temperature:	400°F, not preheated
Shelf Position:	2

3/4 cup soft bread crumbs
1-1/2 cups fine cracker crumbs
3/4 cup (1-1/2 sticks) butter
3 jars (10-oz. each) oysters, drained,
   reserve 2/3 cup liquor

3/4 teaspoon salt
1/8 teaspoon pepper
4 tablespoons minced parsley
1/2 cup cream
1 teaspoon Worcestershire sauce

Combine bread crumbs, cracker crumbs and butter. Spread half crumb mixture in bottom of a lightly buttered 2-quart casserole. Arrange drained oysters over crumbs. Sprinkle with salt, pepper and 2 tablespoons minced parsley. Combine reserved oyster liquor, cream and Worcestershire sauce; pour over oysters. Top with remaining crumbs. Bake at 400° with Microwave on Medium, 18 to 20 minutes or until bubbly. Garnish with remaining parsley. Makes 6 servings.

Tuna-Noodle Casserole

Microwave Power:	High	Low
Oven Selector:	Off	Bake
Oven Temperature:	Off	400°F, not preheated
Shelf Position:	2	2

1 pkg. (8-oz.) medium noodles
1-1/2 cups dairy sour cream
3 tablespoons butter
3/4 cup chopped onion
1/2 cup chopped celery
1/2 cup chopped green pepper
3 tablespoons flour
1 can (10-3/4-oz.) cream of mushroom soup
1/3 cup milk

1/2 teaspoon salt
1/4 teaspoon basil, crushed
1/8 teaspoon pepper
2 to 3 dashes cayenne pepper
2 teaspoons Worcestershire sauce
1/2 cup grated sharp Cheddar cheese
2 cans (6-1/2-oz. each) tuna, drained
1 can (2-1/4-oz.) sliced olives
1 jar (2-oz.) pimiento, drained

Topping:
1 tablespoon butter
1/2 cup bread crumbs

2 tablespoons snipped parsley

On cooktop cook noodles according to package directions. Drain; return to cooking utensil and stir in sour cream. Place butter, onion, celery and green pepper in a 3-quart casserole. Cover; cook with Microwave on High, 4 to 5 minutes or until vegetables are almost limp. Stir in flour, soup, milk, salt, basil, pepper, cayenne and Worcestershire sauce. Cook, uncovered, with Microwave on High, 4 to 5-1/2 minutes or until mixture bubbles and slightly thickens. Add cheese and stir to melt. Add tuna, olives, pimiento and noodles to sauce mixture; stir to combine.

Topping:
Melt butter in a 1-cup glass measure. Add bread crumbs and parsley; set aside.

Bake casserole at 400° with Microwave on Low, 10 minutes. Stir; top with crumb mixture and continue to Bake at 400° with Microwave on Low, 7 to 10 minutes or until heated through. Makes 6 servings.

Seafood Delight

Microwave Power:	Low
Oven Selector:	Bake
Oven Temperature:	400°F, not preheated
Shelf Position:	2

1 can (10-3/4-oz.) cream of mushroom soup
3/4 cup mayonnaise
1/2 cup milk
2 tablespoons lemon juice
2 teaspoons instant minced onion
1 lb. cooked crabmeat, lobster,
   shrimp or combination

5 hard cooked eggs, sliced
1 can (5 to 6-oz.) water chestnuts,
   drained and sliced
1 cup chopped celery
1/2 cup slivered almonds
1/2 cup crushed cornflakes

Combine mushroom soup, mayonnaise, milk, lemon juice and minced onion. Spread a thin layer of sauce over the bottom of a greased 2-quart oblong utility dish. Reserve balance of sauce. Evenly layer seafood, sliced eggs, water chestnuts, celery and almonds. Pour balance of sauce over mixture and gently lift filling ingredients to distribute sauce. Top with cornflakes. Bake at 400° with Microwave on Low, 9 to 13 minutes or until heated through. Makes 6 to 8 servings.

To Make Ahead:
Prepare and store in refrigerator; top with cornflakes just before cooking. Bake at 400° with Microwave on Low, 16 to 19 minutes or until heated through.

Crab Combo

Microwave Power:	High	High
Oven Selector:	Off	Bake
Oven Temperature:	Off	400°F, preheated
Shelf Position:	2	2

1/2 cup minced green onions with tops
1/4 cup chopped parsley
1/2 clove garlic, minced
1/4 cup (1/2 stick) butter
2 cups cooked rice
2 cans (6-oz. each) crab meat,
   drained

1 teaspoon salt
1/8 teaspoon white pepper
2 tablespoons lemon juice
1 egg, beaten
1/4 cup dairy sour cream
1 tablespoon butter, melted
1/4 cup fine dry bread crumbs

In a 2-1/2-quart casserole, combine onions, parsley, garlic and butter. Cook with Microwave on High, 3 to 4 minutes or until transparent; stir once. Preheat oven. Add rice, crab meat, salt, pepper, lemon juice, egg and sour cream to butter mixture, mixing well. Leave in casserole for baking or spoon into 4 or 6 individual ramekins. In a small dish, mix 1 tablespoon melted butter and the bread crumbs. Sprinkle over top of casserole or ramekins. Bake at 400° with Microwave on High, 8 to 12 minutes in casserole, or 7 to 10 minutes in ramekins, until mixture is hot and bread crumbs are brown. Makes 4 to 6 servings.

Pies

Although there is little time saved by baking a pie shell with a combination of heat and micro-waves, the advantage is in a superior finished crust. Microwaves have the effect of producing a very light flaky pastry, and oven heat adds golden brown color. Along with a basic pastry recipe, we have included a selection of interesting, easy to prepare recipes, for single pie shells.

Follow our pastry instructions for a perfect pie shell. Pie shells are often rotated during baking for more even cooking. During the first half of baking, if the pastry puffs up, gently press the puffed area with a fork to allow steam to escape. Chilling the pastry before baking helps to mini-mize puffing and shrinking. Basic pastry is baked with heat and Low microwave power. Crumb crusts are baked with microwave power only, just to set the crust. Browning is not required in a crumb crust.

Two-crust fruit pies bake in half the time of conventional cooking, and the crust is crisp and flaky. Try the Old Fashioned Apple Pie, then use that recipe as a guide for preparing other fruit pies. Two-crust pies using canned fruit or prepared pie filling will require about 5 minutes less baking time than fresh fruit pies.

Custard type fillings are best when partially cooked by microwave power before being poured into a crust. The Pumpkin Pie has a flaky crust even on the bottom because the pastry is baked separately before the filling is added and baked with heat and Low microwave power. However, in Wonderful Walnut Pie, the filling and crust are baked together, because the filling is very liquid and could seep through the fork pricks in a baked crust. Heat and Medium power quickly set the filling and bake the crust.

Cream and chiffon pie fillings are prepared first, then poured into a baked pie shell and topped with whipped cream or meringue. Low microwave power helps set a meringue topping while it is browned by oven heat. For an especially pretty meringue pie, try the Coconut Meringue Pie.

Pastry for One-Crust Pie

Microwave Power:	Low	Off
Oven Selector:	Bake	Bake
Oven Temperature:	475°F, preheated	475°F
Shelf Position:	1	1

1-1/2 cups sifted flour
3/4 teaspoon salt

1/2 cup shortening
3 to 4 tablespoons cold water

Mix flour and salt together. Using a pastry blender, cut in about half the shortening until mixture resembles fine meal. Cut in remaining shortening until about the size of small peas. Sprinkle with water, a tablespoon at a time, tossing lightly with fork until all the flour is evenly moistened. Shape dough into a flat circle, like a pancake, being careful to eliminate all cracks at edge of dough. Roll out on lightly floured surface with lightly floured rolling pin to not quite 1/8-inch thick, large enough to fit a 9-inch glass pie plate. Flour the rolling pin lightly and roll pastry onto pin. Transfer pastry to pie plate and unroll. Avoid stretching dough to help prevent shrinkage. Trim 1-inch beyond edge of plate and fold pastry under to make a standing flute at edge of plate. Hook points of flute under top edge of plate to help prevent shrinking. For a baked crust, prick bottom and sides of pie shell. For an unbaked crust, do not prick. Chill for 20 minutes. Bake at 475° with Microwave on Low, 3 minutes. Rotate dish 1/4 turn. Continue to Bake at 475° with Microwave on Low, 2-1/2 to 3 minutes. Turn Microwave Off and continue to Bake at 475°, 1-1/2 to 3 minutes or until brown. Makes one 9-inch pie crust.

Pastry for Two-Crust Pie

2 cups sifted flour
1 teaspoon salt

2/3 cup shortening
4 to 6 tablespoons cold water

Prepare pastry following directions for one-crust pie, except divide dough into 2 parts, using approximately two-thirds of dough for bottom crust and one-third for top crust. Fit bottom crust into pie plate and trim 1 inch beyond edge of plate. Pour in desired pie filling and top with a circle of pastry. Fit to edge of plate, trim excess. Moisten dough at edge with water and fold over underneath edge. Press firmly to seal and flute edges. Prick top to allow for escape of steam as filling cooks. Bake according to recipes for specific pie fillings. Makes pastry for one 2-crust 9-inch pie.

Sour Cream Crust

Microwave Power:	Low	Off
Oven Selector:	Bake	Bake
Oven Temperature:	475°F, preheated	475°F
Shelf Position:	1	1

1-1/2 cups sifted flour
3/4 teaspoon salt

1/2 cup shortening
4 to 6 tablespoons dairy sour cream

Prepare pastry following directions for one-crust pie. Blend in sour cream 1 tablespoon at a time, adding enough to make the dough workable. For a baked crust, prick bottom of pie shell. For an unbaked crust, do not prick. Chill for 20 minutes. Bake at 475° with Microwave on Low, 3 minutes. Rotate dish 1/4 turn. Continue to Bake at 475° with Microwave on Low, 2-1/2 to 3 minutes. Turn Microwave Off and continue to Bake at 475°, 1-1/2 to 3 minutes, or until brown. Makes one 9-inch pie crust.

Pie Crust Mix

Microwave Power:	Low	Off
Oven Selector:	Bake	Bake
Oven Temperature:	475°F, preheated	475°F
Shelf Position:	2	2

1 pkg. (11-oz.) pie crust mix

Prepare pie crust mix according to package directions. Use entire mix* to make one generous 9-inch pie shell. Fit into 9-inch pie plate. *Do not stretch dough.* Flute edge high and chill pie shell 20 minutes. Prick bottom and sides of dough thoroughly with a fork. Bake at 475° with Microwave on Low, 6 minutes; rotate dish 1/2 turn after 3 minutes. Turn Microwave Off, continue to Bake at 475°, 1 to 3 minutes or until nicely browned.

* In testing, best results were achieved by using all of mix for just one pie shell, rather than the two recommended on the package. This eliminates stretching and helps prevent tearing a too thin dough. Also allows for a high fluted edge.

Graham Cracker Crust

Microwave Power:	High
Oven Selector:	Off
Oven Temperature:	Off
Shelf Position:	2

1/4 cup butter
1-1/4 cups graham cracker crumbs

1/4 cup sugar

Melt butter in 9-inch glass pie plate with Microwave on High, about 45 seconds. Add crumbs and sugar. Combine well and press into pie plate. For a perfectly shaped crust, press a smaller pie plate into crust, sliding it against sides to pack and smooth. Cook with Microwave on High, 4 minutes. Cool before using. Makes one 9-inch pie crust.

Ginger, Chocolate or Vanilla Cookie Crumb Crust:
To make cookie crumb crust, follow the recipe above, substituting desired crumbs. 1-1/4 cups cookie crumbs equals about 4-1/2 ounces. Omit sugar. Prepare as above.

For crumb crust in a 9-inch METAL pie pan, melt butter in a 1-cup liquid measure. Combine all ingredients in METAL pie pan. Prepare as above. Cook with Microwave on High, 6 minutes.

Oatmeal Cookie Crust

Microwave Power:	Low
Oven Selector:	Bake
Oven Temperature:	450°F, preheated
Shelf Position:	2

1/2 cup (1 stick) butter
1/4 cup sugar
1/2 teaspoon vanilla

1/4 teaspoon salt
1 cup sifted flour
3/4 cup rolled oats, quick or regular

Cream together butter, sugar, vanilla and salt. Mix in flour and oats. Chill dough if necessary for easy handling. Gently press into bottom and sides of a 9-inch pie plate. Chill 20 minutes. Bake at 450° with Microwave on Low, 2-1/2 minutes. Rotate 1/4 turn and continue to Bake with Microwave on Low, 2-1/2 to 3-1/2 minutes, or until done. Cool thoroughly before filling. Makes one 9-inch pie crust.

Coconut Crust

Microwave Power:	High	Low	Medium
Oven Selector:	Off	Broil	Off
Oven Temperature:	Off	Medium Broil, preheated	Off
Shelf Position:	3	3	2

1/4 cup (1/2 stick) butter
2 cups coconut

Melt butter in a 9-inch pie plate with Microwave on High, 1/2 to 1 minute. Add coconut; mix well and press into pie plate. Preheat broil element on Medium Broil, 3 minutes, then place pie crust on shelf. Broil on Medium Broil with Microwave on Low, 2 to 3 minutes, or until crust is golden brown. Cool before filling with chiffon, cream filling or ice cream. Chill or freeze. For easy cutting of crust, soften finished pie with Microwave on Medium, 1/2 to 2 minutes, checking each 1/2 minute. Makes one 9-inch pie crust.

Ice Cream Pie

Microwave Power:	Medium
Oven Selector:	Off
Oven Temperature:	Off
Shelf Position:	2

1 half gallon favorite ice cream
1 (9-inch) baked coconut pie crust

2 cups favorite ice cream sundae sauce
1/2 cup chopped nuts (optional)

If necessary, mellow ice cream with Microwave on Medium, checking each 1/2 minute, until easy to handle. Quickly pack ice cream into pie crust. Swirl surface and marble with 1/3 to 1/2 cup sundae sauce. Sprinkle with nuts, if desired. Freeze at least 4 hours before serving. If crust or filling is too hard to serve, mellow with Microwave on Medium, checking each 1/2 minute. Heat ice cream sundae sauce with Microwave on Medium until easily poured. Time depends on amount, 2 cups sauce will take approximately 2 minutes. Top pie with sundae sauce, or cut wedges and pass sauce. Makes 8 servings.

Black Bottom Pie

Microwave Power:	Medium	High
Oven Selector:	Off	Off
Oven Temperature:	Off	Off
Shelf Position:	2	2

1/4 cup water
2 oz. (2 squares) unsweetened chocolate
2 cups half and half
4 egg yolks
1/2 cup sugar
3 tablespoons cornstarch
2 teaspoons vanilla
1 (9-inch) baked pie shell (Pastry, Graham
   Cracker, Ginger Snap or Chocolate Cookie Crust)

2 tablespoons milk
1 tablespoon (1 envelope) unflavored gelatin
2 teaspoons Myers rum or rum extract
4 egg whites
1/8 teaspoon cream of tartar
1/4 cup sugar
Sweetened whipped cream
Chocolate shavings

Combine water and chocolate in 2-cup liquid measure. Cook with Microwave on Medium, 1-1/2 to 2-1/2 minutes, stirring twice, until chocolate is melted. Set aside. In 2-cup liquid measure heat half and half with Microwave on High, 2 to 3 minutes or until hot. In a 1-1/2 quart casserole beat egg yolks with a wire whip; blend in hot half and half. Combine sugar and cornstarch; blend into egg-milk mixture. Cook with Microwave on High, 2 minutes; stir. Continue to cook with Microwave on High, 2 to 3 minutes, stirring every 1/2 minute until thickened. Stir in vanilla. Remove 1 cup of pudding and blend into chocolate; chill then pour into bottom of pie shell. Combine milk and gelatin in custard cup. Dissolve gelatin with Microwave on High, 30 to 45 seconds. Stir to blend, then stir into vanilla pudding. Flavor with rum or extract. Beat egg whites and cream of tartar until frothy, slowly beat in sugar. Beat until stiff peaks form. Stir pudding or beat lightly with mixer if necessary to smooth. Fold in egg whites and spoon over chocolate filling. Top with sweetened whipped cream and chocolate shavings. Makes 8 to 10 servings.

Perfect Lemon Meringue Pie

Microwave Power:	High
Oven Selector:	Off
Oven Temperature:	Off
Shelf Position:	2

1-1/2 cups sugar	1/3 cup lemon juice
1/3 cup cornstarch	2 to 3 drops yellow food coloring
1-1/2 cups boiling water	3 tablespoons butter
4 egg yolks, slightly beaten	1 (9-inch) pastry shell, baked
1-1/2 tablespoons grated lemon peel	Meringue or whipped cream

In a 1-1/2-quart glass casserole, mix together sugar and cornstarch. Add boiling water, mix. Cook with Microwave on High, 4 to 5 minutes, stir after 2 minutes. Cook until thick and translucent. Stir again. Gradually stir some of hot mixture into beaten egg yolks. Then, pour egg mixture into hot cornstarch and sugar. Cook with Microwave on High, 45 seconds to 1 minute, to cook egg yolks. Stir in lemon peel, lemon juice, butter and food coloring. Pour into baked pie shell. Top with meringue and bake according to directions; or cool and serve with whipped cream. Makes 6 to 8 servings.

Meringue

Microwave Power:	Low	Off
Oven Selector:	Bake	Bake
Oven Temperature:	425°F, preheated	425°F
Shelf Position:	3	3

4 egg whites	1/2 cup sugar
1/4 teaspoon cream of tartar	

Beat egg whites with cream of tartar until frothy. Gradually add sugar, 1 tablespoon at a time, while beating with electric mixer. Continue beating until meringue is very stiff and glossy. Spread meringue over warm, cooked pie filling, sealing to edge of crust. Bake at 425° with Microwave on Low, 4 minutes. Turn Microwave Off and continue to Bake at 425°, 1-1/2 minutes or more, until golden brown. Cool on wire rack. Makes enough meringue for one 9-inch pie.

Vanilla Cream Pie

Microwave Power:	High
Oven Selector:	Off
Oven Temperature:	Off
Shelf Position:	2

3/4 cup sugar	1 tablespoon butter
1/4 cup cornstarch	1-1/2 teaspoons vanilla
1/4 teaspoon salt	1 (9-inch) baked pie shell
2-1/2 cups milk	Whipped cream or meringue
4 egg yolks	

In a 2-quart casserole mix together sugar, cornstarch and salt. Gradually add milk, mixing well. Cook with Microwave on High, 4 minutes; stir. Continue to cook with Microwave on High, 4 to 6 minutes or until thick, stirring every minute. Beat egg yolks slightly. Gradually add some of hot mixture to egg yolks, stirring constantly. Add combined egg mixture to hot mixture and mix well. Cook with Microwave on High, 1-1/2 to 2-1/2 minutes until thick, stirring every 30 seconds. Add butter and vanilla. Mix well. Pour hot filling into baked pie shell. Cool. Top with whipped cream or meringue. Makes 6 to 8 servings.

Coconut Meringue Pie

Microwave Power:	Low	Off
Oven Selector:	Bake	Bake
Oven Temperature:	425°F, preheated	425°F
Shelf Position:	2	2

1 recipe Vanilla Cream Pie	1 recipe Meringue
1 cup flaked coconut	

Prepare Vanilla Cream Pie as directed, except stir 3/4 cup flaked coconut into filling along with butter and vanilla. Top with meringue and sprinkle surface with reserved 1/4 cup flaked coconut. Bake at 425° with Microwave on Low, 4 minutes. Turn Microwave Off. Continue to Bake at 425°, 2 to 4 minutes until coconut and meringue are golden. Let cool before serving. Makes 6 to 8 servings.

Banana Cream Pie

Microwave Power:	High
Oven Selector:	Off
Oven Temperature:	Off
Shelf Position:	2

1 recipe Vanilla Cream Pie
4 large bananas

1 cup (1/2-pt.) whipping cream
1/4 cup sifted powdered sugar

Prepare Vanilla Cream Pie as directed, except cool filling. Arrange a layer of sliced bananas 1/2-inch deep (3 large bananas) in bottom of baked pie shell. Pour cream filling over bananas and top with whipped cream sweetened with powdered sugar. Garnish with a ring of sliced bananas. Makes 6 to 8 servings.

Wonderful Walnut Pie

Microwave Power:	High	Medium
Oven Selector:	Off	Bake
Oven Temperature:	Off	425°F, preheated
Shelf Position:	2	2

1/4 cup butter
2 tablespoons flour
1/2 cup dark corn syrup
1 cup sugar
1/3 cup sherry

3 eggs
1-1/4 cups coarsely broken walnuts
1 (9-inch) unbaked pie shell
    in glass pie plate, chilled
Whipped cream or ice cream

In a 2-quart glass casserole melt butter with Microwave on High, 1 to 1-1/2 minutes. Stir in flour, corn syrup, sugar and sherry. Bring to a boil with Microwave on High, 3-1/2 to 4 minutes, stirring twice. Preheat oven. In a 1-1/2-quart casserole, beat eggs with whisk. **Slowly** pour in hot syrup, and continue beating mixture. Add walnuts. Pour into unbaked pie shell. Bake at 425° with Microwave on Medium, 6 minutes. Give dish 1/4 turn. Continue baking 6 to 7 minutes or until knife inserted 1 inch from center comes out clean. Turn Microwave Off. Continue to Bake, if more browning is desired, 2 to 3 minutes. Serve warm or cold, topped with whipped cream or ice cream. Makes 6 to 8 servings.

Grasshopper de Cacao Chiffon Pie

Microwave Power: High
Oven Selector: Off
Oven Temperature: Off
Shelf Position: 2

1 pkg. (1 tablespoon) unflavored gelatin
1/4 cup water
1/2 cup white creme de cacao
1/4 cup green creme de menthe
2 egg whites
1/4 teaspoon salt
1/4 cup sugar

1 cup (1/2 pt.) whipping cream, chilled
1 tablespoon powdered sugar
Few drops green food coloring
1 (9-inch) Chocolate Crumb Crust, baked
Mint leaves, lime wedges and
    sweetened whipped cream for garnish (optional)

Stir together gelatin and water in a 2-cup liquid measure. Heat with Microwave on High, 45 seconds, or until gelatin is dissolved. Cool slightly and stir in liqueurs. Chill, stirring occasionally, until mixture is slightly thicker than an egg white. In a medium bowl, beat egg whites and salt together until frothy. Gradually add sugar beating until very stiff. With same beaters, beat whipping cream, powdered sugar and food coloring until medium mounds can be formed. Fold gelatin mixture into whipped cream; then fold in egg whites. Pour into pie crust and chill about 3 hours or until firm. Garnish, if desired. Makes 8 servings.

Variations:

To make Grasshopper Mint Chiffon Pie follow recipe above, but reverse liqueur amounts using 1/2 cup green creme de menthe and 1/4 cup white creme de cacao.

To make Brandy Alexander Chiffon Pie follow recipe above, but replace liqueurs using 1/3 cup brown creme de cacao and 1/3 cup brandy.

Autumn Apple Pie

Microwave Power:	High	Medium
Oven Selector:	Off	Bake
Oven Temperature:	Off	425°F, preheated
Shelf Position:	2	1

Filling:

6 tart cooking apples
1 cup sugar
2 tablespoons flour
1 teaspoon cinnamon

1 teaspoon grated lemon peel
1/8 teaspoon salt
1/8 teaspoon cloves

1 (9-inch) Sour Cream Crust, unbaked

Topping:

1/4 cup butter, melted
1/2 cup flour
1/2 cup grated Cheddar cheese

1/4 cup sugar
1/8 teaspoon salt
Sour cream

Filling:

Peel, quarter and core apples. Slice thin. Combine sugar, flour, cinnamon, lemon peel, salt and cloves; add apple slices and toss lightly. Pour into unbaked pie shell

Topping:

In a 2-cup liquid measure melt butter with Microwave on High, 30 to 45 seconds. Preheat oven. Combine flour, cheese, sugar, salt and melted butter with a fork. Sprinkle topping over apples. Bake at 425° with Microwave on Medium, 14 to 18 minutes or until the apples are tender and pie is golden. Serve warm with dollops of sour cream on each wedge. Makes 8 servings.

Old Fashioned Apple Pie

Microwave Power:	Medium	Off
Oven Selector:	Bake	Bake
Oven Temperature:	450°F, preheated	450°
Shelf Position:	1	1

Pastry for 2-crust (9-inch) pie
1 cup sugar
1/4 cup flour
1-1/4 teaspoons cinnamon
1/8 teaspoon salt

1-1/2 teaspoons grated lemon peel
6 cups tart cooking apples,
    pared and sliced 1/4-inch thick
2 tablespoons butter, softened

Prepare pastry. Roll out half of the pastry and line 9-inch glass pie plate. Mix together sugar, flour, cinnamon, salt and grated lemon peel. Add to prepared apples, tossing lightly to combine. Turn into pastry-lined pie plate. Dot with butter. Roll remaining pastry. Make several slits near center for steam vents, place over filling. Fold edge of top pastry under edge of bottom pastry. Crimp edges together to seal. Bake at 450° with Microwave on Medium, 10 minutes. Rotate 1/4 turn. Continue to Bake at 450° with Microwave on Medium, 10 to 14 minutes or until apples are tender. If desired, turn Microwave Off and continue baking to finish browning. Makes 6 to 8 servings.

Pumpkin Pie

Microwave Power:	High	Low
Oven Selector:	Off	Bake
Oven Temperature:	Off	450°F, preheated
Shelf Position:	2	2

1-1/2 cups canned pumpkin
1 cup evaporated milk
2 eggs, slightly beaten
3/4 cup sugar
1/4 teaspoon salt

1/2 teaspoon cinnamon
1/2 teaspoon nutmeg
1/2 teaspoon allspice
1/4 teaspoon ginger
1 (9-inch) baked pie shell

In 1-1/2-quart casserole, combine pumpkin and milk. Cook with Microwave on High, 4 minutes. Stir. Preheat oven. Mix eggs with sugar, salt and spices. Add hot pumpkin mixture to eggs slowly, stirring constantly. Combine thoroughly and pour into baked pie shell. Bake at 450° with Microwave on Low, 6 to 9 minutes, until knife inserted 1-1/2 inches from center comes out clean. Cool before serving. Makes 6 to 8 servings.

Fresh Strawberry Pie

Microwave Power:	High
Oven Selector:	Off
Oven Temperature:	Off
Shelf Position:	2

3/4 cup sugar
3 tablespoons cornstarch
5 to 7 cups fresh strawberries
1 cup water
2 to 3 drops red food coloring

1 to 2 tablespoons Cointreau,
   Galliano or orange juice
1 tablespoon grated orange peel (optional)
1 (9-inch) baked pie shell, cooled
Whipped cream, sweetened (optional)

Combine sugar and cornstarch in a 4-cup liquid measure. Crush 1 cup of the smaller berries. Blend into sugar and cornstarch. Stir in water. Cook with Microwave on High, 3 minutes; stir. Continue to cook on High, 3 to 5 minutes, until glaze has come to a boil, stirring occasionally. It should be thick and transparent. Strain, if desired, for a clearer sauce. Add food coloring. Cool slightly. Stir in Cointreau, Galliano or orange juice, and orange peel. Spread 1/3 cup of glaze in bottom of baked pie shell. Arrange remaining berries in pie shell. Pour remaining glaze over berries and chill. Serve plain or with sweetened whipped cream. Makes 6 to 8 servings.

Chocolate-Marshmallow Cream Pie

Microwave Power:	High
Oven Selector:	Off
Oven Temperature:	Off
Shelf Position:	2

1 bar (8-oz.) chocolate with or without almonds
1/2 cup milk
16 marshmallows, regular size
1 cup (1/2 pt.) whipping cream

1 (9-inch) baked pie shell or crumb crust
Whipped cream, whole almonds and/or
   unsweetened chocolate for garnish (optional)

Place chocolate bar, milk and marshmallows in a 2-quart casserole. Cook with Microwave on High, 3-1/2 to 4 minutes, stirring twice. Chill thoroughly. Whip cream and fold into chocolate mixture; pour into pie crust. Chill until firm. Garnish. Makes 6 to 8 servings.

Variation:
To make Rocky Road Chocolate-Marshmallow Pie, follow the recipe above folding in 1 cup miniature marshmallows with whipped cream.

Double Chocolate Mocha Pie

Microwave Power:	High
Oven Selector:	Off
Oven Temperature:	Off
Shelf Position:	2

1 pkg. (3-3/4-oz.) chocolate pudding mix
1 pkg. (1 tablespoon) unflavored gelatin
1 square (1-oz.) unsweetened chocolate, broken
2 cups milk
1/4 cup sugar
1 tablespoon instant coffee powder

2 teaspoons vanilla
Few grains salt
1 cup (1/2 pt.) whipping cream
1 (9-inch) crumb crust
Whipped cream and unsweetened
  chocolate (optional)

Crust:
1 cup finely crushed vanilla wafer crumbs
1/2 cup finely chopped pecans

1/3 cup melted butter

Combine pudding mix, gelatin, chocolate and milk in 2-quart casserole. Heat mixture with Microwave on High, 5 minutes. Continue to cook with Microwave on High for an additional 4 to 6 minutes, stirring occasionally. Mixture should come to a boil according to package directions, but will be slightly thinner. Stir in sugar, instant coffee, vanilla and salt. Cool until mixture will mound from a spoon. Stir frequently. Whip cream with electric mixer, reserve. With same beaters whip chocolate mixture until smooth. Fold whipped cream into chocolate mixture and mound into pie crust. Garnish if desired with reserved whipped cream and grate unsweetened chocolate over top of all. Chill 3 to 4 hours before serving. Makes 6 to 8 servings.

Crust:
Mix crumbs and nuts together in a 9-inch glass pie plate. Melt butter with Microwave on High, 1/2 to 1 minute; add to crumbs and mix well. Press to sides and bottom of pie plate. Chill.

Salads

It is appropriate to include a section on salads in a combination microwave and conventional oven cookbook since many salad ingredients and dressings are cooked. Microwave cooking is handy to simply heat dressings for hot salads or to dissolve gelatin for molded salads. More complicated recipes cook meat or vegetables to be combined in a salad, as in Taco Salad. Use microwave cooking for any salad recipes requiring cooked ingredients.

Hot Chicken Salad

Microwave Power:	Medium
Oven Selector:	Bake
Oven Temperature:	450°F, preheated
Shelf Position:	2

1/2 cup toasted almonds
2 cups diced cooked chicken
2 cups diced celery
1 cup mayonnaise
2 tablespoons lemon juice

3/4 teaspoons salt
3 tablespoons grated onion
3/4 cup grated Cheddar cheese
1 cup crushed potato chips

While preheating the oven toast the almonds, approximately 6 to 9 minutes, or until golden brown. Mix together in a 1-1/2-quart glass casserole the almonds, chicken and celery. In a 1-quart bowl blend the mayonnaise, lemon juice, salt and onion. Combine the mayonnaise mixture with the chicken mixture. Sprinkle grated cheese over top and cover with potato chips. Bake at 450° with Microwave on Medium, 10 to 12 minutes, until bubbly. Makes 4 to 6 servings.

Taco Salad

Microwave Power:	High	Medium
Oven Selector:	Off	Off
Oven Temperature:	Off	Off
Shelf Position:	2	2

1 can (15-1/2-oz.) red kidney beans, drained
1 lb. ground beef
1 pkg. (1-1/4-oz.) taco seasoning mix
1/2 head lettuce, shredded
1 medium red onion, chopped

1 cup grated Cheddar cheese
1 cup Thousand Island Dressing
2 cups tortilla chips
1 large avocado, peeled and sliced
4 medium tomatoes, cut in wedges

Drain kidney beans. Set aside. Crumble ground beef in 1-quart glass casserole. Cook with Microwave on High, 2-1/2 minutes. Stir. Continue cooking with Microwave on High, 2 to 3 minutes or until cooked. Drain fat. Stir in taco seasoning mix; cover. Cook with Microwave on Medium, 3 to 4 minutes to blend flavors. Add beans and mix. Toss together lettuce, onion, cheese, dressing, chips, avocado and tomato, reserving some of the chips, avocado and tomato for garnish. Toss lettuce mixture with meat and beans. Garnish with reserved ingredients. Makes 6 to 8 servings.

Hot Spinach Salad

Microwave Power:	High
Oven Selector:	Off
Oven Temperature:	Off
Shelf Position:	2

1 bunch fresh spinach, washed, dried and stems removed
4 slices bacon
2 tablespoons wine vinegar
2 teaspoons sugar

1/4 teaspoon prepared mustard
1/8 teaspoon seasoned salt
Dash pepper
2 green onions, sliced thin
1 hard cooked egg, chopped

Tear spinach into pieces; place in a salad bowl. Place bacon in a glass-ceramic baking dish; cover with a paper towel. Cook with Microwave on High, 5 to 7 minutes or until crisp. Crumble bacon and set aside. Into bacon drippings stir vinegar, sugar, mustard, salt and pepper. Cook with Microwave on High, 2 to 3 minutes or until mixture boils. Stir in green onions and bacon; cook with Microwave on High, 1 to 1-1/2 minutes to soften. Pour hot dressing over spinach; toss quickly. Sprinkle with chopped egg. Serve immediately. Makes 4 servings.

Marinated Artichoke Salad

Microwave Power:	High
Oven Selector:	Off
Oven Temperature:	Off
Shelf Position:	2

1 pkg. (9-oz.) frozen artichokes, cooked and drained
8 tablespoons oil (olive and salad oil combination)
3 tablespoons grapefruit juice
2 tablespoons white vinegar
1 tablespoon chopped chives
1 teaspoon dry mustard
1-1/4 teaspoons seasoned salt

1/4 teaspoon pepper
1/8 teaspoon garlic powder
2 to 3 chopped green onions, including tops
1/2 green pepper, slivered
1 small cucumber, partially peeled, scored and thinly sliced
4 to 6 cups assorted salad greens

Place hearts in 1-quart covered casserole. Cook with Microwave on High, 8 to 10 minutes, stirring once. Drain well. While hot, toss with oil. Add grapefruit juice, vinegar, chives, dry mustard, salt, pepper and garlic powder. Stir to combine; snipping artichoke hearts into smaller pieces, if desired. Refrigerate for several hours. At serving time, add remaining ingredients and toss with marinated mixture. Makes 6 to 8 servings.

Note:
Bottled or prepared packaged Italian style salad dressing may be substituted for marinade mixture. Toss 3/4 to 1 cup salad dressing with hot, drained artichokes. Follow recipe above.

Hot German Potato Salad with Knockwurst

Microwave Power:	High
Oven Selector:	Off
Oven Temperature:	Off
Shelf Position:	2

3 medium potatoes (1-1/2 lbs.)
3 slices bacon, diced
1 small onion, chopped
1 tablespoon sugar
1 tablespoon flour
1 teaspoon salt
1 teaspoon dry mustard

1/2 teaspoon celery seed
1/4 teaspoon pepper
1/4 cup apple cider vinegar
1/2 cup water
3 knockwurst (8-oz.)
1 tablespoon snipped fresh parsley

Wash potatoes; dry and cut in half; place in a 2-quart casserole. Cover and cook with Microwave on High, 10 to 12 minutes or until tender. Remove skins and slice. Place bacon and onion in a 4-cup liquid measure. Cook with Microwave on High, 5 to 7 minutes or until bacon is cooked and onions are limp. Stir in sugar, flour, salt, dry mustard, celery seed and pepper; mix well. Add vinegar and water. Cook with Microwave on High, 5 to 6 minutes or until dressing has boiled and thickened; stir once. Set aside. Make several cuts into plastic package holding knockwurst; remove metal closures. Heat with Microwave on High, 2 to 2-1/2 minutes or until heated through. Remove from package and cut into 1-inch pieces. Arrange meat and potatoes in a shallow bowl. Pour hot dressing over meat and potatoes and toss lightly. Sprinkle with parsley. Serve hot. Makes 4 servings.

Sauces

Included here are a variety of sauces from basic White Sauce to incredible Super Chocolate Sundae Sauce. Sauces are ideally suited to preparation in the microwave oven. They cook quickly without scorching, but should be stirred during last half of cooking to eliminate lumping. Flour or cornstarch based sauces need to boil on High to thoroughly cook the starch and thicken the sauce. Delicate egg yolk based sauces need to be cooked slowly on Low and should not boil. Most dessert sauces need to cook sufficiently to completely dissolve sugar.

Sauces cook easily in a glass liquid measuring cup or deep bowl. Use a container large enough to allow for boiling.

The Hollandaise and Bearnaise sauces are the traditional longer cooking recipes to show the method for preparing delicate sauces in the Thermatronic II oven. Try your own favorite blender versions of these sauces, using microwave power to melt the butter.

White Sauce

Microwave Power:	High
Oven Selector:	Off
Oven Temperature:	Off
Shelf Position:	2

	Thin	Medium	Thick
Butter	1 tablespoon	2 tablespoons	1/4 cup
Flour	1 tablespoon	2 tablespoons	1/4 cup
Milk	1 cup	1 cup	1 cup
Salt	1/2 teaspoon	1/2 teaspoon	1/2 teaspoon
Pepper	1/8 teaspoon	1/8 teaspoon	1/8 teaspoon

In a 2-quart casserole melt butter with Microwave on High, 30 seconds to 1 minute. Add flour and mix together until smooth. Cook with Microwave on High, 1 minute. Gradually add milk, stirring constantly until smooth. Cook with Microwave on High, 4 to 5 minutes, stirring once or twice. Cook until sauce boils and is thickened and smooth. Season with salt and pepper. Makes 1 cup sauce.

Hollandaise Sauce

Microwave Power:	Low
Oven Selector:	Off
Oven Temperature:	Off
Shelf Position:	2

1/2 cup (1 stick) butter
4 egg yolks
2 tablespoons fresh lemon juice

1/4 to 1/2 teaspoon salt
Dash cayenne
2 tablespoons boiling water

Divide butter into 3 pieces. In a 4-cup liquid measure beat egg yolks and lemon juice together with a wire whip. Cook with Microwave on Low, 1 minute. Beat in one piece of butter with a wire whip. Cook with Microwave on Low, 1/2 minute. Beat in second piece of butter; cook with Microwave on Low, 1/2 minute. Beat in remaining butter, 1/4 teaspoon salt and cayenne, then boiling water. Cook with Microwave on Low, 1-1/2 to 2 minutes, stirring every 1/2 minute until sauce is hot. Avoid overcooking. Add more salt if necessary. Makes about 1-1/2 cups.

Béarnaise Sauce

Microwave Power:	High	Low
Oven Selector:	Off	Off
Oven Temperature:	Off	Off
Shelf Position:	2	2

1/4 cup dry white wine
2 tablespoons white wine vinegar
1 tablespoon minced shallots or green onions
1 teaspoon dried tarragon, crushed
4 egg yolks, beaten

2/3 cup clarified butter
1/4 teaspoon salt
White pepper to taste
Dash cayenne pepper

Combine wine, vinegar, shallots or onions and tarragon in a 2-cup liquid measure. Bring to a boil with Microwave on High and continue cooking until about half of liquid is evaporated, 5 to 7 minutes. Strain liquid. Place beaten egg yolks in a 1-1/2 quart casserole. Slowly pour hot strained liquid into egg yolks, beating constantly with a wire whip. Cook with Microwave on Low, 1-1/2 to 3 minutes, stirring with a wire whip twice during the first minute, then every 15 seconds until sauce is consistency of mayonnaise. Gradually beat in clarified butter. Season with salt, pepper and cayenne. Cover and set dish in bowl of hot, not boiling, water to keep warm. Makes about 1 cup sauce.

Clarified Butter

Microwave Power:	Low
Oven Selector:	Off
Oven Temperature	Off
Shelf Position:	2

1 cup (2 sticks) butter

Melt butter slowly in a 2-cup liquid measure with Microwave on Low, 2 to 3 minutes or until completely melted and oil has started to separate; but butter has not started to bubble or cook. Allow butter to stand a few minutes. Skim off foam, slowly pour off yellow oil—clarified butter—and reserve. Discard leftover whey. Makes about 2/3 cups clarified butter.

Mornay Sauce

Microwave Power:	High
Oven Selector:	Off
Oven Temperature:	Off
Shelf Position:	2

2 tablespoons butter
2 tablespoons flour
1/2 teaspoon salt
1/8 teaspoon cayenne pepper

1 cup half and half
1 cup (4-oz.) grated Cheddar cheese
2 tablespoons sauterne

Melt butter in 4-cup liquid measure with Microwave on High, 1/2 to 1 minute. Mix in flour; cook with Microwave on High, 45 seconds or until bubbly. Blend in salt, pepper, and half and half. Cook with Microwave on High, 3 to 4 minutes, stirring often, until mixture is thickened. Add cheese; cook with Microwave on High, 30 to 45 seconds until cheese is melted. Add wine and beat sauce until light. Makes about 1-1/2 cups. Serve with broccoli or cauliflower.

Mushroom Cheese Sauce

Microwave Power:	High
Oven Selector:	Off
Oven Temperature:	Off
Shelf Position:	2

2 tablespoons flour
Drippings from Chicken Cordon Bleu or
    2 tablespoons melted butter
2 tablespoons grated onion

1/2 cup grated Monterey Jack cheese
1/4 cup milk
2 tablespoons dry white wine, optional
1 can (2-1/2-oz.) sliced mushrooms, drained

Blend flour into fat drippings or melted butter in which Chicken Cordon Bleu was prepared. Mix in onion and cheese, blend in milk and wine. Cook mixture with Microwave on High, 3 to 5 minutes, stirring occasionally, until sauce bubbles and thickens. Stir in mushrooms. Heat with Microwave on High, 1 minute, to heat mushrooms. Spoon over Cordon Bleu.

Sour Cream Mushroom Sauce

Microwave Power:	High
Oven Selector:	Off
Oven Temperature:	Off
Shelf Position:	2

2 tablespoons butter
1/4 cup minced onion
1/2 lb. fresh mushrooms,
   cleaned and halved
2 tablespoons flour

1/2 cup dairy sour cream
1/2 cup whipping cream
1/2 teaspoon salt
1/4 teaspoon pepper
1 tablespoon sherry (optional)

In a 1-1/2-quart casserole, cook butter and onions with Microwave on High, 2-1/2 minutes. Stir in mushrooms and cook with Microwave on High, 1 minute. Blend in flour until smooth. Slowly blend in sour cream and whipping cream; season with salt and pepper. Heat with Microwave on High, 5 to 6 minutes, or until hot; stir once. Blend in sherry, if desired. Serve with Chicken Royal.

Barbecue Sauce

Microwave Power:	High
Oven Selector:	Off
Oven Temperature:	Off
Shelf Position:	2

1 can (8-oz.) tomato sauce
1/4 cup vinegar
2 tablespoons brown sugar, firmly packed
1 tablespoon instant minced onion

1 tablespoon Worcestershire sauce
1 teaspoon prepared mustard
1/4 teaspoon salt
1/8 teaspoon liquid smoke

Combine all ingredients in a 4-cup liquid measure. Cover with plastic wrap. Cook with Microwave on High, 6 to 7 minutes, stirring once. Let stand 20 minutes to blend flavors before using. Serve with ribs, chicken, chops or hamburgers. Makes 1-1/4 cups.

Flaming Brandy Raisin Sauce

Microwave Power:	High
Oven Selector:	Off
Oven Temperature:	Off
Shelf Position:	2

1 cup orange juice
1 tablespoon cornstarch
1/2 cup golden seedless raisins,
   coarsely chopped

1/2 cup orange marmalade
1/2 teaspoon cinnamon
1/3 cup brandy

Mix together orange juice and cornstarch in 1-1/2-quart casserole. Add remaining ingredients, except brandy. Cook with Microwave on High, 4-1/2 minutes; stir. Continue to cook with Microwave on High, 2-1/4 to 3 minutes, stirring every 45 seconds or until thick. When ready to serve, pour sauce over meat, heat brandy in glass cup with Microwave on High, 15 seconds. Flame brandy and pour over top of sauce. Serve at once, with poultry or ham. Makes 1-2/3 cups.

Red Chili Sauce

Microwave Power:	High	Low
Oven Selector:	Off	Off
Oven Temperature:	Off	Off
Shelf Position:	2	2

1/2 cup finely chopped onion
1 large garlic clove, mashed
2 tablespoons oil
1-1/2 tablespoons flour
1 to 2 tablespoons chili powder
1 teaspoon sugar
1 teaspoon salt

1/2 teaspoon oregano, crushed
1/4 teaspoon ground cumin
2 tablespoons diced green chiles
3/4 cup beef bouillion or 1 beef bouillion cube
   dissolved in 3/4 cup water
2 cans (8-oz. each) tomato sauce

Combine onion, garlic and oil in a 2-quart casserole; cover and cook with Microwave on High, 4 to 5 minutes or until onion is tender. Blend in flour, chili powder, sugar, salt, oregano and cumin to make a paste. Stir in chiles, bouillion and tomato sauce. Cover and cook with Microwave on High, 5 minutes. Remove cover and cook with Microwave on Low, 10 minutes, stirring once. Makes about 2-1/2 cups.

Chinese Apricot Glaze

Microwave Power:	High	Low
Oven Selector:	Off	Off
Oven Temperature:	Off	Off
Shelf Position:	2	2

1/2 cup dried apricots
3/4 cup water
1-1/2 teaspoons grated orange peel
1/4 cup orange juice

3 tablespoons dark corn syrup
1 tablespoon cider vinegar
1 tablespoon soy sauce
1/2 teaspoon ground ginger

Combine apricots and water in a 2-cup liquid measure. Cook with Microwave on High, 4 to 5 minutes or until mixture boils. Turn Microwave on Low, continue cooking 3 to 5 minutes or until apricots are soft and plump. Let stand a few minutes, then drain. Combine apricots and remaining ingredients in a blender container, blend at low speed until smooth. Use to baste Cornish Hens according to recipe. Also good on chicken. Makes about 1-1/4 cups.

Apricot Brandy Sauce

Microwave Power:	Medium
Oven Selector:	Off
Oven Temperature:	Off
Shelf Position:	2

3/4 cup apricot preserves
1 tablespoon butter

1/4 cup brandy

In a 2-cup liquid measure heat preserves and butter with Microwave on Medium, 3 to 4 minutes, until butter melts and preserves start to bubble. Stir twice. Stir in brandy. Serve warm over ice cream. Makes about 1 cup.

Chocolate-Bourbon Sauce

Microwave Power:	Low
Oven Selector:	Off
Oven Temperature:	Off
Shelf Position:	2

1/4 cup sugar
1/4 cup corn syrup
Dash salt

2 squares (1-oz. each) unsweetened chocolate
1/3 cup whipping cream
3 tablespoons bourbon

In a 2-cup liquid measure mix sugar, corn syrup and salt. Add chocolate. Heat with Microwave on Low, 2-1/2 to 3-1/2 minutes, stirring once, until sugar and chocolate have melted. Stir until smooth. Gradually stir in cream, then bourbon. Cool. Serve over ice cream. Makes about 1 cup.

Super Chocolate Sundae Sauce

Microwave Power:	High
Oven Selector:	Off
Oven Temperature:	Off
Shelf Position:	2

1 can (15-oz.) sweetened condensed milk
1/4 cup (1/2 stick) butter
1/4 teaspoon salt
1 pkg. (6-oz.) semi-sweet chocolate pieces

1 teaspoon vanilla
1/3 to 1/2 cup very strong coffee,
 brandy or liqueur

Combine milk, butter and salt in a 2-quart casserole. Cook with Microwave on High, 3 to 3-1/2 minutes, stirring once, until butter melts and mixture just comes to a boil. Stir; cook with Microwave on High for an additional 45 seconds. Add chocolate and vanilla. Stir until melted. Slowly stir in liquid. Makes 2-1/2 cups sauce.

Soups

Microwave power is excellent for preparing all kinds of soups. They can be cooked and served in the same casserole dish or tureen, eliminating pot washing. Individual servings of soup can be heated in bowls or mugs.

Many soups in this section are the old fashioned, hearty variety that can be served as a whole meal. Try New England Clam Chowder or Minestrone accompanied by crusty bread.

Soups are cooked on High, except where a slow, simmer type of cooking is desired, as in Split Pea Soup with Ham. There the cooking is started on High, then reduced to Low and simmered. Use this method for cooking dried pea or bean soup.

Reheat soups on High unless it is a small quantity of very thick soup, then use Medium power. Stir soups occasionally during cooking or reheating to distribute heat. Microwave cooking virtually eliminates scorching since food is heated from all sides and heat is not concentrated on the bottom.

Water for dry soups and mix-in-a-cup soups may be heated or boiled on High in the microwave oven, then the soup is prepared according to package directions.

Chicken Soup

Microwave Power:	High
Oven Selector:	Off
Oven Temperature:	Off
Shelf Position:	2

6 cups chicken broth
2 cups diced, cooked chicken
1/2 cup finely chopped celery
1/3 cup diced carrots
1/3 cup finely chopped onion
1/4 cup long grain rice
2 tablespoons finely chopped green pepper

2 sprigs parsley, minced
1 teaspoon salt
1/2 teaspoon pepper
1/4 teaspoon leaf thyme, crushed
1 bay leaf
2 whole cloves

Combine all ingredients in a covered 4-quart casserole. Cover; cook with Microwave on High, 25 to 30 minutes, stirring occasionally. Makes 4 to 6 servings.

Cream of Chicken Soup

Microwave Power:	High
Oven Selector:	Off
Oven Temperature:	Off
Shelf Position:	2

6 tablespoons butter
1 tablespoon finely minced onion
1/3 cup flour
2 cups milk

2 cups chicken broth or bouillon
1/2 teaspoon salt
1/8 teaspoon pepper
2 cups finely chopped cooked chicken

Place butter and onion in 2-1/2-quart casserole. Cover; cook with Microwave on High, 3 to 4 minutes until onions are transparent, stirring once. Stir in flour; cook with Microwave on High, 1 minute. Add milk and broth or bouillon gradually, stirring until smooth. Stir in salt and pepper. Heat with Microwave on High, 9 to 11 minutes until hot, stirring occasionally. Stir in chicken; heat with Microwave on High, 2 to 3 minutes, to serving temperature. Makes 4 to 6 servings.

New England Clam Chowder

Microwave Power:	High
Oven Selector:	Off
Oven Temperature:	Off
Shelf Position:	2

2 slices bacon, diced
1 medium onion, diced
2 medium potatoes, peeled and diced
2 cans (7-1/2-oz. each) minced clams,
  drained (reserving liquid)
Reserved clam liquid plus water to make 2 cups

1/4 cup (1/2 stick) butter, melted
1/4 cup unsifted flour
3 cups milk
3/4 teaspoon salt
1/8 teaspoon pepper

Place bacon in 3-quart casserole, cook with Microwave on High, 3 minutes. Add onion and potatoes; cover. Cook with Microwave on High, 5 minutes. Add clam juice and water; cover. Cook with Microwave on High, 8 to 10 minutes or until potatoes are tender. Melt butter in 2-cup liquid measure. Stir in flour and add to potato mixture, mixing well. Add remaining ingredients. Cover, cook with Microwave on High, 5 minutes or until hot. Makes 6 servings.

Split Pea Soup with Ham

Microwave Power:	High	Low	High
Oven Selector:	Off	Off	Off
Oven Temperature:	Off	Off	Off
Shelf Position:	2	2	2

2 cups (1 lb.) split peas, rinsed and drained
1-1/2 lbs. ham hock or shank
1 small onion, chopped
1 celery stalk with leaves, chopped
1 carrot, chopped

4 whole cloves
1 bay leaf
8 cups (2 qts.) hot tap water
1-1/2 to 2 teaspoons salt
1/8 to 1/4 teaspoon pepper

In a 4-quart casserole combine all ingredients except salt and pepper. Cover; cook with Microwave on High, 20 to 25 minutes or until mixture comes to a full boil. Stir; cover and cook with Microwave on Low, 40 to 50 minutes or until meat is tender and peas are soft. Remove cloves and bay leaf, discard. Remove ham, cut meat from bone and chop; return to soup. Discard bone and fat. Season with salt and pepper. Cook uncovered with Microwave on High, 5 to 8 minutes or until soup is hot and slightly thickened, stirring once. Makes 6 to 8 servings.

French Onion Soup

Microwave Power:	High
Oven Selector:	Off
Oven Temperature:	Off
Shelf Position:	2

3 onions (about 1 lb.), thinly sliced
1/4 cup (1/2 stick) butter
4 cups beef broth or bouillon
1 teaspoon Worcestershire sauce

1/2 teaspoon salt
2 tablespoons dry sherry
5 or 6 slices French bread, toasted
Grated Parmesan cheese

Place onions and butter in a 2-1/2-quart covered casserole. Cook with Microwave on High, 14 to 16 minutes or until onions are cooked, stirring twice. Stir in broth, Worcestershire sauce and salt. Cover; cook with Microwave on High, 7 to 10 minutes or until soup is hot. Stir in sherry. Sprinkle toast with cheese and float on top of soup. Makes 4 to 6 servings.

Hurry-up Onion Soup

Microwave Power:	High
Oven Selector:	Off
Oven Temperature:	Off
Shelf Position:	2

4 tablespoons butter
1/3 cup instant minced onion
4 cups beef bouillon
1/2 teaspoon salt

1/2 bay leaf
1/4 teaspoon seasoned pepper
2 tablespoons sherry (optional)

Melt butter in a 2-quart casserole with Microwave on High, 45 seconds to 1 minute. Add onion and cook with Microwave on High 1-1/2 minutes, stirring once. Add remaining ingredients and bring to a boil with Microwave on High, 9 to 12 minutes. Boil 1 minute. Remove bay leaf and serve with croutons and Parmesan cheese. Makes 4 servings.

Albondigas Soup

Microwave Power: High
Oven Selector: Off
Oven Temperature: Off
Shelf Position: 2

1 egg
1 lb. ground beef
1 small onion, grated
3/4 cup fine dry bread crumbs
3/4 teaspoon salt
3/4 teaspoon chili powder

1/2 cup pine nuts or chopped almonds
6 cups beef consommé
1/4 cup sherry (optional)
1/2 teaspoon oregano leaves, crushed
1 bay leaf

Beat egg slightly in a medium bowl. Mix in beef, onion, bread crumbs, salt, chili powder and nuts. Shape mixture into 1-inch meatballs (about 70-75.) Combine consommé, sherry, oregano and bay leaf in a 3-quart glass casserole. Cover. Heat with Microwave on High, 17 to 20 minutes or until liquid comes to a boil. Drop in meatballs; cover. Continue cooking with Microwave on High, 4 to 6 minutes or until meatballs are done. Makes 6 servings.

Note:
If beef bouillon cubes (7) are used and combined with hot tap water, reduce liquid heating time accordingly.

Minestrone Soup

Microwave Power: High
Oven Selector: Off
Oven Temperature: Off
Shelf Position: 2

1 lb. beef shanks or stew meat
5 cups hot water
1 onion, chopped
1/2 teaspoon basil, crushed
1/4 teaspoon pepper
1/2 cup diced carrots
1 can (16-oz.) tomatoes and juice

1/2 cup uncooked spaghetti,
   broken into 1-inch pieces
1 cup shredded cabbage
2 zucchini, sliced 1/2-inch thick
1 can (16-oz.) kidney beans, drained
1 teaspoon salt
Grated Parmesan or Romano cheese

Place meat in a 4-quart casserole. Add hot water, onion, basil and pepper. Cover; cook with Microwave on High, 30 minutes or until meat is tender, turning or stirring meat once. Remove meat from bone and cut into bite-size pieces. Return meat to broth, add carrots and tomatoes. Cover; cook with Microwave on High, 10 minutes. Stir in spaghetti, cabbage, zucchini, beans and salt. Cover and cook with Microwave on High, 12 to 16 minutes or until vegetables are tender, stirring once. Let stand covered 5 minutes. Sprinkle with cheese. Makes 6 servings.

Potato Soup

Microwave Power:	High
Oven Selector:	Off
Oven Temperature:	Off
Shelf Position:	2

3 cups diced potatoes
1/4 cup chopped onion
3 cups water
6 strips bacon, diced

2 tablespoons flour
2 teaspoons salt
1 teaspoon seasoned pepper

Place potatoes, onions and water in a 2-1/2-quart covered casserole. Cook with Microwave on High, 15 minutes or until potatoes are tender, stirring twice. In an 8-inch round baking dish cook bacon with Microwave on High, 6 to 8 minutes until crisp, stirring once. Mix flour, salt and pepper with undrained bacon. Cook with Microwave on High, 2 minutes, stirring once. Add to potatoes and bring to a boil with Microwave on High, 5 to 6 minutes. Makes 4 servings.

Irish Country Soup

Microwave Power:	High
Oven Selector:	Off
Oven Temperature:	Off
Shelf Position:	2

1 can (10-3/4-oz.) cream of potato soup
1 pkg. (8-oz.) frozen green peas in cream sauce

2 cups milk
2 chicken bouillon cubes

Combine all ingredients in a deep 2-quart casserole. Cover and heat with Microwave on High, 10 to 12 minutes or until bubbly hot; stir often. Pour 1/2 of soup into blender. Cover tightly and blend just until peas are broken into small pieces. Repeat with balance of soup. Reheat with Microwave on High, 3 to 4 minutes. Makes 4 to 6 servings.

Easy Borsch

Microwave Power:	High
Oven Selector:	Off
Oven Temperature:	Off
Shelf Position:	2

1 can (1 lb.) julienne beets, undrained
1 can (10-1/2-oz.) condensed onion soup
3/4 cup dry white wine or water
1/8 teaspoon salt

1/8 teaspoon pepper
2 tablespoons lemon juice
Dairy sour cream

Combine beets, beet juice, soup, wine, salt and pepper in a 2-quart casserole. Cover and heat with Microwave on High, 7 to 9 minutes or until very hot. Stir in lemon juice and ladle into soup bowls. Top each with a dollop of sour cream. Makes 4 to 6 servings.

Tomato Consommé

Microwave Power:	High
Oven Selector:	Off
Oven Temperature:	Off
Shelf Position:	2

2 cans (12-oz. each) tomato juice
1 can (10-1/2-oz.) condensed beef consommé
1/4 teaspoon sugar
1/4 teaspoon salt
1/8 teaspoon seasoned salt

1/8 teaspoon marjoram, crushed
1/8 teaspoon basil, crushed
1/2 bay leaf
4 thin slices lemon
8 whole cloves

Mix tomato juice, consommé, sugar, salt, seasoned salt, marjoram, basil and bay leaf. Stud lemon slices with cloves. Add to soup. Cover and heat with Microwave on High, 9 to 10 minutes or until hot. Remove bay leaf. Makes 4 to 6 servings.

Sandwiches

The sandwiches in this section are traditional hot sandwiches—usually a filling on bread or buns heated with microwave power only. (Other "sandwich type" recipes, such as Mini Pizzas, are found elsewhere in the cookbook.) Drier types of bread, like rye and whole wheat, heat better with microwave power than soft moist white bread. Heat individual sandwiches on a napkin or paper plate to help absorb moisture. When several sandwiches are heated on a plate, place a napkin between sandwiches and dish.

A trick to keep the top slice of bread from overcooking and becoming tough while filling is heating, is to leave it off until the last 1/2 to 1 minute of heating. The filling absorbs most of the microwaves, and helps protect the bottom slice of bread or bottom of bun. Toasted bread or buns may also be used in any of these sandwiches. The bread will not be as crisp as when making a cold sandwich on toast. Fillings may be heated alone then spread on toast, if desired.

Spread fillings evenly over bread and close to the edge. A high mounded filling may not be heated through before the edges begin to dry out. Remember, fillings can get very hot and sandwiches may become awkward to handle when heated with microwaves. Allow a brief standing time for heat to be distributed and filling to set.

Hot Reuben Sandwiches

Microwave Power:	Medium
Oven Selector:	Off
Oven Temperature:	Off
Shelf Position:	2

2 pkg. (3-oz. each) thin sliced pressed
   corned beef or ham, shredded
2 cups grated Swiss cheese
1 cup Bavarian or regular sauerkraut,
   drained

3/4 teaspoon dill weed
1/2 cup Thousand Island Dressing
8 to 12 slices Dill Rye or Rye bread

Combine all ingredients except bread, in a 2-1/2-quart bowl. Toss lightly to mix and coat with dressing. Arrange 4 to 6 slices of bread, depending on size on a serving platter. Spoon filling generously on each slice. Heat with Microwave on Medium, 3 to 5 minutes or until cheese starts to melt. Top with remaining slices of bread. Heat with Microwave on Medium, 1/2 to 1 minute or until bread is warm. Makes 4 to 6 hearty servings.

Heat until cheese just starts to melt, top with remaining bread.

Barbecue Ham Sandwiches

Microwave Power:	High	Medium
Oven Selector:	Off	Off
Oven Temperature:	Off	Off
Shelf Position:	2	2

1/3 to 1/2 cup Barbecue Sauce (see sauces)   2 hamburger buns
6 to 8 thin slices ham (3 to 4 oz.)

Make Barbecue Sauce from recipe in sauce section.

Combine barbecue sauce with ham slices in a glass pie dish. Heat with Microwave on High, 1-1/2 to 2 minutes or until hot. Divide between hamburger buns. Cut in half, if desired and heat with Microwave on Medium, 45 seconds or until buns are warm. Makes 2 servings.

Variation:
Beef, pork or other favorite meat may be substituted for ham.

Spicy Ham Sandwiches

Microwave Power:	Medium
Oven Selector:	Off
Oven Temperature:	Off
Shelf Position:	2

2 cups finely chopped cooked ham   1 tablespoon pickle relish
2 hard cooked eggs   1 teaspoon prepared mustard
3 tablespoons minced green pepper   1 teaspoon cider vinegar
2 tablespoons minced green onion   10 to 12 slices bread
1/2 cup mayonnaise   1 cup (4-oz.) grated Cheddar cheese

Combine ham, chopped egg white (reserve yolk), green pepper and onion; set aside. Mash egg yolks and mix with mayonnaise, pickle relish, mustard and vinegar. Pour dressing over ham mixture, and combine thoroughly. Arrange half of bread slices on serving platter. Spoon filling generously on each slice. Sprinkle with cheese. Heat with Microwave on Medium, 4 to 5 minutes or until cheese just begins to melt. Top with remaining bread; heat with Microwave on Medium, 1/2 to 1 minute, until top bread is warm. Makes 5 to 6 sandwiches.

Tuna Salad Sandwiches

Microwave Power:	Medium
Oven Selector:	Off
Oven Temperature:	Off
Shelf Position:	2

1 can (6-1/2-oz.) tuna, drained
3 tablespoons finely chopped celery
3 tablespoons finely chopped green pepper
1 green onion, finely chopped
1/4 teaspoon salt
1/8 teaspoon paprika

Dash pepper
2 tablespoons mayonnaise
2 tablespoons dairy sour cream
6 slices rye bread
2 medium tomatoes (6 slices)
3/4 cup grated Cheddar cheese

Combine tuna, celery, green pepper, onion, salt, paprika, pepper, mayonnaise and sour cream. Arrange 3 slices bread on serving platter. Spread each with 1/3 cup of filling. Top each with 2 slices of tomato, and cover each with 1/4 cup cheese. Heat with Microwave on Medium, 2-1/2 to 3-1/2 minutes or until cheese begins to melt. Top with remaining bread slices, and heat with Microwave on Medium, 1/2 to 1 minute, until bread is warm. Makes 3 sandwiches.

Hot Swiss-Chicken Sandwiches

Microwave Power:	Medium
Oven Selector:	Off
Oven Temperature:	Off
Shelf Position:	2

1 cup finely diced cooked chicken
2/3 cup finely chopped celery
1/2 cup finely diced Swiss cheese
1/4 teaspoon salt
1/2 teaspoon lemon juice

2 teaspoons grated onion
1 tablespoon dairy sour cream
3 tablespoons mayonnaise
8 slices rye bread

Combine all ingredients, except bread, thoroughly. Arrange 4 slices bread on serving platter. Spread a generous 1/3 cup chicken mixture over bread. Heat with Microwave on Medium, 3 to 4 minutes until cheese just melts. Top with remaining 4 slices bread; heat with Microwave on Medium, 1/2 to 1 minute until bread is warm. Makes 4 generous sandwiches.

Hot Dogs

Microwave Power:	Medium
Oven Selector:	Off
Oven Temperature:	Off
Shelf Position;	2

Amount	Time
1 hot dog	1 to 1-1/4 minutes
2 hot dogs	1-1/2 to 2 minutes
3 hot dogs	2-1/4 to 2-3/4 minutes
4 hot dogs	3-1/4 to 4 minutes

Place wieners in buns on paper or china plate and heat with Microwave on Medium for recommended time. Buns will be hot, soft and moist; wiener will be at eating temperature.

Vegetables

Fresh and frozen vegetables cooked with microwave power may be the best you have ever eaten. Little or no water is required, so vegetables maintain their natural colors and flavors. Broccoli really tastes like broccoli! Try vegetables cooked with microwave power, you may never cook vegetables any other way again.

High microwave power without heat is used for all but very few vegetables. A bake or broil heat is added when crisping is desired, as in baked potatoes, or to melt cheese or brown a vegetable dish, such as Stuffed Crookneck Squash.

Cook vegetables in a casserole with a glass lid or covered with plastic wrap. Serve in the same casserole, no pan to wash. If vegetables are cooked whole, like potatoes or acorn squash, pierce the skin to allow steam to escape. Cook corn right in its husk.

To cook vegetables in pouches, cut an "X" slit in the bag, so steam can escape.

FROZEN VEGETABLES

Frozen vegetables usually need no additional moisture. Place vegetables in a casserole; if solidly frozen, place icy side up. For best results, do not cook vegetables in the package unless it is a cooking pouch. Always use a tight fitting cover to retain moisture. If the casserole does not have a cover, substitute plastic wrap. The times given will produce tender crisp vegetables. If a softer vegetable is preferred, increase microwave time. Special attention must be given when adding additional time! Vegetables become dehydrated and tough very quickly. Vegetables should be stirred at least once or turned over during cooking. Allow all vegetables to have 3 to 5 minutes of standing time in covered casserole before increasing recommended cooking time.

If frozen vegetables are purchased in the bulk-pack, about 1-1/2 cups will be equal to an 8 to 10 ounce package.

To cook vegetables in plastic cooking pouch, make an "X" slit in the bag, otherwise the pouch could burst as steam builds up inside. The pouch should be placed in a dish for cooking, not on the oven shelf. See further instructions in Convenience Food Section.

Frozen Vegetable Chart

VEGETABLE	PACKAGE SIZE	COOKING PROCEDURE	MINUTES
Artichokes Hearts	9-ounce	1-quart covered casserole	8 to 10
Asparagus	10-ounce	1-quart covered casserole	6 to 8
Beans—Green Wax, Italian	9-ounce	1-quart covered casserole	6 to 9
Beans—Lima	10-ounce	1-quart covered casserole	7 to 9
Broccoli	10-ounce	1-quart covered casserole	6 to 8
Brussels Sprouts	10-ounce	1-1/2-quart covered casserole	6 to 8
Carrots	10-ounce	1-1/2-quart covered casserole	10 to 12
Cauliflower	10-ounce	1-quart covered casserole	6 to 8
Corn—cut from cob	10-ounce	1-quart covered casserole	5 to 7
Mixed Vegetables	10-ounce	1-quart covered casserole	7 to 9
Okra	10-ounce	2 tablespoons water in 1-quart covered casserole	5 to 7
Peas—Green	10-ounce	2 tablespoons water in 1-quart covered casserole	6 to 8
—Petit	10-ounce	2 tablespoons water in 1-quart covered casserole	5 to 7
Pea Pods	6-ounce	1-quart covered casserole	5 to 7
Peas and Carrots	10-ounce	2 tablespoons water in 1-quart covered casserole	6 to 8
Peas—Black-eyed	10-ounce	1/2-cup water in 1-1/2-quart covered casserole	12 to 15
Spinich—leaf or chopped	10-ounce	1-quart covered casserole	6 to 8
Squash—Summer (Zucchini)	10-ounce	1-quart covered casserole	6 to 8
Squash—Winter (Hubbard)	12-ounce	2 tablespoons butter in 1-quart covered casserole	7 to 9

Frozen Vegetable Combinations

TYPE	PACKAGE SIZE	COOKING PROCEDURE	MINUTES
Rice with Vegetables	11 ounces in pouch	Slit pouch, place in 1-1/2-quart covered casserole	7 to 10
Rice with Vegetables	7-ounce	Follow package directions for amount of water and butter. Place in 1-1/2-quart covered casserole.	9 to 11
Americana Vegetable Combinations	10-ounce	Follow package directions for amount of water and butter. Place in 1-1/2-quart covered casserole.	5 to 7
International Vegetable Combinations	10-ounce	Follow package directions for amount of water and butter. Place in 1-1/2-quart covered casserole.	6 to 8

CANNED VEGETABLES

These vegetable need only to be heated before serving. Empty contents into a casserole, cover and heat. Do not heat vegetables in the can. Drain excess liquid after heating and add seasonings. Canned vegetables from a No. 303 can (15 to 17 ounces) will take 3 to 5 minutes to heat with Microwave on High. Stir at the end of cooking time. Allow a few minutes of standing time in the covered casserole before serving. Home canned foods should be thoroughly boiled on the cooktop for 10 to 20 minutes.

FRESH VEGETABLES

The amount specified for fresh vegetables is as purchased at the market, before any preparation has been done, except root vegetables (beets, carrots, etc.) which were weighed without tops (greens). The times given are approximate and should only be used as a guide. It may be necessary to increase or decrease the time as would be done when cooking conventionally.

Fresh vegetables may vary in tenderness due to freshness and age. Individual preferences as to doneness desired are also a factor in timing. Check vegetables for doneness halfway through the cooking time, when stirring. If vegetables are whole, turn over after half of cooking time.

For many fresh vegetables, the water that clings after washing is enough to provide the moisture needed for cooking in a covered casserole. Add seasonings as desired, but salt after cooking.

If left whole, thick stem ends of some vegetables require longer cooking than the flower end. If whole pieces are being cooked, slit heavy stalks and place the stem ends toward the outside of the dish with the flower ends in the center. Or, stalks may be chopped and flowerets left in large pieces so that all parts will cook at the same time.

Remove vegetables from oven when almost cooked to the desired doneness; a standing time of 3 to 5 minutes will finish the cooking.

Fresh Artichokes

Microwave Power: High
Oven Selector: Off
Oven Temperature: Off
Shelf Position: 2

Allow 1 artichoke per serving

Amount	Container	Time
1	1-quart	6 to 7 minutes
2	1-1/2-quart	9 to 11 minutes
4	3-quart	15 to 18 minutes

Cut 1 inch off the top, trim stem. Remove tough outside leaves. With scissors, snip off thorny leaf tips. Rinse well. Place upside down in 1 inch of water with 2 teaspoon lemon juice, a garlic clove, add a small piece of bay leaf, if desired, in covered container. Cook with Microwave on High until leaf can be pulled easily from stalk, or stem can be easily pierced with a fork. Drain. Serve with hot melted butter, mayonnaise, or Hollandaise sauce.

Graceful eating:
Pull off leaf. Dip wide end into preferred sauce. Scrape soft pulp from base with teeth. Discard the rest. With knife and fork, remove prickly area in center "choke" and discard. Cut up heart and dip into sauce.

Fresh Asparagus

Microwave Power: High
Oven Selector: Off
Oven Temperature: Off
Shelf Position: 2

Allow 1/2 lb. asparagus for each serving

Amount	Container	Time
1 lb.	1-1/2-quart	4 to 6 minutes
2 lbs.	2-quart	6 to 8 minutes

Snap off tough end and discard. Wash tips and tender stalks very thoroughly. Remove any loose scales. Leave stalks whole or cut into pieces. If stalks are thick, slit half of length. Cook whole stalks in oblong baking dish covered with plastic wrap; or cook pieces in a covered casserole. Serve at once with salt, pepper and melted butter.

Frosted Asparagus

Microwave Power:	High	Low
Oven Selector:	Off	Broil
Oven Temperature:	Off	High Broil, not preheated
Shelf Position:	2	4

2 lbs. fresh asparagus	6 tablespoons mayonnaise
3 egg whites	1/8 teaspoon seasoned salt

Wash asparagus, snap off tough ends. Slit thick stalks in half. Place in a 2-quart oblong utility dish. Cover; cook with Microwave on High, 6 to 8 minutes, until tender crisp. Beat egg whites until stiff, but not dry, gently stir in mayonnaise and seasoned salt. Spread over asparagus. Move shelf up to 4th position. Broil at High Broil with Microwave on Low, 2 to 2-1/2 minutes or until cooked. Turn Microwave Off. Continue at High Broil, 1-1/2 to 2 minutes or until browned. Serve immediately. Makes 4 to 6 servings.

Fresh Beans — Green, Wax

Microwave Power:	High
Oven Selector:	Off
Oven Temperature:	Off
Shelf Position:	2

1-1/2 lbs. beans
1/3 cup water

Wash, snap off ends. Leave whole, or cut crosswise into 1-inch lengths, or cut French-style into lengthwise pieces. Place in 2-1/2-quart covered casserole, with water. Cook with Microwave on High, 18 to 20 minutes. To serve, season with salt, pepper and butter. For variety, add bacon or ham drippings or crumbled bacon. Makes 4 servings.

Note:

Green beans when cooked with microwave do not become as tender as when simmered for a long time. The result is a tender-crisp bean which should not be overcooked in an effort to make it tender.

Parisian Beans

Microwave Power:	High
Oven Selector:	Off
Oven Temperature:	Off
Shelf Position:	2

2 pkgs. (9-oz. each) frozen French cut
   green beans
1 can (10-3/4-oz.) condensed cream of
   mushroom soup

1 can (3-oz.) French fried onion rings

Cook green beans in 2-quart covered glass casserole. Drain; stir in mushroom soup. Cover; cook with Microwave on High, 3 minutes; stir. Sprinkle onions on top and continue cooking uncovered with Microwave on High, 4 to 5 minutes. Makes 6 to 8 servings.

Bean & Cabbage Scramble

Microwave Power:	High
Oven Selector:	Off
Oven Temperature:	Off
Shelf Position:	2

2 to 3 slices bacon, cut into 1-inch pieces
1 pkg. (10-oz.) frozen French-cut green beans
3 to 4 tablespoons chopped onion
3 to 4 cups coarse shredded cabbage

Salt and pepper
Wine vinegar
Sugar

Place bacon in a 2-quart casserole. Cook with Microwave on High, 2 to 3 minutes or until bacon is crisp. Remove bacon and set aside. Add green beans and onion to bacon drippings. Cover and cook with Microwave on High, 5 minutes. Stir in cabbage and sprinkle with salt and pepper. Cover and cook with Microwave on High, 6 to 9 minutes or until vegetables are cooked; stir once. Season with vinegar and sugar if desired and top with bacon. Makes 4 to 6 servings.

Fresh Beets

Microwave Power:	High
Oven Selector:	Off
Oven Temperature:	Off
Shelf Position:	2

1 lb. (1 bunch) fresh beets
1-1/2 cups water

Scrub beets with brush. Cut off all but 1 inch of tops, save the tops if desired and cook separately. Leave beets whole. Place in a 2-quart covered casserole with water. Cook with Microwave on High, 15 to 20 minutes, until tender. Let stand 5 minutes; drain and run cold water over beets. Slip off skins and root ends. Slice, dice or leave small beets whole to prepare for serving. Reheat with butter, salt, pepper and a little fresh lemon juice. Makes 2 servings.

Beets in Orange Sauce

Microwave Power:	High
Oven Selector:	Off
Oven Temperature:	Off
Shelf Position:	2

1 tablespoon butter
2 tablespoons granulated sugar
1 tablespoon brown sugar
2 teaspoons cornstarch
1/8 teaspoon salt

1/8 teaspoon pepper
3/4 cup orange juice
2 to 2-1/2 cups diced cooked beets
1 teaspoon grated orange peel

Melt butter in 4-cup liquid measure, with Microwave on High, 1 minute or until melted. Mix sugars and cornstarch. Blend into butter; stir in salt, pepper and orange juice. Cook with Microwave on High, 4 to 5 minutes, stirring once or twice, until thickened. Pour over beets in 1-quart casserole. Cover and heat with Microwave on High, 3 to 5 minutes, until beets are hot. Sprinkle with grated orange peel. Makes 4 to 6 servings.

Fresh Broccoli

Microwave power:	High
Oven Selector:	Off
Oven Temperature:	Off
Shelf Position:	2

1-1/2 lbs. broccoli

Wash well, trim ends off the stems, but do not remove entire stems. The whole stalk is edible. If any of the stems are more than 1 inch in diameter, make several slits through the stem or peel thick portion. Place in 2-quart covered casserole; cook with Microwave on High, 10 to 15 minutes, until just tender; or chop broccoli stem, leave flowerets whole, cook in a covered casserole, 8 to 12 minutes. Serve at once with salt, pepper, and melted butter. Makes 4 servings.

Variation:
Pour Mornay Sauce over hot, drained broccoli for a new flavor treat.

Fresh Brussels Sprouts

Microwave Power:	High
Oven Selector:	Off
Oven Temperature:	Off
Shelf Position:	2

1-1/2 lbs. brussels sprouts
2 tablespoons water

Remove loose or discolored outer leaves. Cut off stem. Wash thoroughly in cold water. Place in 2-quart covered casserole with water. Cook with Microwave on High, 10 to 15 minutes or until tender. Serve at once seasoned with salt and pepper and a generous amount of melted butter. Makes 4 servings.

German Style Brussels Sprouts

Microwave Power:	High
Oven Selector:	Off
Oven Temperature:	Off
Shelf Position:	2

1 pkg. (10-oz.) frozen brussels sprouts
1 tablespoon brown sugar
2 tablespoons butter or margarine

2 teaspoons wine vinegar
1/8 teaspoon dill weed
1 slice bacon, cooked and finely crumbled

Cook brussels sprouts in a 1-1/2-quart covered casserole with Microwave on High, 6 to 8 minutes or until tender. Drain. In a 2-cup measure combine remaining ingredients. Cook with Microwave on High, 1-1/2 to 2 minutes or until hot and bubbly. Pour over brussels sprouts, stir and serve. Makes 4 servings.

Sour Cream Brussels Sprouts Casserole

Microwave Power:	High	Low
Oven Selector:	Off	Bake
Oven Temperature:	Off	400° F, preheated
Shelf Position:	2	2

1 pkg. (10-oz.) frozen brussels sprouts
1 tablespoon butter or margarine
1 tablespoon flour

1/4 teaspoon nutmeg
1/2 cup chicken broth
1/2 cup dairy sour cream

Topping:
1 tablespoon butter, melted

3 tablespoons plain bread crumbs

Cook brussels sprouts in a 1-1/2-quart covered casserole with Microwave on High, 6 to 8 minutes or until tender. Drain. In a 4-cup measure melt 1 tablespoon butter with Microwave on High, about 1 minute. Stir in flour and nutmeg to make a smooth paste; stir in chicken broth. Cook with Microwave on High, 2 to 2-1/2 minutes, stirring often, until hot and thickened. Quickly stir in sour cream using a wire whisk. Pour over brussels sprouts in casserole. Melt 1 tablespoon butter. Preheat oven. Stir butter into bread crumbs until moistened. Sprinkle evenly over sauce. Bake, uncovered, at 400° with Microwave on Low, 5 to 8 minutes until bubbly and lightly browned. Let stand 5 minutes. Makes 4 servings.

Fresh Cabbage

Microwave Power:	High
Oven Selector:	Off
Oven Temperature:	Off
Shelf Position:	2

1 lb. fresh cabbage
2 tablespoons water

Wash well. Remove core and shred for cooking. Place in a covered 10-inch glass-ceramic skillet with water. Cook with Microwave on High, 8 to 10 minutes or until just barely tender. Serve at once while hot. Season with salt, pepper and butter. Makes 4 servings.

Variations:
For Red Cabbage, follow directions for Green Cabbage, but add 2 tablespoons fresh lemon juice to cooking water to retain red color.

Confetti Cabbage

Microwave Power:	High
Oven Selector:	Off
Oven Temperature:	Off
Shelf Position:	2

1 small head (1-lb.) cabbage, shredded
  (approximately 8 cups)
2 tablespoons water
1/4 cup (1/2 stick) butter
1/4 cup chopped onion
1/4 cup chopped green pepper

1/2 teaspoon salt
1/4 teaspoon pepper
1-1/2 tablespoons flour
1/2 cup milk
2 tablespoons sauterne
2 tablespoons chopped pimiento

Place shredded cabbage and water in 10-inch glass-ceramic skillet; cover. Cook with Microwave on High, 9 to 11 minutes or until cooked. Leave covered while making sauce. Place butter, onion and green pepper in a 2-cup liquid measure; cook with Microwave on High, 3 to 4 minutes, until vegetables are transparent. Add salt, pepper and flour; cook with Microwave on High, 30 seconds. Stir well and add milk, and stir again. Cook with Microwave on High, 1 to 2 minutes, until slightly thickened. Stir in sauterne and pimiento. Drain cabbage and mix with sauce, stirring until cabbage is coated. Makes 4 to 6 servings.

Fresh Carrots

Microwave Power:	High
Oven Selector:	Off
Oven Temperature:	Off
Shelf Position:	2

1 lb. carrots
2 tablespoons water

Remove tops. Scrape or pare with a knife or scrub well with a stiff brush. Cut into 1-inch slices or thin strips. Place in a 1-1/2-quart covered casserole, with water. Cook with Microwave on High, 9 to 12 minutes. Be careful not to overcook. For variety, add finely chopped green onions while carrots are cooking. Serve hot with a sprinkling of snipped parsley, season with salt, pepper and butter. Makes 4 servings.

Pecan Carrots

Microwave Power:	High
Oven Selector:	Off
Oven Temperature:	Off
Shelf Position:	2

6 medium carrots (about 12 oz.),
   pared and sliced
2 tablespoons water
2 tablespoons butter

2 teaspoons lemon juice
1 tablespoon brown sugar
1/8 teaspoon nutmeg
2 tablespoons chopped pecans

Combine carrots and water in a 1-quart casserole. Cover; cook with Microwave on High, 5 to 8 minutes or until carrots are just tender, stirring once. Do not overcook; carrots toughen easily. Drain. Combine butter, lemon juice, brown sugar and nutmeg in a 2-cup liquid measure. Cook with Microwave on High, 1 to 2 minutes or until hot and bubbling. Stir into cooked carrots. Sprinkle with pecans. Makes 4 servings.

Honey-Glazed Carrots

Microwave Power:	High
Oven Selector:	Off
Oven Temperature:	Off
Shelf Position:	2

2 tablespoons butter
1/4 cup honey
1/8 teaspoon nutmeg

1 pkg. (10-oz.) frozen sliced carrots,
   cooked and drained

Combine butter, honey and nutmeg in 2-cup liquid measure, heat with Microwave on High, 2 to 2-1/2 minutes, to melt butter and bring just to a boil, stirring once. Pour over cooked carrots; stir to cover well. Heat with Microwave on High, 1 to 2 minutes until carrots are hot. Makes 4 servings.

Fresh Cauliflower

Microwave Power:	High
Oven Selector:	Off
Oven Temperature:	Off
Shelf Position:	2

Allow 1/2 lb. cauliflower per serving

Amount	Container	Time
1 small head (1 lb.)	1-1/2-quart	7 to 9 minutes
1 medium head (2 lbs.)	2-quart	11 to 14 minutes

Wash well. Remove any green stalks. Separate into flowerets. Cook according to chart, in covered casserole, until tender when tested with a fork. Stir once. Serve hot with butter, salt and pepper.

Cauliflower Casserole

Microwave Power:	Low
Oven Selector:	Broil
Oven Temperature:	High Broil, not preheated
Shelf Position:	4

1 pkg. (10-oz.) frozen cauliflower,
  cooked and drained
3/4 cup (1/2 recipe) Mornay Sauce

2 tablespoons freshly grated Parmesan
  or Romano cheese

Cook cauliflower in a 1-quart, covered, glass-ceramic casserole as directed in vegetable chart. Let stand covered while making Mornay Sauce. See Sauce Section. Pour sauce over cauliflower and sprinkle with cheese. Broil at High Broil with Microwave on Low, 3 to 4 minutes, until lightly browned on top. Makes 4 servings.

Hungarian Cauliflower

Microwave Power:	High
Oven Selector:	Off
Oven Temperature:	Off
Shelf Position:	2

2 tablespoons butter
2 tablespoons flour
1/2 cup dairy sour cream
1/2 cup water

1/2 teaspoon dill weed
2 lbs. cauliflower floweretes,
  cooked and drained

In 4-cup liquid measure melt butter with Microwave on High, 45 seconds to 1 minute. Stir in flour; cook with Microwave on High, 1 minute. Mix together sour cream and water. Gradually stir into butter-flour mixture until smooth. Add dill weed. Cook with Microwave on High, 4 to 5 minutes until thickened and smooth, stirring twice. Pour over hot cauliflower. Makes 4 servings.

Fresh Celery

Microwave Power:	High
Oven Selector:	Off
Oven Temperature:	Off
Shelf Position:	2

1 medium bunch celery

Remove leaves and trim roots. Wash thoroughly, use a brush to remove sand. Dice outer stalks. Reserve inner stalks to serve raw. Place diced celery, 4 cups, in a 1-1/2-quart covered casserole. Cook with Microwave on High, 10 to 14 minutes, until tender. Season with salt, pepper and melted butter. Makes 4 servings.

Fresh Corn-on-the-Cob

Microwave Power:	High
Oven Selector:	Off
Oven Temperature:	Off
Shelf Position:	2

Allow 1 or 2 ears per person

Amount	Time
1	2 to 3 minutes
2	4 to 5 minutes
3	6 to 8 minutes
4	8 to 10 minutes
6	12 to 14 minutes

Do not husk. Buy fresh ears with husks intact for best flavor. Cut off silk and stem, remove outer husks, but leave a covering over all corn. Place ears on paper towel, on shelf. Turn ears over and rearrange after half of the cooking time. After cooking, wrap corn in a kitchen towel or foil and let stand 5 minutes. When ready to serve, remove remaining silk and husk. Serve with salt, pepper and butter.

Fresh Eggplant

Microwave Power:	Low	Off
Oven Selector:	Broil	Broil
Oven Temperature:	High Broil	High Broil
Shelf Position:	4	4

1 medium eggplant (1-3/4 lb.)
Parmesan cheese

It is not necessary to peel eggplant unless the skin is tough. Do not soak in salt or salt water before cooking. Wash well. Cut eggplant into 3/4-inch slices. Brush with melted butter or bacon drippings, brush again after 5 minutes of cooking. Place in glass-ceramic open roaster. Use shelf position 4, Broil on High Broil with Microwave on Low, 7 to 9 minutes or until brown. Sprinkle with Parmesan cheese. Turn Microwave Off and Broil on High Broil, 30 seconds to 1 minute until cheese is bubbly. Season with salt and pepper and serve hot. Makes 4 servings.

Far East Eggplant

Microwave Power:	High	Low
Oven Selector:	Off	Broil
Oven Temperature	Off	High Broil
Shelf Position:	2	2

1/4 cup olive oil	2 teaspoons salt
1 clove garlic, minced	1/4 teaspoon pepper
1 green pepper, chopped	3 tomatoes, cut into eighths
1 medium onion, chopped	3 tablespoons Parmesan cheese
1 medium (1-lb.) eggplant, cubed	6 slices bacon, cooked crisp and crumbled

Combine oil, garlic, green pepper, onion, and eggplant in 3-quart casserole. Cover; cook with Microwave on High, 12 to 15 minutes or until eggplant is tender. Stir in salt and pepper. Add tomatoes, sprinkle with Parmesan cheese and bacon. Broil on High Broil with Microwave on Low, 4 to 5 minutes until cheese is melted and tomatoes are hot. Makes 4 servings.

Fresh Onions

Microwave Power:	High
Oven Selector:	Off
Oven Temperature:	Off
Shelf Position:	2

1-1/2 pounds onions (about 4)
2 tablespoons water

Peel. Place in a 1-1/2-quart shallow casserole with water. Cover; cook with Microwave on High, 8 to 12 minutes until tender. Serve with salt, pepper and butter or cream sauce. Makes 4 servings.

Fresh Parsnips

Microwave Power:	High
Oven Selector:	Off
Oven Temperature:	Off
Shelf Position:	2

1-1/2 pounds parsnips
1/4 cup water

Scrape or peel. Slice into 1-inch pieces. Place in 2-quart covered casserole with water. Cook with Microwave on High, 11 to 14 minutes or until tender. To serve, season with salt, pepper, butter and a sprinkling of minced parsley. Makes 4 servings.

Fresh Peas

Microwave Power:	Medium
Oven Selector:	Off
Oven Temperature:	Off
Shelf Position:	2

Amount	Container	Time
1-1/2 cups shelled peas	1-quart with 3 tablespoons water	6 to 8 minutes
3 cups shelled peas	1-1/2-quart with 1/3 cup water	11 to 13 minutes

Shell and wash just before cooking. Save a few pods to cook with the peas. Place in covered casserole. Cook according to chart until just tender. Remove pods. To serve, season with salt, pepper, and butter. Add a sprinkling of chopped fresh mint for variety. Allow 3/4 lb. per person—1 lb. unshelled mature peas should equal 1 cup shelled.

Fresh Peppers — Green

Microwave Power:	High
Oven Selector:	Off
Oven Temperature:	Off
Shelf Position:	2

4 medium green peppers—allow 1 whole pepper for each serving

Wash, remove stem and seeds. Leave peppers whole. Place in a 2-quart casserole. Cover; cook with Microwave on High, 4 to 7 minutes until tender. Let stand, covered, 5 minutes before using. Makes 4 servings.

Southern Black-Eyed Peas

Microwave Power:	High	Low
Oven Selector:	Off	Off
Oven Temperature:	Off	Off
Shelf Position:	2	2

1 pkg. (11-oz.) fresh black-eyed peas	1/4 cup chopped green pepper
1-1/2 cups water	1/2 cup diced ham or 3 slices bacon, diced
1 medium onion, chopped	1/2 teaspoon salt
1/2 cup chopped celery	1/4 teaspoon pepper

Rinse peas, place all ingredients in 1-3/4-quart covered casserole. Bring to a boil with Microwave on High, 8 to 10 minutes. Then simmer with Microwave on Low, 50 to 55 minutes or until peas are tender, stirring occasionally. Makes 4 to 6 servings.

Fresh Baked Potatoes

Allow 1 potato per serving

MICROWAVE ONLY

Microwave Power:	High
Oven Selector:	Off
Oven Temperature:	Off
Shelf Position:	2

Amount	Time
1	6 to 7-1/2 minutes
2	8 to 10 minutes
4	14 to 16 minutes
6	18 to 21 minutes

MICROWAVE AND HEAT

Microwave Power:	High
Oven Selector:	Bake
Oven Temperature:	450°F, not preheated
Shelf Position:	2

Amount	Time
1	6 to 7-1/2 minutes
2	8 to 10 minutes
4	11 to 14 minutes
6	16 to 19 minutes

Scrub potatoes thoroughly, do not peel. Pierce with a fork in 2 or 3 places. Place directly on oven shelf. Recommended times are based on 7-ounce potatoes; adjust time accordingly. Potatoes may be baked with or without heat. When heat is added the interior is drier and the skin is more crisp. Allow a standing time of at least 5 minutes before cutting potatoes open. Wrap in foil while standing to keep hot up to 30 minutes. Serve hot with salt, pepper and butter.

Fresh Boiled Potatoes

Microwave Power:	High
Oven Selector:	Off
Oven Temperature:	Off
Shelf Position:	2

Amount	Cooking Container	Time
1 (8 oz.)	20-ounces	3 to 3-1/2 minutes
2 (1 lb.)	1-1/2-quart	5 to 6 minutes
3 (1-1/2 lbs.)	2-quart	9 to 10 minutes

Wash potatoes; cut in half. Place in covered casserole. Cook for recommended time and let stand covered a few minutes before peeling. Serve as boiled potatoes or cooked potatoes, for salads or mashed potatoes.

Mashed Potatoes

Microwave Power:	High	Medium
Oven Selector:	Off	Off
Oven Temperature:	Off	Off
Shelf Position:	2	2

3 medium potatoes (1-1/2 lbs.)	1/4 teaspoon salt
2 to 3 tablespoons butter	Pepper
1/4 to 1/3 cup milk	

Wash potatoes; cut in half and place in a 2-quart covered casserole. Cook with Microwave on High, 10 to 12 minutes. Drain, peel and mash potatoes. Stir in butter and milk. Season with salt and pepper. If necessary before serving, reheat with Microwave on Medium, 2 to 3 minutes or until hot. Makes 2 to 2-1/4 cups, mashed potatoes or 4 to 6 servings.

Chantilly Potatoes

Microwave Power:	Medium	Off
Oven Selector:	Broil	Broil
Oven Temperature:	Medium Broil, not preheated	Medium Broil
Shelf Position:	2	2

2 to 2-1/2 cups stiffly mashed potatoes
1/2 cup whipping cream

1/2 to 1 cup grated sharp Cheddar cheese
1/8 to 1/4 teaspoon pepper

Spread potatoes into a 1-1/2-quart round cake dish. Whip cream and fold in cheese and pepper. Spread over potatoes. Broil on Medium Broil with Microwave on Medium, 6 to 7 minutes or until heated through and slightly golden on top. If additional browning is desired, turn Microwave Off and continue to Broil watching surface carefully. Makes 5 to 6 servings.

Variation:
Use instant potatoes, omit salt and reduce liquid slightly.

Saucy Scalloped Potatoes

Microwave Power:	High
Oven Selector:	Bake
Oven Temperature:	375°F, not preheated
Shelf Position:	2

1 can (10-3/4-oz.) cream of mushroom soup
1-1/4 cups milk
4 medium potatoes, peeled and thinly sliced
1/2 medium onion, thinly sliced

Salt and pepper to taste
4 slices bacon, cooked crisp and crumbled
1/3 cup dry bread crumbs
2 tablespoons butter, melted

Combine soup and milk; pour 1/4 cup into the bottom of a greased 2-quart casserole. Layer about half of potatoes and onions; season with salt and pepper. Sprinkle with half of bacon and pour on 3/4 cup of milk-soup mixture. Repeat layering process; pour remaining milk-soup mixture over all. Cover; Bake at 375° with Microwave on High, 25 minutes. Combine bread crumbs and melted butter. Sprinkle potato mixture with buttered bread crumbs, continue to bake, uncovered, at 375° with Microwave on High, 5 to 10 minutes or until potatoes are tender. Makes 6 to 8 servings.

Variation:
Scalloped Potatoes may be prepared without bread-crumb topping. Remove cover after 25 minutes and continue to bake as above.

Fresh Baked Sweet Potatoes or Yams

Allow 1/2 yam per serving

MICROWAVE ONLY

Microwave Power:	High
Oven Selector:	Off
Oven Temperature:	Off
Shelf Position:	2

Amount	Time
1	6 to 8 minutes
2	8 to 11 minutes
4	13 to 17 minutes
6	17 to 22 minutes

MICROWAVE AND HEAT

Microwave Power:	High
Oven Selector:	Bake
Oven Temperature:	450°F, not preheated
Shelf Position:	2

Amount	Time
1	6 to 8 minutes
2	8 to 11 minuets
4	11 to 14 minutes
6	15 to 20 minutes

Scrub yams, cut off any very long narrow ends, pierce with a fork in 3 or 4 places, do not peel. Place yams directly on oven shelf, avoiding recessed area. Cook according to chart. Recommended times are based on 12-ounce yams; adjust time accordingly. Allow yams to stand 10 minutes after cooking or wrap in foil to stay hot 30 minutes.

Sweet Potatoes Hawaiian

Microwave Power:	High	Medium
Oven Selector:	Off	Broil
Oven Temperature:	Off	Medium Broil, not preheated
Shelf Position	3	3

1/4 cup (1/2 stick) butter
2 cups flaked coconut
1 can (29-oz.) sweet potatoes, drained

1 to 2 tablespoons brown sugar
1/2 cup half and half

Melt butter in a 2-cup liquid measure with Microwave on High, 45 seconds to 1 minute. Add 1 cup of coconut and toss with butter. Set aside for topping. Whip potatoes until fluffy. Add remaining coconut, sugar and half and half. Beat until creamy. Spoon into a 1-quart buttered casserole. Sprinkle with coconut-butter topping. Broil on Medium Broil with Microwave on Medium, 7 to 10 minutes or until golden brown and heated through. Makes 6 to 8 servings.

Orange-Glazed Sweet Potatoes

Microwave Power:	High
Oven Selector:	Off
Oven Temperature:	Off
Shelf Position:	2

1/3 cup sugar
1-1/2 teaspoons cornstarch
1/4 teaspoon salt
1/2 teaspoon grated orange peel

1/2 cup orange juice
2 tablespoons butter
1 can (29-oz.) sweet potatoes, drained
1/3 cup chopped pecans

In 4-cup liquid measure combine sugar, cornstarch and salt. Stir in orange peel and orange juice. Cook with Microwave on High, 3 to 4 minutes or until clear, stirring after 2 minutes. Add butter, stirring to melt. Arrange sweet potatoes in 1-1/2 quart casserole. Pour sauce over sweet potatoes. Cover and cook with Microwave on High, 3 minutes. Stir, sprinkle with pecans, cook uncovered with Microwave on High, 3 to 5 minutes, until hot. Makes 4 servings.

Fresh Spinach

Microwave Position:	High
Oven Selector:	Off
Oven Temperature:	Off
Shelf Position:	2

2 lbs. spinach

Cut off stems, remove damaged leaves. Wash thoroughly to remove sand. Place in 4-quart covered casserole using only the water that clings to the leaves after washing. Cook with Microwave on High, 13 to 15 minutes, stirring twice. Serve at once seasoned with salt, pepper, butter and fresh lemon juice. Makes 4 servings.

Creamed Spinach

Microwave Power:	High
Oven Selector:	Off
Oven Temperature:	Off
Shelf Position:	2

3 tablespoons butter	1/4 teaspoon nutmeg
3 tablespoons flour	3/4 cup milk
1/2 teaspoon sugar	3/4 teaspoon lemon juice
1/2 teaspoon salt	2 lbs. spinach, cooked, chopped and drained

Melt butter in 2-cup liquid measure with Microwave on High, 45 seconds to 1 minute. Add flour, sugar, salt and nutmeg; mix together until smooth. Cook with Microwave on High, 1 minute. Gradually add milk, stirring constantly until smooth. Cook with Microwave on High, 2 to 3 minutes, until sauce boils and is thickened and smooth, stirring twice. Stir in lemon juice. Pour over spinach and mix thoroughly. Cover and heat with Microwave on High, 2 to 3 minutes, until serving temperature. Makes 6 to 8 servings.

Fresh Squash — Summer

Microwave Power:	High
Oven Selector:	Off
Oven Temperature:	Off
Shelf Position:	2

2 lbs. summer squash

Wash, but do not pare. Remove stem and blossom ends. Cut into 1/2-inch slices. Place in 3-quart covered casserole. Cook with Microwave on High, 13 to 15 minutes until tender. Serve seasoned with salt, pepper and butter. Makes 4 to 6 servings.

Stuffed Crookneck Squash

Microwave Power:	High	Low
Oven Selector:	Off	Broil
Oven Temperature:	Off	High Broil, not preheated
Shelf Position:	2	3

2 lbs. yellow crookneck squash	Dash white pepper
1/2 small onion, chopped	1/8 teaspoon nutmeg
1/4 cup butter	1/2 cup grated Cheddar cheese
1/3 cup dry bread crumbs	1/4 cup dry bread crumbs
1/4 teaspoon seasoned salt	

Wash squash, remove stem and blossom ends. Place in a 3-quart casserole; cover. Cook with Microwave on High, 10 to 12 minutes or until tender-crisp. In a 1-1/2-quart casserole, combine onion and butter. Cook with Microwave on High, 2 minutes. Cut squash in half lengthwise, scoop out soft seed pulp and combine with onion. Stir in 1/3 cup bread crumbs, seasoned salt, pepper and nutmeg. Arrange squash shells in a 2-3/4-quart oblong glass-ceramic baking dish. Stuff each with filling mixture. Combine grated cheese and 1/4 cup bread crumbs. Sprinkle mixture on top of each squash half. Move oven shelf to position 3. Broil on High Broil with Microwave on Low, 4 to 6 minutes or until filling is nicely browned. Makes 6 servings.

Marie's Tomato Stack-ups

Microwave Power: High
Oven Selector: Broil
Oven Temperature: High Broil
Shelf Position: 3

2 pkgs. (10-oz.) chopped spinach or   3 large tomatoes
   chopped broccoli, cooked and drained   1/4 teaspoon salt
1 cup grated Swiss cheese   Pepper
1/3 to 1/2 cup finely chopped onion

Cook spinach or broccoli according to directions under Vegetables. Drain thoroughly. Combine with 2/3 cup cheese and onion. Slice tomatoes in half and place in a shallow baking dish, cut side up. Sprinkle with salt and pepper. Spoon vegetable mixture onto tomatoes and top with remaining cheese. Broil on High Broil with Microwave on High, 4 to 6 minutes or until heated through. Makes 3 to 6 servings.

Stewed Tomatoes

Microwave Power: High
Oven Selector: Off
Oven Temperature: Off
Shelf Position: 2

1/4 cup finely chopped green pepper   1 teaspoon sugar
2 tablespoons finely chopped onion   1 teaspoon salt
1 tablespoon butter   1/8 teaspoon pepper
4 medium tomatoes (about 1 lb.),
   peeled and quartered

Place green pepper, onion and butter in 1-1/2-quart covered casserole. Cook with Microwave on High, 2 to 3 minutes, until transparent. Add remaining ingredients; cover; cook with Microwave on High, 5 to 6 minutes, or until cooked through. Makes 4 servings.

Zucchini Continental

Microwave Power:	High
Oven Selector:	Off
Oven Temperature:	Off
Shelf Position:	2

1 lb. zucchini, washed and grated   1/2 teaspoon salt
1/2 cup dairy sour cream   Dash pepper

Place zucchini in a 1-1/2-quart casserole; cover. Cook with Microwave on High, 6 to 8 minutes or until tender-crisp; stir once. Drain well; stir in sour cream and season with salt and pepper. Makes 3 to 4 servings.

Italian Style Zucchini

Microwave Power:	High
Oven Selector:	Off
Oven Temperature:	Off
Shelf Position:	2

1 lb. zucchini, sliced   1/2 teaspoon oregano
1 medium onion, sliced thin   1/8 teaspoon pepper
3/4 teaspoon salt   1 cup tomato juice

Scrub zucchini, do not pare. Slice crosswide, 1/4-inch thick (approximately 4 cups.) Place zucchini in 1-1/2 quart glass casserole. Place sliced onion on top of zucchini. Mix salt, oregano and pepper with tomato juice and pour over all. Cover; cook with Microwave on High, 11 to 14 minutes or until fork tender. Makes 4 servings.

Fresh Squash — Winter

Microwave Power:	High
Oven Selector:	Off
Oven Temperature:	Off
Shelf Position:	2

ACORN SQUASH

2 whole squash about 1 lb. each

Place whole squash in a shallow casserole. Cook with Microwave on High, 12 to 15 minutes, until squash can be pierced easily with a fork. Let stand 5 minutes. Cut in half, scoop out seeds, season with salt, pepper and butter. Makes 4 servings.

If desired, while squash is standing, prepare a 10-ounce package of frozen peas. Fill centers of squash with cooked peas, drizzle with 2 tablespoons melted butter mixed with 1 tablespoon brown sugar. Sprinkle with seasoned salt.

BANANA SQUASH

3 lbs. banana squash

Wash, do not peel. Cut into individual servings; remove seeds. Place in a 3-quart oblong baking dish, skin side down. Cover with plastic wrap. Cook with Microwave on High, 12 to 16 minutes or until tender. To serve, remove from rind and mash or serve individual pieces in the shell. Season with salt, pepper and butter. Makes 4 to 6 servings.

Sugar Glazed Banana Squash

Microwave Power:	High	Low
Oven Selector:	Off	Broil
Oven Temperature:	Off	High Broil, not preheated
Shelf Position:	2	4

3 lbs. banana squash	1/4 teaspoon nutmeg
2 tablespoons butter	Seasoned salt
2 tablespoons brown sugar	

Cut squash into 4 or 6 pieces, remove seeds. Place skin side down in a 3-quart oblong baking dish. Cover with plastic wrap; cook with Microwave on High, 12 to 16 minutes or until tender. Dot top of squash with butter, sprinkle with brown sugar, nutmeg and seasoned salt. Move oven shelf to position 4. Broil on High Broil with Microwave on Low, 3 to 4 minutes, until sugar melts and bubbles. Serve in whole pieces with skin intact. Makes 4 to 6 servings.

Fresh Tomatoes

Microwave Power:	High
Oven Selector:	Off
Oven Temperature:	Off
Shelf Position:	2

4 large tomatoes (1 lb.)—allow 1/2 pound per serving

Wash, peel if desired, and halve. Place in a 1-1/2-quart casserole. Cover and cook with Microwave on High, 4 to 6 minutes. Season with minced onion, salt, pepper and butter. Makes 2 to 4 servings.

* To peel easily, plunge tomatoes in boiling water, slips off skins.

Fresh Turnips

Microwave Power:	High
Oven Selector:	Off
Oven Temperature:	Off
Shelf Position:	2

Allow 1/2 pound per serving

Amount	Container	Liquid	Time
1 lb. (3 medium)	1-1/2-quart	3 tablespoons water	6 to 8 minutes
2 lbs. (4 large)	2-quart	1/3 cup water	9 to 11 minutes

Wash, peel, and cube. Place in covered casserole. Cook according to chart until tender. Season with salt, pepper and butter.

Defrosting

Microwave energy defrosts meat in a fraction of the time it takes to defrost in the refrigerator or on the kitchen counter. Meat no longer has to start thawing a day ahead, but can be ready to prepare usually with only 15 to 30 minutes notice. Please read the tips below, then refer to the Meat Defrosting Chart for specific meat items and instructions.

Low power is used for defrosting for the best, most uniform results.

Meat wrapped in paper, plastic wrap or freezer bags can be defrosted in the package. Remove metal clips or wires. The package is usually placed in a dish to catch drippings. The chart may recommend transferring a meat from the package for easier handling as it defrosts, ground beef, for example. A covered dish may be used when meat defrosts and cooks in the same dish.

Meat wrapped in foil must be removed from the packaging.

Pieces of aluminum foil are used to shield areas that defrost faster than other areas. For example, leg ends and some other areas of a turkey are covered with foil to prevent them from defrosting too quickly. See specific turkey information in chart.

Calculate the minimum to maximum defrosting time recommended in the chart by multiplying the minutes-per-pound of defrost time by the weight of the meat. For example, ground beef defrosts in 6 to 7 minutes-per-pound and is broken apart with a fork after 1/2 to 2/3 of the defrost time. One and a half pounds of ground beef should defrost in a minimum of about 9 minutes to a maximum of about 10-1/2 minutes. It should be defrosted enough to break apart after about 4-1/2 to 7 minutes. Use minimum timings first, increasing time gradually as needed.

Standing time is very important in defrosting to equalize the temperature of the meat. Allow meat to stand the recommended time before adding more defrost time. Some meats, especially large bulky items, require a standing time between intervals of defrost time. Follow directions in the chart.

After standing time, additional defrost time may be necessary if meat is still too cold or icy to use. Additional defrost and standing times are suggested in the chart, but may only be needed occasionally after defrosting techniques become familiar.

Do not over defrost; meat will start to cook. Signs of over defrosting include hot or cooked spots on edges and translucent fat. Cover these areas with foil if continued defrosting is needed.

Thin pieces of meat defrost faster than thick, bulky pieces. Separate or break apart pieces of meat as soon as possible, to hasten defrosting.

Turn most meats over at least once during defrosting.

Prepare meat for cooking immediately after standing time. If meat is to be cooked later, refrigerate until ready to use.

Seafood and fish should be very cold or even icy after defrosting time. After standing, add defrosting time with care. Fish starts cooking very easily.

If meat is to be sliced, defrost only part of the time indicated. Partially thawed meat is easier to slice than completely thawed. Continue to defrost after slicing.

Use the following settings for defrosting:

Microwave Power:	Low
Oven Selector:	Off
Oven Temperature:	Off
Shelf Position:	2

MEAT DEFROSTING CHART

Food Item	Defrosting Container	Specific Instructions	Defrost Time	Standing Time	Additional Defrost Time if necessary	Additional Standing Time
BEEF, LAMB, PORK, VEAL						
Bacon (1 pound)	Package on oven shelf	Defrost until slices can be separated easily with a knife.	2 to 3 min. per pound			
Chops (1 to 3 pounds)	Package placed in dish	Turn over after 1/2 of defrost time. After minimum defrost time, remove wrapper, separate chops, let stand. If necessary, defrost additional time.	6 to 7 min. per pound	10 to 15 min.	1 to 1-1/2 min. per pound	5 to 10 min.
Glandular Meats— liver, kidney, brains (3/4 to 2 pounds)	Covered dish	Transfer meat from container to dish. Plastic cartons may melt from microwave energy. Defrost until it can be separated, will still be icy. Rinse, let stand.	4 to 5 min. per pound	10 to 15 min.		
Ground Meat (1/2 to 3 pounds)	Covered dish	After 1/2 to 2/3 of defrost time break meat apart with fork. Ground beef can be cooked from frozen on High power for casseroles, if desired.	6 to 7 min. per pound	10 min.	1 to 2 min.	5 min.
Ground Meat Patties (1 to 3 pounds)	Loosen wrapper, place package on plate	Defrost until meat can be separated, place in single layer on plate. Continue to defrost 2 to 3 minutes, let stand.	6 to 7 min. per pound	15 min.	1 to 2 min.	5 min.
Ham Slice (1 to 3 pounds)	Package	Turn over after 1/2 of defrost time. Shield fat with foil. If additional defrost time is necessary, shield all but coldest area.	6 to 7 min. per pound	15 to 20 min.	1 to 2 min. per pound	10 min.
Italian Sausage (1 to 2 pounds)	Package in dish	Turn over after 1/2 of defrost time. Separate sausages before standing time.	6 to 7 min. per pound	10 min.	1 to 2 min.	5 min.
Round & Chuck Steak (1 to 5 pounds)	Package	Turn over after 1/2 of defrost time. Shield fat and warm areas with foil if necessary. Cover with foil while standing.	6 to 7 min. per pound	15 min., covered	1 to 2 min. per pound	10 min.
Roast Chuck (2 to 6 pounds)	Loosen wrapper, place package in dish	Turn over after 1/2 of defrost time. Shield fat and warm areas. Let stand, add additional defrost time if necessary	6 to 7 min. per pound	15 min., covered	1 to 2 min. per pound	10 min.
Rump (2 to 6 pounds)	Loosen wrapper, place package in dish	Turn several times during defrosting. Shield fat and warm areas with foil. Let stand, add additional defrost time if necessary.	6 to 7 min. per pound	15 min., covered	1 to 2 min. per pound	10 min.
Sirloin (2 to 6 pounds)	Loosen wrapper, place package in dish	Turn several times during defrosting. Shield fat and warm areas with foil. Let stand, add additional defrost time if necessary.	6 to 7 min. per pound	15 min., covered	1 to 2 min. per pound	10 min.

MEAT DEFROSTING CHART

Food Item	Defrosting Container	Specific Instructions	Defrost Time	Standing Time	Additional Defrost Time if necessary	Additional Standing Time
Sausage links (8 oz. to 1 pound)	Package	Defrost just until links can be separated. Remove outer links if defrosted faster than center.	3 to 4 min. per pound	5 to 10 min.	1/2 min.	2 min.
Spareribs (1 to 5 pounds)	Package	Turn over 2 to 3 times during defrosting. Remove wrapper and spread ribs out on dish when workable. Shield ends and warm areas with foil.	5 to 6 min. per pound	10 min.	1 to 2 min. per pound	5 to 10 min.
Stew Meat (1 to 4 pounds)	Covered dish	Separate pieces when workable.	6 to 7 min. per pound	10 to 15 min.	1 to 1-1/2 min. per pound	5 to 10 min.
Wieners (1 pound)	Package	Defrost just until wieners can be separated. Spread out on plate, shield ends with foil if more defrosting is desired.	4 to 5 min. per pound	5 to 10 min.		
POULTRY Chicken Cut-up (1-1/2 to 4 pounds)	Loosen wrapper, place package in dish	Turn over after 1/2 of defrost time. Defrost until pieces can be separated. Let stand. Rinse. Defrost additional time if necessary.	5 to 7 min. per pound	15 min.	1 to 2 min. per pound	10 min.
Whole (2 to 5 pounds)	Loosen wrapper, place package in dish	Turn over after 1/2 of defrost time. Defrost until giblets can be removed from cavity. Shield let and wing ends as needed. Let stand. Rinse. Defrost additional time if necessary.	5 to 7 min. per pound	15 to 20 min.	1 to 2 min. per pound	10 min.
Cornish Hens (1 to 4— 1 pound each)	Package, remove metal clip, place in dish	Turn over after 1/2 of defrost time. Let stand, remove giblets, rinse.	5 to 6 min. per pound	15 min.	1 min. per pound	5 min.
Turkey (6 to 12 pounds)	Package, remove metal clip, place in large dish; then unwrapped in dish	Defrost large turkey on shelf position #1. Defrost 10 minutes, turn over, defrost 10 minutes. Let stand 10 minutes. Remove wrapper. With foil, shield leg ends, wings, neck opening and any areas starting to cook. Continue to defrost. Turn turkey over every 10 minutes, let	4 to 5 min. per pound	10 min. after every 20 min. of defrost	1/2 to 1 min. per pound	1 hour
(13 pounds and up)		stand 10 minutes after each 20 minutes of defrost time. Shield any hot areas. Defrost until giblets can be removed from cavity. Rinse. Let stand. Continue to defrost if icy. Before roasting, let stand 1 hour or overnight in refrigerator. For best results, be sure turkey is thoroughly defrosted before roasting.	3 to 4 min. per pound	10 min. after every 20 min. of defrost	1 to 1-1/2 min. per pound	1 hour

MEAT DEFROSTING CHART

Food Item	Defrosting Container	Specific Instructions	Defrost Time	Standing Time	Additional Defrost Time if necessary	Additional Standing Time
FISH Fillets (1 to 2 pounds)	Package placed in dish	Turn over after 2 minutes. Defrost just until fillets can be separated. Do not over defrost. Fillets should still be very cold after defrosting.	3 to 4 min. per pound	10 min.	1/2 to 1 min. per pound	5 min.
Steaks (1 to 3 pounds)	Package placed in dish	Turn over after 1/2 of defrost time. Defrost until steaks can be separated. Arrange thick steaks on dish and continue to defrost if necessary. Do not over defrost. Steaks should still be very cold after defrosting.	3 to 4 min. per pound	10 to 15 min.	1/2 to 1 min. per pound	5 to 10 min.
Whole (1 to 6 pounds)	Package placed in dish	Turn over after 1/4 of defrost time. Remove wrapper after 1/2 of defrost time. Shield ends with foil. Continue to defrost and turn over until a metal skewer can be inserted through fish. Center will still be very cold. Let stand. Continue to defrost if necessary. Do not over defrost.	3 to 4 min. per pound	10 to 20 min.	1 min. per pound	10 min.
SEAFOOD Lobster— whole or tails (8 ounces to 2 pounds)	Package placed in dish	Turn over after 1/2 of defrost time. Do not over defrost.	2 to 3 min. per pound	10 min.	1/2 min. per pound	5 min.
Oysters (8 to 12 ounces)	In jar, remove lid. If canned, transfer to dish.	Separate with fork after 3 or 4 minutes. Continue to defrost if necessary.	4 to 5 min.	10 min.	1/2 to 1 min. total	
Scallops (8 ounces to 2 pounds)	In dish, covered	Separate with fork after 2/3 of defrost time. Do not over defrost, scallops will still be icy before standing time.	3 to 4 min. per pound	10 min.	1/2 to 1 min. total	5 min.
Shrimp (8 ounces to 2 pounds)	In dish, covered	Separate with fork after 1/2 of defrost time. Do not over defrost. Raw shrimp may be cooked from frozen.	3 to 4 min. per pound	10 min.	1/2 to 1 min. total	

Convenience Foods

The convenience foods featured in this section include frozen, prepared main dishes, TV dinners, meats, vegetables, desserts, breads, appetizers and refrigerated, ready to bake rolls. There is considerable time to be saved defrosting and cooking frozen convenience foods. However, the fastest is not always the best. High power usually cooks frozen foods too fast, except vegetables. Low and Medium power offer more versatility for gentle cooking and defrosting with or without added heat.

A combination of heat and microwave energy is excellent for preparing convenience food items that would be heated or cooked in a conventional oven. Low or Medium power is usually used to hasten defrosting and cooking, while Bake or Broil heat browns and crisps the food. The oven is preheated except for a few specific foods. The Bake temperature is often 25° to 50°F higher than the temperature recommended on the package.

Microwave only is used to defrost and heat or cook foods that would be prepared on the cooktop conventionally, for example foods in boilable cooking pouches. Entrées and precooked meat items in cooking pouches are cooked on Medium in much less time than it takes to boil them. Vegetables in cooking pouches are cooked on High power as are other frozen vegetables. See further cooking pouch instructions in the Convenience Food Chart.

Many convenience food items that are just thawed before eating, for example frozen prepared desserts, can be quickly defrosted on Low power without oven heat and served in minimum time. Donuts, coffeecakes and rolls are defrosted and warmed on Medium.

A few convenience foods do not adapt well to microwave or combination cooking. These include "toaster" foods, such as waffles and french toast which are best prepared in the toaster.

The techniques described here for cooking commercially frozen, prepared foods, can also be applied to similar home prepared and frozen foods.

Freeze homemade casseroles in freezer-to-oven dishes or shaped to fit glass-ceramic casseroles and dishes that will withstand sudden temperature changes. Freeze individual pieces of food, like appetizers, cooked chicken and meatballs, on a tray. After frozen, slip food into a plastic bag to keep in freezer. When ready to cook, take out as many pieces as needed and return the rest to the freezer. Cooking times will be based on the quantity of food. Try to prepare quantities that correspond to the chart.

Tips:

Below are some general guidelines to follow for cooking frozen prepared convenience foods in the Thermatronic II oven:

Use shelf position #2 unless Preparation Instructions indicate otherwise.

Casseroles and main dishes with a sauce—such as cabbage rolls, sliced meat in gravy—bake 25°F higher than package recommends with Microwave on Medium, in a covered casserole. If some drying of the surface is desired, as in lasagna, remove the lid the last 5 to 10 minutes of cooking.

Casseroles and main dishes containing a large proportion of cheese—such as macaroni and cheese, rarebit—bake at temperature recommended on package with microwave on Low. Cover, unless crisping of top is desired, as in macaroni and cheese.

Individual pieces of food with a crisp coating—fried chicken, fish sticks—bake in a preheated oven, 50°F higher than package recommends with Microwave on Low, uncovered, in a shallow glass dish.

Do not cook more than 2 TV dinner trays or 3 entreé trays at a time. Allow at least one inch of space all around each tray. Too many foil trays can block microwaves and slow cooking. Food cooked in a shallow foil container takes slightly longer to cook than if the food is transferred to a glass dish.

Baked products—breads, pizza rolls, fruit desserts—bake, in a preheated oven, 25° to 50°F higher than package recommends, with Microwave on Low or Medium, uncovered, in a glass baking dish.

Most frozen convenience food in a foil container, except a TV dinner tray or a shallow foil pie pan, is transferred to a casserole dish similar in size and shape to the food. If food being cooked with microwave and heat needs to be covered, it should be transferred to a glass casserole dish with a lid. Plastic wrap cannot be used with thermal heat, and a foil cover would deflect microwave energy away from the food.

Frozen casseroles should be stirred during cooking, if possible. Entrées that cannot be stirred, for example stuffed peppers, should be tested for doneness with a fork. Poke down into filling or center of casserole to see if it is hot. Sauces will defrost and heat more quickly than the bulk of the food, so baste colder areas with heated sauce when possible.

Covering food helps it heat faster, however this is not always possible if a browned, crisp surface or coating is desired. Some casseroles and entrées may be covered during most of cooking, then uncovered the last few minutes for crisping.

Many frozen convenience food packages now give microwave cooking instructions. These instructions are intended for a 600 to 675 watt portable microwave oven used with High power and no thermal heat. For best results, consult the Convenience Food Chart for microwave setting, cooking time, and temperature. The combination of heat and Low or Medium microwave power produces a better end product in frozen foods that would otherwise be baked conventionally. Total cooking time will be slightly longer than High microwave only cooking, yet significantly shorter than conventional cooking.

Cooking times have been determined using food from the freezer compartment of an upright refrigerator. Foods frozen below $0°F$ which are very solid may take a few extra minutes to defrost and cook.

The Convenience Food Chart gives a general sampling of most frozen food items available in the supermarket. It would be difficult to include here all convenience foods, but this chart will serve as a guide in the preparation of the most popular. If a favorite food is not listed, follow the preparation instructions for a similar food.

The chart has three sections: 1. Microwave Only to Defrost, 2. Microwave Only, to Defrost and Cook—Boilable Cooking Bags or Pouches. 3. Microwave and Heat to Defrost and Cook. The chart indicates the Food Item with quantity (weight); Cooking Container, whether original foil pan or transferred to another dish; Preparation Instructions with any special comments for a particular dish; Microwave Power, Oven Selector and Oven Temperature if heat is combined with microwave energy; Cooking Time and Standing Time.

After cooking, allow the specified standing time to finish cooking and equalize the internal temperature of the food. Occasionally after standing, some foods may require additional cooking time. It is easy to add a few extra minutes of microwave cooking. If heat has also been used, do not preheat the oven again, simply reset it to the desired temperature, or use the residual heat still in the oven combined with microwave power.

Check the preparation instructions carefully for each item. It will say whether a food should be transferred from its foil container, covered, stirred or cooked on a shelf position other than #2. Occasionally the instructions will say to finish cooking with Bake only. This will also be indicated in the Cooking Time.

POPCORN

We do not recommend popping corn in the microwave oven. Even if the corn is just purchased, it could have been on the market shelf for awhile. Moisture in the kernels is what makes it pop. Keeping popcorn in the refrigerator or sprinkling the kernels with water does not increase the moisture in the popcorn. Extended cooking times do not yield more popped corn, but can cause a fire or make the dish too hot to handle or even break. Never even attempt to pop corn in a paper bag.

CONVENIENCE FOODS

Food Items *(Typical)*	Cooking Container	Preparation Instructions	Microwave Power	Oven Selector	Oven Temperature	Cooking Time	Standing Time
MICROWAVE ONLY TO DEFROST AND/OR WARM							
PIE							
Cream Pie, 26 oz. *(lemon, coconut, chocolate)*	8" pie dish	Transfer frozen pie to glass pie dish. If left in foil container, top melts before center is defrosted. Slice immediately after heating, then allow standing time.	Low	Off	Off	2 min., rotate dish 1/2 turn, plus 2 to 2-1/2 min.	15 min.
Cream Cheese Pie or Cake 19 oz. *(plain or fruit topped)*	Foil container	Remove cover.	Low	Off.	Off	2-1/2 min., rotate dish 1/2 turn, plus 2-1/2 min.	10 min.
CAKE							
Cupcakes and Crumb Cakes (6/pkg) 10 to 12 oz.	Glass or ceramic plate	Transfer from foil container to plate. Arrange in a circle or square.	Low	Off	Off	1 to 2 min.	3 to 5 min.
Single Layer Cake 13 to 19 oz. *(chocolate, orange, banana)*	Glass dish or plate	Transfer cake to serving plate. If left in foil container, frosting melts.	Low	Off	Off	2 min.	10 min.
Small Layer Cake 8-1/2 to 11-1/2 oz. *(chocolate, golden, white)*	Styrofoam tray	Defrost just until frosting begins to look glossy.	Low	Off	Off	1-1/2 to 2 min.	10 min.
Layer Cake 17 to 19 oz. *(chocolate, coconut)*	Styrofoam tray	Defrost just until frosting begins to look glossy.	Low	Off	Off	2 to 2-1/2 min.	10 to 15 min.
Donuts (6/pkg) 9 oz. (glazed, *chocolate, cake)*	Plate or pie dish	Cook just until slightly warm. See also coffeecakes and rolls in separate table in this section.	Medium	Off	Off	1-1/2 to 2 min.	3 to 5 min.
Pound Cake, 11-1/4 oz.	Plate or loaf dish	Transfer from foil container Slice immediately after cooking, then continue to cook an additional 1 to 2 minutes, if necessary, then let stand.	Low	Off	Off	2-1/2 to 3 min.	10 to 15 min.
Brownies, 13 oz.	Plate or oblong glass dish	Transfer from foil container. Defrost, but do not heat.	Low	Off	Off	1-1/2 to 2-1/2 min.	5 to 10 min.

COFFEECAKES AND DINNER ROLLS
Consult Defrosting and Reheating Charts and Information in this section for already baked coffeecakes, coffee rolls, dinner rolls and French rolls.

261

Food Items (Typical)	Cooking Container	Preparation Instructions	Microwave Power	Oven Selector	Oven Temperature	Cooking Time	Standing Time
MICROWAVE ONLY TO DEFROST AND COOK							
BOILABLE COOKING BAGS OR POUCHES							
Sliced Beef in Gravy or Barbecue Sauce with Sliced Beef, 5 oz.		General instructions for all cooking pouches: Place pouch in bowl large enough to hold entire bag without overlapping. Make an "X" slit in top side of bag. Cook with microwave power only according to time given below. "Stir" by manipulating bag gently from side to side after about 2/3 of cooking. Do not turn bag over. Allow to stand recommended time. With kitchen scissors, cut completely across one end of bag, grasp and pull opposite end of bag and slide food into bowl. If preferred, frozen food may be removed from cooking pouch and cooked in a covered casserole. Cooking time will be slightly longer.	Medium	Off	Off	4 to 6 min.	3 min.
Chicken a la King, 5 oz.			Medium	Off	Off	4 to 6 min.	5 min.
Chow Mein, 12 to 15 oz.			Medium	Off	Off	9 to 13 min.	6 min.
Creamed Chip Beef, 11 oz.			Medium	Off	Off	8 to 10	6 min.
Pepper Oriental, 15 oz.			Medium	Off	Off	10 to 13 min.	6 min.
Salisbury Steak in Gravy, 5 oz.			Medium	Off	Off	4 to 6 min.	3 min.
Spaghetti with Meat Sauce, 14 oz.			Medium	Off	Off	9 to 12 min.	5 min.
Sweet & Sour Pork, 14 oz.			Medium	Off	Off	9 to 12 min.	5 min.
Giblet Gravy and Sliced Turkey, 5 oz.			Medium	Off	Off	4 to 6 min.	3 min.
Vegetables in Sauce, 9 to 10 oz. (broccoli, cauliflower, peas, spinach in butter, cheese or cream sauce)			High	Off	Off	5 to 7 min.	4 min.
MICROWAVE AND HEAT TO DEFROST AND COOK							
APPETIZERS Egg Rolls, 6 oz.	2 qt. oblong glass dish	Preheat oven. Stir and turn after 3 minutes of cooking. Increase cooking time 1 to 2 minutes for 2 packages.	Low	Bake	475°F	5 to 6 min.	3 min.
Pizza Rolls, 6 oz.	2 qt. oblong glass dish	Preheat oven. Stir and turn after 3 minutes of cooking. Increase cooking time 1 to 2 minutes for 2 packages.	Low	Bake	475°F	5 to 6 min.	3 min.
Fish Kabobs, 16 oz.	3 qt. oblong glass dish	Preheat oven. Stir gently after 5 minutes.	Low	Bake	450°F	9 to 11 min.	3 min.

CONVENIENCE FOODS

Food Items (Typical)	Cooking Container	Preparation Instructions	Microwave Power	Oven Selector	Oven Temperature	Cooking Time	Standing Time
BREAD AND ROLLS							
Consult information and chart in this section for Baking Packaged Refrigerated Roll Doughs.							
Hot Slices, 15-1/2 oz. 1 loaf	1-1/2 qt. glass dish	Preheat oven. After microwaves go off, continue to bake until browned as desired.	Low	Bake	450°F	5 min. plus 2 min. Bake only	5 min.
2 loaves	2 qt. glass dish	Preheat oven. After microwaves go off, continue to bake until browned as desired.	Low	Bake	450°F	6 to 7 min. plus 2 min. Bake only	5 min.
Brown & Serve Rolls, not frozen (12/pkg) 12 oz.	3 qt. oblong glass dish	Preheat oven. Separate rolls. After microwaves go off, continue to bake until browned as desired.	Low	Bake	450°F	4 min. plus 3 min. Bake only	Serve immediately
Garlic Bread	2 qt. oblong dish	Shelf position # 3. After microwaves go off, continue to broil until browned as desired.	Low	Broil	High	3 min. plus 2 to 4 min. Broil only	3 min.
DESSERTS AND PASTRY							
Pecan Coffee Cake 11-1/4 oz.	9" pie dish	Preheat oven. Transfer from foil container.	Low	Bake	400°F	4 to 5 min.	5 min.
Carmel Pecan Rolls 10-1/2 oz.	2 qt. oblong dish	Preheat oven. Transfer from foil container. Place in dish, nut-side up.	Low	Bake	400°F	5 to 6 min.	5 min.
Croissants, 5-1/4 oz.	2 qt. oblong dish	Preheat oven. Transfer from foil container.	Low	Bake	450°F	2 to 3 min.	Serve immediately.
Muffins, frozen (6/pkg) 9 oz. (blueberry, bran, corn)	2 qt. oblong glass dish	Preheat oven. Transfer from foil container.	Low	Bake	425°F	4 to 6 min.	3 to 5 min.
Criss-Cross Pastry (with fruit filling) 14 oz.	3 qt. oblong glass dish	Preheat oven. After microwaves go off, continue to bake until browned as desired.	Medium	Bake	475°F	8 min. plus 4 to 6 min. Bake only	10 min.
Cobbler, fruit (blueberry, peach) 32 oz.	2 qt. square casserole	Preheat oven. Transfer from foil container. Bake until crust is browned and crisp and fruit thickens.	Low	Bake	425°F	20 to 25 min.	15 min.
Fruit and Danish (apple, cherry) 13 oz.	In foil container	Preheat oven.	Low	Bake	425°F	5 to 6 min.	2 to 3 min.
Fruit Turnovers, 12-1/4 oz.		See specific baking information in this section.					
MAIN DISHES							
CHEESE							
Macaroni & Cheese 8 to 10 oz.	Foil container	Preheat oven. Do not cover. Stir after 10 minutes, continue to bake only.	Low	Bake	425°F	10 min., stir, plus 5 to 6 min. Bake only	5 min.
Macaroni & Cheese, 20 oz.	Foil container	Preheat oven. Do not cover. Stir after 15 minutes, continue to bake only.	Low	Bake	425°F	15 min., plus 5 to 7 min. Bake only	5 min.

CONVENIENCE FOODS

Food Items (Typical)	Cooking Container	Preparation Instructions	Microwave Power	Oven Selector	Oven Temperature	Cooking Time	Standing Time
Welsh Rarebit, 10 oz.	1 qt. casserole	Preheat oven. Transfer from foil container. Cover. Stir with fork after 5 minutes.	Low	Bake	400° F	5 min., stir plus 3 to 5 min.	3 min.
MEAT, FISH, POULTRY Cabbage Rolls with Beef in Tomato Sauce, 14 oz.	1 or 1-1/2 qt. shallow casserole	Preheat oven. Transfer from foil container. Cover. Baste rolls with sauce after cooking. Cover, let stand.	Medium	Bake	425° F	14 to 16 min.	8 min.
Stuffed Green Peppers, 14 oz.	1-1/2 qt. casserole	Preheat oven. Transfer from foil container. Cover.	Medium	Bake	425° F	16 to 18 min.	8 min.
Stuffed Pasta Shells, 16-3/4 oz. (chicken & cheese, beef & spinach)	1-1/2 qt. shallow casserole	Preheat oven. Transfer from foil container. Cover. After 15 minutes, spoon sauce over shells, cover and continue to bake only.	Low	Bake	400° F	15 min. plus 3 to 5 min. Bake only	8 min.
Lasagna with Meat Sauce 21 oz.	2 qt. shallow casserole	Preheat oven. Transfer from foil container. Cover. After 16 minutes, spoon sauce over all, continue to bake only, uncovered.	Low	Bake	400° F	16 min., uncover, plus 5 to 8 min. Bake only	8 min.
Breaded Veal Parmigiana, 14 oz.	1-1/2 qt. casserole	Preheat oven. Transfer from foil container. Cover.	Medium	Bake	400° F	12 to 14 min.	8 min.
Salisbury Steak, 12 oz.	1-1/2 qt. casserole	Preheat oven. Transfer from foil container. Cover.	Medium	Bake	400° F	10 to 12 min.	8 min.
Roast Beef Hash, 11-1/2 oz.	1-1/2-qt. casserole	Preheat oven. Transfer from foil container. Cover.	Medium	Bake	425° F	8 min., uncover, plus 5 to 6 min.	6 min.
Fish Sticks, 14 oz.	3 qt. oblong dish	Preheat oven. Arrange in single layer in dish. Do not cover.	Low	Bake	450° F	8 to 10 min.	5 min.
Fish Fillets, 24 oz.	3 qt. oblong dish	Preheat oven. Arrange in single layer in dish. Do not cover.	Low	Bake	450° F	10 to 12 min.	5 min.
Fried Chicken, 32 oz.	3 qt. oblong dish	Preheat oven. Arrange in single layer in dish. Do not cover.	Low	Bake	450° F	13 to 15 min.	5 min.
Corn Dogs, (hot dogs on a stick) 16 oz., 6/pkg	3 qt. oblong dish	Preheat oven.	Medium	Bake	450° F	5 to 7 min.	5 min.
FAMILY SIZE ENTREES Sliced Turkey in Gravy, 32 oz.	2-1/2 qt. shallow casserole	Preheat oven. Transfer from foil container. Cover. Spoon gravy over meat after 15 minutes.	Medium	Bake	400° F	20 to 23 min.	10 min.
Sliced Beef in Gravy, 32 oz.	2-1/2 qt. shallow casserole	Preheat oven. Transfer from foil container. Cover. Spoon gravy over meat after 15 minutes.	Medium	Bake	400° F	20 to 23 min.	10 min.
Meat Loaf with Tomato Sauce, 32 oz.	2-1/2 qt. shallow casserole	Preheat oven. Transfer from foil container. Cover. Spoon gravy over meat after 15 minutes.	Medium	Bake	400° F	20 to 23 min.	10 min.

CONVENIENCE FOODS

Food Items (Typical)	Cooking Container	Preparation Instructions	Microwave Power	Oven Selector	Oven Temperature	Cooking Time	Standing Time
Salisbury Steak in Gravy, 32 oz.	2-1/2 qt. shallow casserole	Preheat oven. Transfer from foil container. Cover. Spoon gravy over meat after 15 minutes.	Medium	Bake	400° F	20 to 23 min.	10 min.
Cabbage Rolls in Sauce, 32 oz.	2-1/2 qt. shallow casserole	Preheat oven. Transfer from foil container. Cover. Spoon sauce over meat after 18 minutes. Make sure centers are hot at end of cooking.	Medium	Bake	400° F	23 to 28 min.	10 min.
Stuffed Peppers in Sauce, 32 oz.	2-1/2 qt. shallow casserole	Preheat oven. Transfer from foil container. Cover. Spoon sauce over meat after 18 minutes. Make sure centers are hot at end of cooking.	Medium	Bake	400° F	23 to 28 min.	10 min.
VEGETABLES AND SIDE DISHES Corn or Spinach Soufflé, 12 oz.	1 qt. shallow casserole	Preheat oven. Transfer from foil container. Cover. Remove cover after 10 minutes.	Low	Bake	400° F	10 min., remove cover, plus 3 to 5 min.	5 min.
Escalloped Apples, 12 oz.	1 qt. shallow casserole	Preheat oven. Transfer from foil container. Cover. Remove cover after 10 minutes.	Medium	Bake	425° F	10 min., remove cover, plus 3 to 5 min.	5 min.
Potatoes Au Gratin, 11-1/2 oz.	1 qt. shallow casserole	Preheat oven. Transfer from foil container. Cover.	Medium	Bake	425° F	12 to 14 min.	5 min.
Scalloped Potatoes, 12 oz.	1 qt. shallow casserole	Preheat oven. Transfer from foil container. Cover.	Medium	Bake	425° F	12 to 14 min.	5 min.
Vegetable Au Gratin, 10 oz. (broccoli, cauliflower)	1 qt. shallow casserole	Preheat oven. Transfer from foil container. Cover. Stir gently after 10 minutes.	Medium	Bake	400° F	12 to 14 min.	5 min.
2 Stuffed Potatoes, 12 oz.	Foil containers	Preheat oven.	Medium	Bake	450° F	12 to 14 min.	10 min.
French Fries or Taters, 16 oz.	3 qt. oblong dish	Preheat oven. Arrange in a single layer in dish. Stir and rearrange after 4 minutes.	Low	Bake	500° F	5 to 7 min.	5 min.
Onion Rings, 7 oz.	2-3/4 glass-ceramic dish	Shelf position # 3. Turn over after 3 minutes.	Low	Broil	High Broil	5 to 6 min.	3 min.

CONVENIENCE FOODS

Food Items (Typical)	Cooking Container	Preparation Instructions	Microwave Power	Oven Selector	Oven Temperature	Cooking Time	Standing Time
MEAT PIES (CHICKEN, TURKEY, BEEF)							
1 Double Crust Pie 8 oz.	Foil container	Preheat oven. Shelf position #1. Prick top crust. Place on ceramic insert.	Low	Bake	475° F	14 to 16 min.	10 min.
2 Double Crust Pie 8 oz. each	Foil container	Preheat oven. Shelf position #1. Prick top crust.	Low	Bake	475° F	16 to 18 min.	10 min.
1 single crust pie 16 oz. each	Foil container	Preheat oven. Prick crust.	Low	Bake	450° F	16 to 18 min.	10 min.
TV DINNERS & ENTRÉES Entrees 5-1/2 to 8-3/4 oz. (meat & potato, beans or spaghetti)	Foil container	Preheat oven. Remove foil cover. Stir mashed potatoes, beans or spaghetti with a fork after 5 minutes. When preparing 2 or 3, allow at least one inch of space all around each container. Do not prepare more than 3 at a time.	Medium	Bake	450° F	1 — 6 to 8 min. 2 — 7 to 10 min. 3 — 9 to 12 min.	5 min. 5 min. 5 min.
Breakfasts, 4-1/2 to 6-1/2 oz.	Foil container	Preheat oven. Remove foil cover. When preparing 2 or 3 allow at least one inch of space all around each container. Do not prepare more than 3 at a time.	Medium	Bake	475° F	1 — 4 to 6 min. 2 — 5 to 8 min. 3 — 7 to 9 min.	5 min. 5 min. 5 min.
TV Dinners, 11-1/2 to 14 oz. (fried chicken, turkey, roast loin of pork, beef)	Foil container	Preheat oven. Remove foil cover. Do not prepare more than 2 at a time. Allow at least one inch of space all around each container. Stir mashed potatoes after 6 or 8 minutes.	Medium	Bake	450° F	1 — 9 to 12 min. 2 — 11 to 15 min.	5 min. 5 min.
Mexican Style Dinners, 12 to 16 oz. (enchiladas or tamale, beans & rice)	Foil container	Preheat oven. Remove foil cover. Do not prepare more than 2 at a time. Allow at least one inch of space all around each container. Stir beans after 6 or 8 minutes.	Medium	Bake	450° F	1 — 9 to 11 min. 2 — 12 to 15 min.	5 min. 5 min.
Man-sized Dinners, 16 to 20 oz.	Foil container	Preheat oven. Remove foil cover. Do not prepare more than 2 at a time. Allow at least one inch of space all around each container. Stir mashed potatoes or spaghetti after 8 minutes.	Medium	Bake	450° F	1 — 11 to 14 min. 2 — 13 to 18 min.	5 min. 5 min.

Frozen Two-Crust Fruit Pie

Microwave Power:	Low
Oven Selector :	Bake
Oven Temperature:	See Below, not preheated
Shelf Position:	1

1 frozen fruit pie (36 to 38-oz.)

Slit crust as package directs. Place shelf in bottom position and set foil container in glass pie plate. Bake at 500° with Microwave on Low, 15 minutes. Reduce the temperature to 425°. Continue to bake with Microwave on Low, 12 to 15 minutes or until crust is golden brown and filling cooked.

Frozen Two-Crust Mini Fruit Pie

Microwave Power:	Low
Oven Selector:	Bake
Oven Temperature:	500°F, preheated
Shelf Position:	1

1 frozen fruit pie (8-oz.)

Leave in foil pie pan. Set pan in glass pie plate. Bake at 500° with Microwave on Low, 14 to 16 minutes, until crust is golden and pie is bubbly.

Frozen Fruit Turnovers

Microwave Power:	Low
Oven Selector:	Bake
Oven Temperature:	475°F, preheated
Shelf Position:	1

1 pkg. frozen fruit turnovers (4 in 12-1/4-oz. pkg.)

Unwrap pastry and space evenly in 3-quart oblong baking dish. Place folded edge of pastry towards outside of dish. Place on shelf with handles right to left. Bake at 475°, with Microwave on Low, 10 to 12 minutes.

Frozen Pizza

Microwave Power:	Low
Oven Selector:	Bake
Oven Temperature:	500°F, preheated
Shelf Position:	1

PIZZA	DIRECTIONS
10-inch pizza (20 ounces)	Brush off loose cheese from underside; place directly on oven rack. Bake at 500° with Microwave on Low, 5 to 6 minutes, or until heated through and cheese is melted.
12 pack pizza (24 ounces)	Heat 4 or 5 at a time in a 3-quart oblong baking dish. Bake at 500° with Microwave on Low, 5 to 6 minutes, or until heated through and cheese is melted.
15 pack pizza snacks (7-1/4 ounces)	Remove from foil tray and place in a 3-quart oblong baking dish. Bake at 500° with Microwave on Low, 4-1/2 to 5-1/2 minutes, or until heated through and cheese is melted.

Baking Packaged Refrigerated Roll Dough

Microwave Power:	Low	Off
Oven Selector:	Bake	Bake
Oven Temperature:	See Chart, preheated	See Chart
Shelf Position:	2	2

Food Item	Baking Dish	Oven Temperature	Bake and Microwave Time	Bake Only Time
Buttermilk Biscuits (7-oz.)	1-1/2-quart round cake dish	475°F	2 min.	4-1/2 to 5 min.
Hungry Jack Flakey Biscuits (10-oz.)	1-1/2-quart round cake dish or 3-quart oblong baking dish	475°F	3-1/2 to 4 min. 3-1/2 min.	3 to 3-1/2 min. 3-1/2 to 4 min.
Butterflake Rolls (8-oz.)	6-cup metal muffin pan	425°F	3 min.	4-1/2 to 5 min.
Crescent Rolls (8-oz.)	3-quart oblong baking dish	475°F	3 min.	2-1/2 to 3 min.
Cinnamon Rolls (9-1/2-oz.)	1-1/2-quart round cake dish	475°F	3 min.	3 to 3-1/2 min.
Orange Danish Rolls (11-oz.)	1-1/2-quart round cake dish	475°F	2-1/2 min.	3 to 3-1/2 min.
Danish Carmel Rolls (11-oz.)	1-1/2-quart round cake dish	475°F	3 min.	3 to 3-1/2 min.

Place dough in baking dish according to chart. Bake with Microwave on Low for recommended time. Turn Microwave Off and continue to Bake at suggested temperature for recommended time or until golden brown.

Defrosting & Heating Frozen Coffeecakes & Rolls

Microwave Power: Medium
Oven Selector: Off
Oven Temperature: Off
Shelf Position: 2

FROZEN COFFEECAKES (defrosted and heated)

Quantity	Time
1 whole coffeecake (9 to 12 ounces)	2 to 4 minutes
4 coffee rolls (9 to 12 ounces)	2 to 3 minutes
2 coffee rolls (4 to 6 ounces)	1 to 2 minutes
1 coffee roll (2 to 4 ounces)	1/2 to 1 minute

FROZEN DINNER ROLLS

Quantity	Time
8 rolls	2 to 3 minutes
6 rolls	1-1/2 to 2-1/2 minutes
4 rolls	1 to 1-1/2 minutes
2 rolls	1/2 to 1 minute

Place rolls on paper plate or serving dish. Remove coffeecake from foil-lined package* and place on plate. Heat with Microwave on Medium according to chart. Do not cover.

Foil-lined package should not be used as it may cause arcing.

Heating Room Temperature Coffeecakes & Rolls

Microwave Power:	Medium
Oven Selector:	Off
Oven Temperature:	Off
Shelf Position:	2

Quantity	Time
1 whole coffeecake (9 to 12 ounces)	1 to 2 minutes
4 individual coffee rolls (9 to 12 ounces)	1 to 2 minutes
2 individual coffee rolls (4 to 6 ounces)	1/2 to 1 minute
1 individual coffee roll (2 to 4 ounces)	1/4 to 3/4 minute
8 dinner rolls	1 to 2 minutes
6 dinner rolls	3/4 to 1-1/2 minutes
4 dinner rolls	1/2 to 1 minute
2 dinner rolls	1/4 to 3/4 minute

Place coffeecake* or rolls on paper plate or serving dish. Heat with Microwave on Medium according to chart. Do not cover.**

*   Remove coffeecake from foil-lined package. *Do not use any foil-lined package in Thermatronic II as it may cause arcing.*

** A cover may be used if very moist rolls are desired.

Heating French Rolls

Microwave Power:	Low
Oven Selector:	Off
Oven Temperature:	Off
Shelf Position:	2

Quantity	Time
1 roll	30 seconds
2 rolls	40 - 45 seconds
3 rolls	50 - 55 seconds
4 rolls	55 - 60 seconds
6 rolls	60 - 65 seconds

Times based on 1 package (13 ounces) containing 10 rolls. Heat with Microwave on Low in basket or plate, not in a plastic bag.

Jams & Relishes

We have prepared a few recipes as examples of the types of jams and relishes that can be prepared in the microwave oven. Fresh jams are a delicious accompaniment to fresh bread baked in the combination oven. Microwave cooking makes it easy to prepare small batches (when fresh fruits and vegetables are available) which can be stored in the refrigerator without undertaking a big canning project. However, if jams and relishes are to be canned and stored in the cupboard, they must be processed on a conventional cooktop according to jar manufacturer's instructions.

There are two principle brands of powdered pectin available. They vary in ounces, 1-3/4 ounces and 2 ounces. Directions are NOT interchangeable from one brand to the other. Be sure to check the package size and follow the directions for that size package.

Freezer Strawberry Jam I

Microwave Power:	High
Oven Selector:	Off
Oven Temperature:	Off
Shelf Position:	2

3-1/4 cups crushed strawberries
1/4 cup lemon juice
1 pkg. (2-oz.) powdered pectin

1 cup light corn syrup
4-1/2 cups sugar

Wash, stem and crush berries completely. Place berries in a 3-quart bowl, add lemon juice and stir well. Slowly pour powdered pectin into berries, stirring vigorously. Set aside 30 minutes, stirring occasionally. Add corn syrup, mix well. Gradually stir sugar into berries. Warm with Microwave on High, 3 to 4 minutes, to dissolve sugar. Warm only to 100°F, no hotter. Stir to dissolve sugar. Pour into suitable freezer containers with tight lids . Conventional jam glasses with lids may also be used in freezing. Store in freezer. Makes 7 cups.

Freezer Strawberry Jam II

Microwave Power:	High
Oven Selector:	Off
Oven Temperature:	Off
Shelf Position:	2

2 cups crushed strawberries
4 cups sugar

3/4 cup water
1 pkg. (1-3/4-oz.) powdered pectin

Wash, stem and crush berries completely. Place berries in 3-quart bowl. Thoroughly mix sugar into fruit; let stand 10 minutes. Mix water and pectin in 4-cup liquid measure. Bring to a boil with Microwave on High, 3 to 4 minutes, stirring once. Then boil 1 minute; stir. Pour into fruit and stir for 3 minutes. Pour into suitable freezer containers with tight lids. Conventional jam glasses with lids may also be used for freezing. Let set up at room temperature—can take up to 24 hours. Store in freezer. Makes 5-1/2 cups.

Cooked Strawberry Jam

Microwave Power:	High
Oven Selector:	Off
Oven Temperature:	Off
Shelf Position:	2

5-3/4 cups crushed strawberries
1/4 cup lemon juice

1 pkg. (2-oz.) powdered pectin
8-1/2 cups sugar

Wash, stem and crush berries completely. Put prepared, crushed berries and lemon juice in a 4-1/2-quart or larger casserole. Add pectin and stir well. Cover and cook with Microwave on High, 15 to 17 minutes; to bring to a boil. Stir once. Add sugar; mix well. Cook uncovered with Microwave on High, 14 to 16 minutes, stirring twice until jam comes to a rolling boil. Boil 4 minutes, stirring every 1-1/2 minutes. Watch very carefully so jam does not boil over. Remove from oven and stir and skim several times for 5 minutes, cooling slightly to prevent floating fruit. Stir again just before pouring into scalded glasses. Seal with 2 thin layers of melted paraffin. Cover. Store in a cool place. Makes fourteen 6-ounce glasses.

Boysenberry Jam

Microwave Power:	High
Oven Selector:	Off
Oven Temperature:	Off
Shelf Position:	2

5 cups crushed boysenberries
1 pkg. (1-3/4-oz.) powdered pectin

7 cups sugar

Sieve half of pulp* to remove some of seeds. Put crushed berries in a 4-1/2-quart casserole. Add pectin and stir well. Bring to a hard boil with Microwave on High, 9 to 11 minutes. Add sugar; mix well. Cook with Microwave on High, 14 to 16 minutes, stirring twice, until jam comes to a full rolling boil. Boil hard for 1 minute. Remove from oven and stir and skim several times for 5 minutes, to cool slightly and prevent floating fruit. Ladle into scalded glasses. Seal with 2 thin layers of melted parafin, cover. Store in cool place. Makes 7 cups.

*Save pulp for Boysenberry Refresher in Beverage Section.

Pennsylvania Dutch Corn Relish

Microwave Power:	High
Oven Selector:	Off
Oven Temperature:	Off
Shelf Position:	2

2 pkgs. (10-oz. each) frozen corn
1/2 tablespoon flour
1/2 tablespoon dry mustard
3/4 cup sugar

3/4 cup cider vinegar
1/2 cup chopped green pepper
1 jar (2-oz.) pimientos, rinsed, drained, chopped
2 cups finely shredded cabbage

Place packages of corn on oven shelf. Cook with Microwave on High, 2 minutes. Set aside. In a 4-quart bowl combine flour, dry mustard and sugar; stir in vinegar. Cook with Microwave on High, 3 to 5 minutes or until mixture boils. Add corn, green pepper, pimientos and cabbage. Cook with Microwave on High, 5 to 7 minutes or until mixture boils. Cool. Store in jars in refrigerator. Makes 4 cups.

Tips

Salting: Avoid sprinkling salt on the surface of food. Salt has a tendency to toughen and dehydrate the surface of the food. If salt is mixed and dissolved in the food, it can be added during preparation. It can be sprinkled on the surface near the end of the cooking time or after cooking is completed.

Heat baby's bottle: Loosen cap on bottle; heat 8 ounces with Microwave on High, 45 seconds to 1 minute; then test to see if additional heating is necessary.

Flaming desserts: Heat 1/3 cup brandy or rum in a glass measuring cup with Microwave on High, 15 to 20 seconds.

Blanch nuts: Bring 1 cup water to a boil in 4-cup liquid measure with Microwave on High. Drop 1/2 cup nuts into boiling water. Cook about 1 minute; drain. Let cool and slip skins off.

Roasted almonds: Melt 1 tablespoon butter in a glass cake dish. Add 1/2 cup almonds. Heat with Microwave on High, 8 to 10 minutes, stirring occasionally. Sprinkle with onion or garlic salt. Let cool before serving.

Dry herbs: Wash and let dry completely. Place a few sprigs or 1/2 cup leaves in a single layer between paper towels. Heat with Microwave on High, 3 to 5 minutes or until dry and crumbly. Exact time depends on type and amount of herb.

Dry bread crumbs: Place 4 cups fresh bread cubes in 3-quart baking dish. Heat with Microwave on High, 8 to 10 minutes, stirring every 2 minutes, until crisp and dry. Crush for coating such things as chicken or fish.

Fresh croutons: Place 4 cups fresh bread cubes in 3-quart baking dish. Heat with Microwave on High, 2 minutes. Drizzle with 1/2 cup melted butter, sprinkle with garlic salt and 1 to 2 teaspoons Italian or other seasonings, toss to coat all cubes. Continue heating 6 to 8 minutes until crisp and dry, stirring every 2 minutes.

Shell nuts: To shell nuts easily and with less breakage place 1/2 pound nuts and 1 cup water in 1-quart covered casserole. Heat with Microwave on High, 5 to 6 minutes. Drain. Let cool before shelling.

Warm syrup: In a pitcher warm 1/2 cup syrup with Microwave on High, about 1 minute. Add a pat of butter for buttery syrup.

Defrost fruit juice: To mix frozen concentrate fruit juice quickly, remove top metal lid on cardboard container, heat with Microwave on High, 1 to 2 minutes or until soft enough to pour into pitcher; add water and mix.

Quick mint icing: Place about 16 chocolate coated mint patties on a single layer of cake. Soften with Microwave on Medium, 2-1/2 to 3 minutes. Let stand 1 to 2 minutes, then swirl to cover top evenly.

Hot fudge sundae: Heat 1/2 cup fudge sauce with Microwave on Medium, about 2 minutes or until hot. Pour over ice cream.

Ice cream sundae: Heat refrigerated sundae toppings for easy pouring. Heat 1/2 cup sauce with Microwave on Medium, 30 seconds to 1 minute, to take the chill off and to ease pouring.

Frozen cookie dough: Make a double batch of cookie dough, then freeze half. Use Microwave on Low and thaw only until soft enough to handle. Time will depend on amount and type of dough.

Speedy cheese sauce: Place 5-ounce jar processed Cheddar cheese spread in a bowl. Melt with Microwave on Medium, 2 to 3 minutes, stirring occasionally. Pour over cauliflower or broccoli.

Heat tortillas: Leave in plastic bag or wrap in a damp towel. Heat with Microwave on High, 1-1/2 to 2 minutes or until pliable. Turn over after 1 minute.

Melt marshmallows: Add a large marshmallow to a cup of hot chocolate the last 15 to 30 seconds it heats.

Chocolate curls: For fast and easy chocolate curls, **heat unwrapped bar of chocolate with Microwave on Medium,** about 10 seconds. Immediately scrape over flat side with a vegetable peeler.

Melt butter: In glass measuring cup with Microwave on High melt 2 tablespoons butter 30 seconds to 1 minute; 1/4 cup in 45 seconds to 1-1/4 minutes.

Soften butter: In a glass dish with Microwave on Low soften 1/4 cup in 30 to 45 seconds.

Melt chocolate: In glass dish melt 1 square with Microwave on High, 3 to 3-1/2 minutes.

Soften cream cheese: Remove from foil and place in small bowl. Soften with Microwave on Low; one 3-oz. package, 30 to 45 seconds; one 8-oz. package, 1 to 1-1/2 minutes.

Staggered dinner hours: When everyone arrives home at different times, make individual servings on dinner plates; cover and heat each one with Microwave on Medium as needed.

Heat crepes: Wrap in a damp towel. Heat with Microwave on High, 45 seconds or longer, depending on amount. Warm just until flexible.

276

Index

Part Number 14-10-675